THE RIALTO IN RICHMOND RECONSTRUCTED

Confederates, Canada, and Carpetbaggers

JOSEPH P. FARRELL

Adventures Unlimited Press

Other Books by Joseph P. Farrell:

The Rialto in Richmond
Hess and the Penguins
Hidden Finance
The Third Way
Nazi International
Thrice Great Hermetica and the Janus Age
Covert Wars and the Clash of Civilizations
Saucers, Swastikas and Psyops
Covert Wars and Breakaway Civilizations
LBJ and the Conspiracy to Kill Kennedy
Roswell and the Reich
Reich of the Black Sun
The S.S. Brotherhood of the Bell
Babylon's Banksters
The Philosopher's Stone
The Vipers of Venice
Secrets of the Unified Field
The Cosmic War
The Giza Death Star Revisited
The Demon in the Ekur
Transhumanism (with Scott deHart)
The Grid of the Gods (with Scott deHart)

THE RIALTO IN RICHMOND RECONSTRUCTED

Confederates, Canada, and Carpetbaggers

The Rialto in Richmond Reconstructed

by Joseph P. Farrell

ISBN: 978-1-948803-78-6

Published by:
Adventures Unlimited Press
One Adventure Place
Kempton, Illinois 60946 USA

auphq@frontiernet.net

www.adventuresunlimitedpress.com

Cover by Joe Boyer

10 9 8 7 6 5 4 3 2 1

THE RIALTO IN RICHMOND RECONSTRUCTED

For all the Gizars, in thanks for the wonderful
conversation of the past several years,
and especially to Chuck McCorkle
and Catherine Austin Fitts and all the good people
who brought music back into my life with "Bruno,
And to Walter Bosley who boldly went where no
man had gone before,
To T.S.F. and G.A.H. and M.T.C.
Who made it all possible,
And to Shiloh
Who encouraged in the writing of this book with the
well-placed wag-of-tail, barks, whines, and canine
kisses; each and all a
DUR-AN-KI...

TABLE OF CONTENTS

PART ONE:
THE FIRST LAYER:
TWO MORE PRESIDENTS AND THE RACKET OF RECONSTRUCTION

PART TWO: THE SECOND, DEEPER LAYER: THE DISASTROUS RAID, THE FOILED PEACE, AND MURDERED MERCY

PART THREE: THE THIRD AND DEEPEST LAYER: THE SERPENTS OF THE CITY, THE WEASELS OF WALL STREET, AND BISMARCK'S BANKSTERS

1
INTRODUCTION: A CATALOGUE OF QUESTIONS
AND THE PLAYERS AND LAYERS OF A DEEP CONSPIRACY

"...(The) years from 1865 to 1880 were dreary years in which there was no peace. The war had ended only on the battlefield. In the minds of men it still persisted."
Paul H. Buck[1]

NOTHING SAYS "CRIMINAL PROTECTION RACKET," international espionage, geopolitical conspiracy, and "hall of mirrors" as clearly and distinctly as the "Reconstruction of the South" following the American War Between the States. To this day, most Americans are ignorant of the policies of Reconstruction, and of the deep and abiding effects they had in dramatically exacerbating racial tensions where they already existed in the country, and creating and nursing them where they did not. Minefields thus await on every side of anyone venturing to write about the period.

I have attempted to remedy this difficulty by appealing to scholars I have adjudged to be either profoundly pro-Union and abolitionist, or to that certain stripe of recent revisionist scholarship on reconstruction that can only be qualified as "Southern" or "Confederate apologetics."[2]

---

[1] Paul H. Buck, *The Road to Reunion 1865-1900* (Boston: Little, Brown and Company, no date nor ISBN), p. 45.

[2] Historian and lawyer David O. Stewart, in his well-written and deeply researched book *Impeached: The Trial of Andrew Johnson and the Fight for Lincoln's Legacy*, (New York, Simon and Schuster: 2009, ISBN 978-1-4165-4750-1) notes this historiographical contradiction at work in the ways one of the

This cumbersome methodology is adopted because one of the central focuses of this book is not upon the rapid deterioration of race relations in the *post bellum* period, but rather on *why* it happened. That "why" is encapsulated in the characterization of Reconstruction that I have given it. To put it bluntly, *Reconstruction was a racket, and a* ***protection*** *racket at that.*

As such, the post bellum South was the first, and incidentally, largest example of what a modern politician or developer would call an "opportunity zone," those coveted areas of urban "blight" or rural "emptiness" that have been

---

components of our study, President Andrew Johnson's impeachments and Senate trial, have been interpreted:

"Beginning in the early years of the twentieth century, Andrew Johnson was celebrated as a healer of the sectional divisions of the war, while the impeachers were depicted as hate-filled gorgons who wished only to oppress noble Southern whites. Many writers insisted that Johnson saved the nation from congressional Radicals who lusted to destroy the presidency and Southern culture....

"By mid-century, the emergence of the civil rights movement began to change perspectives on Reconstruction. Johnson's solicitude for white Southerners seemed less admirable. His abandonment of the freedmen seemed misbegotten. His stubborn belief in the states' rights values of the pre-Civil War Constitution began to look like a bullheaded failure to notice how the war had revolutionized the nation....

"The impeachment trial of 1868 seethes with contradictions that have fostered equally contradictory views." (pp. 315-316) Stewart's book is a valuable work as it is written by a lawyer willing to explore the nuances of both sides' legal and constitutional arguments, and we shall follow his review of the three impeachment efforts against President Andrew Johnson closely, later in this book.

targeted for "renewal" and "infrastructure improvement" which, "coincidentally" happens after large scale riots or other catastrophes (like civil war) have destroyed private and business property values, making assets easily purchased for carpetbagging pennies on the dollar—*per* the analysis of former Assistant Secretary of Housing and Urban Development Catherine Austin Fitts in her extensive interviews and writings.[3]

The states of the defeated Confederacy constituted nothing but one big Opportunity Zone. Indeed and as we shall see, for many of the Radical Republicans, the states of the Confederacy were no longer even "states" at all. They were simply conquered and occupied territories with a subject and defeated people to be ruled by the federal military. The poverty and debt peonage inflicted on Southern blacks and whites as a result of "Congress Reconstruction" and its Jim Crow backlash lasted well into the beginning of the twentieth century and in many places much later, as did the tendency among some people within each race to blame the other for its own woes, while the poorest among both populations lived and worked and struggled together as best as circumstances would permit. Utterly forgotten were Mr. Lincoln's own views and policies on Reconstruction, or Mr. Davis' or other Southerners' pre-bellum advocacy of the "high road to emancipation."[4] The one—with his policies—was literally

---

[3] Fitts articulated this thesis in particular reference to the George Floyd riots and burning in Minneapolis which, she discovered, "coincidentally" corresponded with the "opportunity zones" for business development that the government had declared in that city.

[4] There were, of course, cruelties and barbarisms practiced against black slaves on many Southern plantations, as attested by none other than Frederick Douglass himself. There were also,

murdered by a deep multi-layered conspiracy, and the other was left to live out the remainder of his life sharing some of the poverty that had descended upon his beloved Dixie.

But we're getting ahead of ourselves.

Thus did the War Between the States become a template for similarly cynical and future American plunder initiatives, hiding the plunder program behind the moralizing posturing of northern (or American) "virtue" and a demonized enemy, in this case, southern "vice," "stubbornness" or "conservatism." All one needed was (1) the plunder opportunity itself (in this case, a civil war and an enabling assassination), (2) a narrative of virtue and morality behind which to disguise the real plunder operation, in this case, abolition of slavery and/or the narrative that the soldiers and leaders of the Confederacy were all traitors, and/or that the inherently depraved and evil "mentality" of the white southerner itself had to be "reconstructed" according to virtuous New England Yankee secularized Calvinist-

---

however, Southerners who knew the institution would eventually have to be abolished, and that blacks would have to take their place in the Southern population as free members of society, and accordingly attempted to prepare their own slaves for the eventuality. Davis was one of such figures in the South who advocated the "high road" to emancipation, and followed up on his principles by action, training his slaves to read, write, administer his plantation—Briarwood—and run its day to day finances, requiring the slaves themselves to hear and try cases and to decide on punishments, and absolutely forbidding whipping or flogging as forms of punishment. During the war, the Davis family adopted a little boy of mixed black and white parentage—"Jim Limber" or James Henry Brooks - out of an abusive family relationship. (Q.v. Felicity Allen, *Jefferson Davis: Unconquerable Heart* [Columbia: University of Missouri Press, 1999, ISBN 0-8262-1219-0], pp. 6, 373-374.)

Unitarian lines, and so on; and (3) a "demonized" and "evil" enemy (the slave-holding South) against which to practice "nation-building," in the guise of "reconstruction." Thus were the modern American template of imperialistic "nation-building" and its moralizing justifications born in, and nurtured by, the War Between the States.

The War Between the States is thus not simply a "unit" in a history class or graduate school elective for it permanently altered and shaped the American culture and character, both for good and ill, and through it, the wider world influenced by America. For the deeper and deepest players and layers that fought it, it constituted a template for political action, social engineering, and a road map to the acquisition and maintenance of power. In its preparation, ending, and aftermath one finds the real founding of the American Empire, and its template of geopolitical action ever since in its "defenses of democracy," moralizing vilification of an enemy, asset seizure (through a variety of byzantine and in many cases barbaric and cruel means), and "nation-building."

No one seems to have noticed the unpleasant fact that the assassination of Mr. Lincoln's reconstruction policies and the failure of his luckless and bumbling successor, Tennessee Democrat Andrew Johnson, to enact them drove the southerner, both black and white, into decades of mutually crippling poverty, depredation, mutual recriminations and bigotry, and a host of "Jim Crow" laws administered by a superintending (and very *un*reconstructed) plutocracy and oligarchy, the center of which was headquartered in New England but whose tentacles reached far and wide into "elsewhere."

It's that "elsewhere" that is the *other* central and highly speculative theme of this book, a book which I fully intended to do after completing *The Rialto in Richmond,* when it became apparent that some of the threads, questions, and indicators that I had literally stumbled over in the writing of that book deserved a fuller exposition. Those threads, questions, and indicators may be conveniently summarized as a series of questions that this book intends to raise, and to answer, even if only as speculation:

1) Is it true that the reconstruction policies of President Andrew Johnson were more or less those of Abraham Lincoln?
2) If so, then why would the alleged Radical Republican component of the conspiracy responsible for President Lincoln's murder and the attempted murder of his Secretary of State William Seward not have attempted to assassinate Johnson as well?
3) What role does the little-known Hampton Roads peace conference at the end of the war, between Union President Lincoln, his Secretary of State William Seward, and the Southern delegation led by Confederate Vice President Alexander Hamilton Stevens, play in these assessments?
4) A related question to the previous point is this: what, if any, role might the Hampton Roads conference between Lincoln and Stephens have played in Jefferson Davis' flight from Richmond and his abortive "Continuity of Government" operation?[5] And what might this, in turn, have to do with the geopolitical scheme being discussed at Hampton Roads to bring the war to an end?

---

[5] Q.v. Joseph P. Farrell, *The Rialto in Richmond: the Money War Between the States and Other Mysteries of the Civil War* (Kempton, Illinois: Adventures Unlimited Press, 2025), pp. 50-60f.

5) What details in the Dahlgren Raid might point to hidden players in the high stakes drama playing out in the final months of the war?
6) Why do end-of-war covert operations all seem to come to a common point of contact in John Wilkes Booth, and, more importantly, in Montreal, Canada? Does that Canadian connection have anything to do with the British and European subscribers to the Erlanger Cotton Loan bonds of the Confederacy? Was British Chancellor of the Exchequer William Gladstone *really* involved? If so, to what extent does that involvement reflect or indicate a semi-official position of the Britsh government?
7) What, if anything, might the hypothesized European financial connection to the Confederacy have to do with Reconstruction of the southern "Opportunity Zone"? Are there *any* indicators that Chancellor von Bismarck's apocryphal statements about the European financial powers being behind the American Civil War might in fact be true? And if so, what are they?
8) Were these same hidden financial operators active covertly *before* the war, and did their activities deliberately precipitate the war? Might these operators have been active in the financial and political schemes of the "Secret Six," the financiers behind the terror campaigns of radical abolitionist John Brown and his murderous raids in Kansas and Harpers' Ferry? And finally,
9) Is there any indicator that there *is* a reason to suspect that there is a "geopolifinance" behind it all? Was that war's "Impresario of Imposture" merely a very skilled and able swindler and grifter, or does the pattern of his

activities suggest something far different and more sinister?

It will be obvious from careful consideration of the above catalogue of questions that I intend in this book to "view things whole" and to "re-think" the end of the war and its aftermath.

This will become particularly clear once the reader is enmeshed within the body of this work, for it will become evident that each chapter of this book concentrates, though not exclusively, on one or two recent scholarly treatments of the incident or event under examination. The great value of these works lies precisely in their concentration on the event under consideration. But this is also their great weakness, *for as this book argues, it is when only when one views them synthetically, as an interconnected whole, that the pattern and possibilities of a much wider and deeper geopolitical and financial conspiracy with all its players and covert agendas becomes evident. I call this complex interplay of deep players, deep politics, deep geopolitics, and deep finance "geopolifinance."* It is thus to be emphasized that this book is *not* a book of scholarship or "proof" of that wider and deeper conspiracy. It is rather an argued speculation that such a conspiracy remains one possible interpretation of the pattern of evidence presented herein. It thus argues a *prima facie* case, as if before a grand jury. Whether or not to return an indictment, or a "no bill," is entirely up to the reader – the grand jury – to decide.

In addition to being like trying to argue a *prima facie* case before a grand jury, this book is also a bit like an archaeologist trying to make sense of a discovery of strange bones deep within the strata of the earth. From the Radical Republicans and "Congress Reconstruction," to the resulting debacle for race relations and Jim Crow laws, from the debt peonage of the post bellum South, to the hidden players and their financial plunder operations, from the unsuccessful impeachment trial of President Andrew Johnson to the seemingly bottomless corruption of the administrations of Ulysses S. Grant or, even more suggestively, his post-political world travels, from the prewar financial machinations of the radical New England Abolitionists, to the looming geopolitics during the war and its end, to the bewildering array of currency and finance legislation during and after the war, it is all one big fossilized organism, teeth bared in a frozen snarl, that must be carefully reassembled into some sort of skeleton, bone by bone, chapter by chapter. This dissection lies somewhere between forensic autopsy and historiography, for the organism is long dead, and some of the archival bones of proof, if they ever existed at all, are buried still. Notwithstanding these difficulties, every effort is made herein to advance plausible pathologies for its demise. As one digs deeper and deeper into the strata of each chapter, the frightening geopolifinancial fossil within them becomes more apparent.

The plausibility of these pathologies are, again, for the reader to determine, and to determine with as much caution, circumspection, and wisdom as can be mustered. The pathologies are not merely academic, for the eggs laid and hatched from that old organism are with us still, in the form of its long lasting consequences in the templates and formulae of contemporary oligarchical and plutocratic power and geopolitics.

Or to put it much more succinctly, globalogna has very ancient roots, and very perceptible patterns.

Joseph P. Farrell
From Somewhere, 202

New England Calvinist-Puritan Jonathan Edwards, whose famous sermon "Sinners in the hands of an angry God" touched off the first wave of many New England "Revivals." Edwards was a slave-holder.

Part One: Two More Presidents, and the Racket of Reconstruction: (The First Layer)

"Mr. Johnson was so proud of the dignity into which fate had thrust him that he boasted of it in the language of a clown and with the manners of a costermonger."
—The London Times

"Two weeks after assuming office, President Grant signed the first bill Congress sent him, which became the Public Credit Act.... Specifically, the act pledged to redeem the Civil War public debt in gold although nearly all holders of such bonds (including Grant) purchased them with paper currency..."
—Philip Leigh,
The Failed Presidency of U.S. Grant, pp. 44-45

Andrew Johnson,
Seventeenth President of the United States
And First Post-Bellum President

2
RIGGING JOHNSON'S JURY

"And then there was Johnson himself. For many Northerners, his most basic qualities made him seem unworthy of the presidency at that moment in history. He was a Southerner, but the South had lost the war. He was a Democrat, but that party had not supported the war. He defended states' rights theories that had supported secession and civil war. He was rigid and angry, unwilling to compromise, at a time when the nation had to be united. And many thought of him as a drunkard. It was a ruinous combination."

David O. Steward[1]

ON MARCH 4, 1865, THE SOON-TO-BE NEW VICE PRESIDENT of the United States of America, Democrat Andrew Johnson of Tennessee, walked—or rather, more probably *wobbled*—to a podium inside the U.S. capitol building to take the oath of office. It is, however, somewhat of a misnomer to label him a "Democrat," since he was a calculated part of President Abraham Lincoln's effort to reach out to northern and southern Democrats in the crucial 1864 election, and retain office. Accordingly, the name of the Republican Party was changed to the "Union party" for the election and Lincoln reached across the political divide to secure a second term in office, a term during which he and other Union leaders fully expected to see the end of the war.

The 1864 election was itself by no means a foregone conclusion when the year began. Both belligerents' populations were increasingly restive and tired of the war,

---

[1] David O. Stewart, *Impeached: The Trial of President Andrew Johnson & the Fight for Lincoln's Legacy* (New York, Simon and Schuster, 2009), p. 73.

and peace feelers had already been initiated by both sides. For the Union in particular, the high casualties of ever more costly and bloody campaigns only intensified the desires for peace. The early campaigns of 1864 added further fuels to the peace fires. Confederate General Robert E. Lee consistently stymied Union General Ulysses S. Grant's numerically superior forces in the Wilderness campaign in Virginia, while the armies of the equally capable Joseph Johnston slowed, and sometimes halted, Union General William Tecumseh Sherman's army's slow crawl toward Atlanta.

The Confederacy, in other words, was down, but definitely not out. Indeed, the slow military progress and the failure of superior Union forces to deal any decisive blows against Johnston and Lee was a crucial factor in the political and military calculus of 1864. Mr. Lincoln needed a clear and decisive return to power in the election. In order to achieve that, he needed clear, visible, and decisive progress on the battlefields. The decision was taken to wage a total war of attrition and logistics, to literally bleed the Confederate armies white. There was not much tactical or strategic finesse or nuance in such a strategy, but it played to the Union's strengths and the Confederacy's weaknesses. The Union could afford thousands of casualties per battle; the Confederacy could not.

Lincoln was not aided by his own track record of managing the war. For most civilians in the Union, Lincoln's search to find a general capable of commanding the Army of the Potomac was a recent memory, and he had tried nearly everything and every*one* without much success: McDowell, McClellan, Burnside, Hooker. Even Meade, who had won the Battle of Gettysburg, could not convert that victory into a rigorous pursuit of Lee. Worst of all, McClellan, a northern Democrat, had led the Army of the Potomac in 1862, and urged the policy of attritional and logistical warfare even then, and begged Lincoln for the supplies and manpower to do so. Lincoln, his war department under the ever-dubious Edwin Stanton, and some in the Northern press, denounced McClellan as too slow and cautious, forgetting that McClellan had actually handed the Union its first "victory" against Lee at Antietam, and providing Lincoln with the opportunity to promulgate his Emancipation Proclamation. McClellan was replaced by Burnside, and then Hooker, who handed the Union two of its bloodiest and worst defeats in 1863 at Fredericksburg and Chancellorsville. And while Grant proved capable of beating Lee, the public perception was that he could only do so by the tactical expedient of throwing lots of men and material at him.

All of this was recent memory in early 1864, and all of it played against Lincoln's hopes for re-election, especially since the nominee of the northern Democrats was likely to be the very same General George Brinton McClellan, which eventually it was.

The political calculus that brought Lincoln—and Johnson—to power in 1864's elections was thus a delicate one, one calculated upon Union victories in the field, a direct and open appeal to Northern Democrats (and an implied appeal to Southerners) via Johnson's presence on the ticket, and a quietly advocated policy of a lenient peace. [2] When Sherman handed Lincoln the capture of Atlanta in September of that year, the delicate nature of the political calculus

---

[2] Lincoln had dropped his first term vice president, Hannibal Hamlin, from the ticket in order to reach across the aisle of partisan politics to embrace Johnson on the ticket, and had thus used his presence to re-brand the Republican Party as the "Union" party, in an attempt to shed the "sectionalist" perception of the Republicans as an exclusively north-eastern industrial, radical abolitionist, and railroad party. The change was also necessitated, in Lincoln's and some of his advisors' minds, by the need to appeal to a non-sectional politics, one emphasizing national and cultural unity.

suddenly changed because a Union victory now seemed all but certain.

Lincoln was voted overwhelmingly back into office for a second term, while McClellan carried only the few northern slave states that had remained in the Union. Lincoln, who by December of 1862 was also advocating openly in Congress for a policy of compensated manumission of slaves, and his "lenient" policy of southern Reconstruction, seemed to be on track to accomplish both.

Consequently a mood of sober optimism prevailed in the inauguration ceremonies of 1865, and Johnson, the lone southern senator in 1861 to vote against his state's secession, and to remain in the Union, and who had been the Union's military governor of occupied Tennessee since 1862, was a contributing factor to the election victory of 1864. Johnson thus had a certain cachet in the Union as the Southern Democrat who had remained loyal and not joined the rebellion. That very same cachet would soon turn against him.

But on March 4, 1865, when he entered the Senate chamber to take the oath of office, it quickly became clear to the assembled senators and cabinet members that the new vice president had been "celebrating," for as Johnson stood—one may assume somewhat uneasily—to address (or rather, to harangue) them, he began by denouncing both his boss, Abraham Lincoln, and himself as being nothing but "plebeians," and, moreover (Johnson drawled) he, a Tennessean, was proud of it. Then, turning to the cabinet members, he addressed each one individually, reminding them that their power came from the people. When he came to the Secretary of the Navy, however, he could not remember his name.

The whole miserable and shabby performance was, fortunately, blotted out by Lincoln's inaugural address with its memorable lines: "with malice toward none, with charity toward all…to bind up the nation's wounds." But some were not having it. Michigan Senator Zachariah Chandler, a radical Republican whom we shall encounter later in this book, wrote his wife that "The Vice President was too drunk to perform his duties (and) disgraced himself (and) the Senate by making a drunken foolish speech."[3] The *London Times* had a reporter on the scene who recorded the performance with no attempt to play down the enormous gaffe: "All eyes were turned," he wrote,

> to Mr. Johnson as he started, rather than rose, from his chair, and, with wild gesticulations and shrieks, strangely and weirdly intermingled with audible stage whispers, began (his) address…. (Johnson's) behavior was that of an illiterate, vulgar, and drunken rowdy, and could it have been displayed before any other legislative assembly in the world, would have led him to his arrest by the sergeant-at-arms…. Mr. Johnson was so proud of the dignity into which fate had thrust him that he boasted of it in the language of a clown and with the manners of a coastermonger.[4]

David O. Stewart, who wrote the most recent and perhaps most valuable examination of President Johnson's record and impeachments and whose work on Johnson's three impeachments we shall follow closely here, observed that Johnson's performance on the day of his inauguration forever damaged him to the extent that whenever he made a strong, or controversial statement, "many assumed he had been drunk."[5]

---

[3] David O. Stewart, *Impeached: The Trial of President Andrew Johnson and the Fight for Lincoln's Legacy* (New York: Simon and Schuster, 2009, ISBN 978-1-4165-4749-5), p. 11.

[4] Ibid. I am reminded of the screaming fist-pounding, and red-wrapped harangues of a recent Democratic avatar president.

[5] Ibid., p. 12.

Drunk or not, however, Johnson was still the Vice President, a member of Mr. Lincoln's administration, and all the delicate political and military calculus that put him into that position would change again—dramatically—when Lincoln was murdered a little more than a month later, on April 14, 1865, leaving Johnson, a Southern Democrat, who had remained alone among all Southern U.S. Senators loyal to the Union, former Military Governor of Tennessee, thrust suddenly and unexpectedly into the summit of American executive power as the heir and executor of Lincoln's reconstruction policies for the South. The very calculus that worked to re-elect Lincoln and endorse his policies, would thus now work *against* Johnson and his efforts to enact them, at least, they would as far as the Radical Republicans in Congress, and their powerful ally in the War Department, Edwin Stanton, would have it. They would try no less than three times to bring articles of impeachment against him to prevent him from carrying them out.

Behind these efforts, like the rings or layers of an onion, are ever deeper and more hidden players, agendas, and motivations, and all of them are financial, and geopolitical. And Andrew Johnson's blighted presidency is both the locked door concealing, and the key to open and reveal, them.

A. A Brief Introduction to the Principals of the First Layer.

1. The Basic Political Problem of Reconstruction

In order to understand the political and financial machinations surrounding "reconstruction," one need only understand one simple thing, the simple thing that set all those political and financial machinations—and ultimately racial tensions—into motion. This was the fact that the war brought an end to the 3/5ths apportionment rule of the Philadelphia Constitution of 1787-89. That end posed a significant, almost insurmountable, problem for the northern Republicans, and particularly for the radical abolitionist wing of the party. That wing, after all, was the wing that brought Lincoln into power, and that wing also represented the majority position of his own cabinet. The problem was that the original constitution defined the slaves held in the slave states as "3/5ths" of a person for the purpose of deciding the representation of those states in the House of Representatives and the presidential electoral College. It was a purely political calculation, but, by the standards of that time, a necessary one, for if on the one hand slaves were not to be regarded as full persons in law, then this would artificially reduce the population of southern states to their freed white and black men, while at the same time making the slave owner responsible for the feeding, clothing, and housing of his slaves. It would thus place an undue economic and political burden on those states while simultaneously and artificially reducing the political power of those states below the actual reality. Conversely, if the slaves were to be considered full persons, yet without any political franchise, then this would artificially *elevate* the political power of those states and the slave-holding oligarchies running them out of proportion to the reality.

Thus the compromise of the "3/5ths" apportionment rule was adopted at the Philadelphia constitutional convention and later ratified by the states ratifying that constitution: slaves would count as 3/5^{ths} of a person for the purposes of population counts, representative apportionment, and the electoral college, yet, this same fiction of quantization would assure that recognition as "full persons" in law, and therefore, a franchise, was not included.

This in turn highlights precisely the problem posed by the policies of postwar "reconstruction" of the South. If, on the one hand, one advocated full emancipation—which

Lincoln had decreed and later insisted upon—this meant that the franchise for freed blacks and former slaves would result in higher population counts for the former states of the Confederacy, their delegations would be returned to the federal congress *with even more representation in the U.S. House of Representatives than they had before their secession.* Moreover, this also meant that the same southern Democratic oligarchs would emerge as the de facto controllers of the only party machinery in the South, and thus perhaps even able to manipulate the new incoming bloc of black voters, many of who remained, to the Yankee North, "inexplicably loyal" to their former owners. The way to *break* this looming relationship and political problem was to view the southern free population—both white and black[6]—as a *conquered* population subject to military rule and jurisdiction, and ipso facto, as disenfranchised. Thus the newly emancipated black population was to be enfranchised, promoted to political power, and be secured and maintained by Union occupying military forces, while the Southern white population was treated as a conquered and *dis*enfranchised people. This, in fact, was the "solution" advocated by the Radical Republicans, and it was this solution that Johnson resisted.

The clash that would determine the course of American politics in the second half of the nineteenth century was thus inevitable, and about to begin.

That this formula is a recipe not only for disaster but for exacerbation—if not outright sewing—of racial tensions in

[6] To the modern mind—so badly propagandized as it has been—the notion of free blacks in the ante-bellum South seems like a complete fiction. While there were few such freed black people, they nonetheless existed in, for example, Louisiana and Virginia. While not much remembered today, the first victim of John Brown's murderous raid on Harper's Ferry, Virginia, and for which he was apprehended (by Robert E. Lee!) and eventually tried and hung for murder, was a freed black man.

the post-bellum South between blacks and whites is a given. As we saw in the previous volume of this series, *The Rialto in Richmond*, President Lincoln proposed a *compensated manumission* policy to the Union congress in December of 1862. In other words, the slaves were to be freed, and presumably, some form of assistance provided to them for land, equipment, and education to allow them to be self-sustaining and productive, and their former owners also compensated for loss of lands and labor. What actually happened during the course of Johnson's administration, however, was that the plan of compensated manumission was—at best—lost in all the political machinations surrounding Johnson's impeachments and the seemingly endless clashes with the Radical Republicans over the direction and scope of post-war Southern reconstruction. With one large exception, what resulted was emancipation without any compensation for anybody, a situation that drove both blacks and most southern whites into desperate sharecropping poverty lasting well into the next century, with mutual recriminations as each group blamed the other for their desperate circumstances. But we are getting ahead of ourselves, and must return to the other aspect of this post-war problematic of reconstruction policy and politics: the Politics of the "Bloody Shirt."

2. The Radical Republican Abolitionists and the Politics of the Bloody Shirt

a. Features of Radical Republicanism

When dealing with this period of American political, cultural, and financial history one often encounters the label "Radical Republicans" to designate a certain class of political player—whether an office holder or not—united more or less around a certain constellation of ideas. Oftentimes this label is used by scholars of various tendencies, without much attempt to summarize just exactly what constitutes a "Radical Republican" (or a "Radical Republican abolitionist") of that era. Throughout this book, I will continue to use the familiar term since it has acquired the characteristic of a stable name or feature in most scholarship of the period. For our purposes here, however, I intend "Radical Republican" or "Radical Republican Abolitionist" to mean a combination of one or more of the following agendas, motivations, or policies:

1) In the pre-bellum period, a total and complete abolition of all slavery and enfranchisement as soon as possible and without regard to any effects or consequences on the populations concerned, whether former slaves or slave owners, i.e., the "purely moral" approach of uncompensated manumission;
2) In the pre-bellum period, a willingness to finance or pursue the above agenda by the promotion of violence, terror, and violent *agents provocateur* such as John Brown;
3) a willingness in the post bellum period to pursue similar objectives without consideration of the long-term effects on the populations concerned;
4) a willingness in the post bellum period to pursue the "purely moral" solution of uncompensated manumission; and/or,
5) a willingness to regard the defeated states of the Confederacy and their populations as conquered territories, conquered peoples, and thus subject to military jurisdiction, and their leaders as having committed treason and subject to the full penalities thereof, i.e., death by hanging; and

6) a willingness to promote newly enfranchised blacks to political office and power in spite of any competency for office, and in some cases over the objections of their own leaders;
7) a willingness to promote the interests of freed black populations and leaders over those of local Indian or white populations and leaders,

and so on. That such policies are bound to produce resentments in both southern white and black populations not only toward each other, but toward their conquerors, should be evident. *Why* such manifestly self-destructive policies should eventually have been pursued suggests that there may have been "hidden hands" at work in the policies of Southern "reconstruction," an hypothesis that will become increasingly clear as the layers of the onion are peeled back and exposed.

b. The Politics of the "Bloody Shirt"

The fact that Abraham Lincoln was assassinated on Good Friday, April 14, 1865, and died the following Holy Saturday morning, gave control of the first reactions to the news to the clergy throughout the Union, and as a result, the role of Lincoln as a kind of secular savior and martyr was quickly emphasized, to become a component of the American civil religion ever after:

> It so happened in this "unfolding web" of history that because Lincoln was shot on Good Friday and died on Saturday morning, the clergymen in Sunday sermons had first opportunity to express and mold public opinion, and the newspapers on Monday, in widely spreading the preachers' gospel, let themselves be guided by the men of God. It was Easter Sunday the sermons were preached, the great feast day of the Christian calendar. Never did pulpits

> consecrated to the Prince of Peace take on grimmer aspect than on this Easter Day of 1865. Not the Christ of sacrifice and forgive-ness but the God of righteousness and vengeance was preached to a saddened people.[7]

With this comment, one must again pause and take note of circumstances that can be interpreted in one of two ways, either (1) as an unfortunate yet predictable circumstance, as is the interpretation suggested by the quotation above, or (2) one may view it against the backdrop of a wider conspiracy. In the latter respect, it must be remembered that virtually the entire Union press was under the watchful and controlling eye of the Union Secretary of War, Edwin Stanton. When Mr. Lincoln announced his intention to attend the play that evening in the company of Mr. and Mrs. Ulysses Grant, the Union's victorious general,[8] it was the perfect opportunity to "shape the narrative," for even without direct and covert influence, the predominantly abolitionist clergy of the North could be counted upon to craft a narrative beneficial to those opposed to Lincoln's more lenient reconstructionist inclinations.

The effect of the assassination, in other words, dug the Radical Abolitionists in like ticks, deep into the body politic of the North, cloaking their extreme reconstruction policies with the robes of morality and righteousness:

> The great body of Northern clergymen passed through the experience to a result disastrous to any hope of

---

[7] Paul H. Buck, *The Road to Reunion, 1865-1900* (Boston: Little, Brown and Company, 1907), p. 12. Buck's work, while now over a century old, is a very worthwhile cultural study of the effects of reconstruction policies and the decades of "bloody shirt" politics that followed.

[8] Q.v. the previous volume in this study, *The Rialto in Richmond* (Kempton, Illinois: Adventures Unlimited Press, 2025), pp. 112-120.

> reconciliation. The defeat of the South came more than ever to signify a moral victory. The ability to understand, much less to sympathize, with the problems of Southern life grew more impossible.[9]

While this process of transforming the Abolitionist and Radical Republican cause into a kind of "secular righteousness" was well under way before the Southern secession and resulting war, the assassination of Lincoln sealed the process in a way that the hypocritical "martyrdom" of John Brown and his murderous raids could not.[10] In a peculiar fashion, the northern and Radical Abolitionist cause thus became identified with the Republican Party, to such an extent that writers like James Russell Lowell argued that the South must be swiftly, and forcibly, "Americanized" with the spread of Northern institutions.[11] Whatever the South had been *prior* to the war, it was not, on Lowell's view, genuinely "American."

It was in this crucible of the cultural reaction to the assassination, combined with the political realities engendered by the emancipation and the collapse of the 3/5ths apportionment rule that the politics of the "Bloody Shirt" was born, for if the Republican North stood to lose political power to a Southern bloc in congress, should the southern apportionment be calculated on the basis of both black and

---

[9] Paul H. Buck, *The Road to Reunion*, p. 14.

[10] As is my habit while writing books, during the writing of this chapter I was listening to a well-known national "conservative" talk radio show, and the hosts—who should have known better—repeated the "narrative" of the "martyred" John Brown and how he hastened the cause of abolition and freeing the slaves. Utterly unmentioned in this invocation of a secular saint was the fact that the first man murdered by Brown's raid on Harpers' Ferry was a freed Black Virginian. His name was Heyward Shepherd.

[11] Buck, op. cit., p. 23.

white southern populations, that very same *cultural* attitude provided a basis to sidestep and offset the implications. One had merely to "wave the bloody shirt" and remind the North that hundreds of thousands of "Billy Yanks" had died in the war to restore the Union and free the slaves. A return to the status quo *ante bellum* should accordingly be unthinkable to any loyal "American" (of the Lowell school).

Indeed, the chief waver of the bloody shirt at the beginning of 1866, less than a year into the wobbly Johnson administration, was none other than his inherited Secretary of War, Edwin Stanton, who continued to seek the conviction of Jefferson Davis, accusing him of having plotted the assassination of Lincoln, and murdering "Union prisoners of war by starvation and other barbarous and cruel treatment."[12] Of course, while Stanton was trying to maneuver Davis to the trap door on a gallows publicly, he was equally trying to avoid ever having to put Davis to a trial where he would be able to mount his own defense. The additional problem was that, even had Davis been guilty of the things Stanton was accusing him, the only result would have been to make Davis a martyr, and to solidify even more deeply the sectional strife and divisions of reconstruction.[13]

The politics of "the Bloody Shirt" were consequently less about "justice" then about maintaining the sectional disunity of the country, and maintaining the Republicans in power. As a result, the politics of "the Bloody Shirt" became a consistent underlying feature of post-bellum politics until long after the war had ended, at least to the beginning of the twentieth century if not much further. Paul H. Buck very aptly summarizes the binary and dualistic nature of the

---

[12] Paul H. Buck, *The Road to Reunion*, pp. 50-51.

[13] Ibid., p. 52.

political and cultural dilemma of American politics in the post bellum nineteenth century:

> The Republican party was born in strife on issues that won support only in the North. The tactics of the party had always been to appeal on strictly sectional lines to the numerically stronger portion of the Union, realizing that there were electoral and Congressional votes enough in a united North to control the national government. It was a party of sectional-consciousness. As such it operated to split asunder the fabric of national life….
>
> …
>
> Thus it became the interest of the Democratic party to "forget" the war and to patch up quickly a truce which would re-admit their Southern allies to the political contest. But it was equally important to Republicans that the past be not forgotten and that a reunion which would increase the strength of their opponents should be postponed. The process of reconciliation was fatefully involved in this counterpurpose of party aims. When one party recommended peace it seemed as though it was prostituting a nation's interests for selfish ends. When the other party clung to the memory of past feuds hatred and suspicion lingered longer than conditions warranted.[14]

Johnson, as Lincoln's 1864 "Union" party running mate, and a Southern Democrat who had voted *against* his state's secession and remained loyal to the Union, thus became the heir and executor of Lincoln's reconstruction policy, and though for a short period he seemed to be on board with the Radical Republicans in Congress and their "reconstruction-by-retribution" agenda, he eventually broke with Congress, and set up not only his own three impeachment crises, but the politics of the Bloody Shirt.

---

[14] Paul H. Buck, *The Road to Reunion*, pp. 72-73.

For the Radical Republicans in the Congress, the principals in the unfolding drama—the Benjamin Wades, Zechariah Chandlers, Charles Sumners, Thaddeus Stevens, Benjamin Butlers, and George Julians—it was they, and not Democrat Andrew Johnson, who were the true heirs of the "spirit," of the mind and mentality and policies, of Abraham Lincoln. "The Reconstruction program originated by the Radicals became the test of party loyalty with hatred of the white South and distrust of Democrats as fixed tenets of the creed."[15]

The result of these creedal tenets was that Congress, through their ally in the executive, Secretary of War Edwin Stanton, took control of Reconstruction and wrested it from the hands of Johnson, setting up an immediate post-war constitutional crisis that would tarnish the entirety of his administration, and determine the course of American culture, finance, and politics for the rest of the century. Once again

> ... the North sent its armies into the South, this time to overthrow the moderate Reconstruction governments established under the auspices of Lincoln and Johnson, and to rule by martial law until new structures based upon Negro rule and directed by Republican cheiftans might make a conquest of the Southern spirit. The result was a disorder worse than war, and oppression unequaled in American annals.
>
> Yet the North continued to cherish a belief in its own supposed leniency. The record of having taken no lives in execution and virtually no property in confiscation as punishment for the "crimes of treason and rebellion" was pointed to with pride.[16]

---

[15] Paul H. Buck, *The Road to Reunion*, p. 87.
[16] Ibid., pp. 24-25.

And in the meantime, if it could not bring Jefferson Davis to the gallows, it could get Southerner Andrew Johnson removed from the White House, and install one of their own, the Radical Republican Senator from Ohio, Benjamin Franklin Wade, who, as president pro tempore of the Senate, would succeed him by the laws of the day.

If there were hidden intrigues and covert and occulted hands at work in splitting the country to begin with, it was almost as if they were continuing to operate.

3. The Principals of the Three Impeachments

So we must now take a look at who the principals in that unfolding drama were, for in what now follows, it would be useful for the reader to have a "face" to attach to the character in the narrative.

Secretary of War Edwin Stanton,
Whose role in the Lincoln Assassination remains suspicious; President Andrew Johnson inherited him from Lincoln, and his efforts to force Stanton's Resignation played directly into the hands of the Radical Republicans, their attempts to control Reconstruction, and to get rid of Johnson

Judge Advocate General Joseph Holt
Led the military tribunal that convicted and hung four Lincoln conspirators, and who attempted to aid Stanton. As will be seen in subsequent chapters, as another Radical Republican, he actively and knowingly suppressed evidence and possibly suborned perjury

Radical Republican Abolitionist Pennsylvania Congressman Thaddeus Stevens; he led the House of Representatives' three impeachment efforts against President Andrew Johnson, and was part of the House's seven managers of Johnson's impeachment trial in the Senate. He played an active role in drafting the articles of impeachment for all three impeachment efforts against Johnson.

Union General Benjamin F. Butler in uniform; Another Radical Republican, Butler became one of the House's chief prosecutors during Johnson's impeachment trial in the Senate.

The House Impeachment Managers' Delegation to Johnson's Senate Impeachment Trial;
Benjamin Butler (R- Massachusetts), and Thaddeus Stevens (R-Pennsylvania) are seated on the left, and behind them, standing between them, is Iowa representative James Wilson. The other are, seated, Thomas Williams (R-Pennsylvania, next to Thaddeus Stevens), and on the right, John Bingham (R-Ohio). Standing in the center is George Boutwell, (R-Massachusetts) and on the right, John Logan (R-Illinois)

Republican Senator Hiram Revels of Mississippi, first black U.S. Senator; originally from South Carolina, Revels was highly educated in theology, and was one of the early post-war black leaders calling for a more sane and rational and less vengeful reconstruction policy than the Radical Republicans and predicted the racial tensions the radical policy would cause. His pleas went largely and sadly unheeded.

Stanton loyalist Major Thomas Eckert ran the War Department cipher and telegraph room. As was seen in The Rialto in Richmond, *it was Eckert whom Lincoln requested as his security on the night of his assassination, and whose services Stanton denied; it was Eckert who personally stood guard over convicted assassin Lewis Paine/Powell, and who will appear again and again in the current book in a variety of dubious and suspicious circumstances.*

Union Colonel Lafayette Baker, Stanton's police, intelligence, and counter-intelligence chief. Like Eckert, he appeared in The Rialto in Richmond *and reprises his role in the current book.*

Radical Republican power broker and Michigan Union Senator Zachariah Chandler, Lincoln's Campaign manager before the war, Chandler was a key leader of the Senate opposition to Johnson, and, tellingly, President Ulysses S. Grant's Secretary of the Interior

Radical Republican and Ohio U.S. Senator Benjamin Franklin Wade. As president Pro Tempore of the Senate, he was next in line for the Presidency after Johnson by the law of that time. His "patriot" credentials included an ancestor that had fought in the American Revolutionary War at the Battle of Bunker Hill. Nonetheless, Wade was controversial, and some did not want Johnson convicted because they did not want a President Wade

*The Usually Unmentioned Principal in the story:
Former Confederate President Jefferson Davis and
Confederate First Lady Varina Howell Davis,
In Montreal Canada ca. 1867-68, at the approximate time of
Johnson's Second and Third Impeachments and trial.*

Radical Republican Abolitionist U.S Senator from Massachusetts, Charles Sumner

Andrew Johnson,
17th President of the United States of America

Waiting in the Wings:
General in Chief,
And The 18th President of the United States of America,
Ulysses S. Grant;
His careful and calculated politics during the tumultuous Johnson Administration kept him out of the crossfire and enabled his ascension to the leadership of the Republican Party.

B. The Three Impeachment Crises

1. The Background to the First Impeachment Crisis: The Suicide Pact of the Metaphysics of the "Indussoluble Union"

If the War Between the States exposed the fundamental flaws in the original Philadelphia constitution of 1787—slavery and its 3/5th apportionment rule among them[17] —the "resolution" by the victory of Union arms exposed new ones, not the least of which was the Lincolnian view of "the Union" as a kind of indissoluble "Roman Catholic marriage" which, once entered, was never to be left no matter what the circumstances. It was a kind of "suicide pact" that states entering it simply had to endure; if a section of the country became infected with lunacy of one form or another, and seized control of the federal government to impose the lunacy on everyone else, there was no recourse but endurance, on the Lincolnian view of "indissoluble marriage." Such a view made an incomprehensible hash of the original treaty with Great Britain that recognized the independence and successful secession of the original colonies from the British Empire, for that treaty was signed with the thirteen colonies, now recognized as states, and moreover, they were recognized specifically, and by name. This, plus the fact that some of the states, when ratifying the original Philadelphia constitution, made their relationship with the general government clear by specifying that their ratification could, at any time, be withdrawn and with it, their independence and sovereignty reasserted.[18] These facts were well known to southern polemicists who had no difficulty in asserting the philosophy behind nullification and secession.

---

[17] David O. Stewart, *Impeached: The Trial of President Andrew Johnson and the Fight for Lincoln's Legacy*, p. 1.

[18] Early in the history of the country, it will be recalled, Massachusetts threatened precisely such a secession.

On the other hand, however, whatever one may think about the notions of "indissoluble union" (whether political or marital), the position did have a point, for if on every minor disagreement partners in a union should threaten to walk out, then it was a weak and perhaps even undesirable thing. This problem constitutes the central core difficulty of the constitution of 1787, and it *remains* a difficulty. Settling it by force of arms and imposing one or another view by that means only exposes the unresolved nature of the problem.

Indeed, the conflict between the Radical Republican Union Congress and the Southern Democrat Andrew Johnson nearly tore the country apart once again, within less than half a decade after the "conclusion" of the War.[19] One might even go so far as to say that the impeachments and trial of Johnson were but the continuation of that war by political rather than military means. One need go no further than Johnson's, and the Radical Republicans', views on the nature of the Union than to see that the one, indeed, was attempting to preserve the interpretation of the Union according to the original view of the constitution, that the general government was established by the sovereign states, with the implicit understanding that that grant of general authority could be withdrawn. Johnson, a Southern Democrat, adhered to this view. The Republicans opposing him, on the other hand, "insisted that the Constitution, and the Union, had to change."[20]

All of this occurred against the backdrop of other equally profound arguments over reconstruction policy, and the difficulties caused to Republicans by the collapse of the 3/5ths apportionment rule of the original constitution. They were thus also opposed to Johnson's policy of readmission of southern states to the Union with little to no alteration of their

---

[19] David O. Stewart, *Impeached*, p. 2.

[20] Ibid., p. 3.

state governments. The unresolved nature of the problem is aptly summarized by David O. Stewart in his landmark study of the Johnson impeachments:

> The argument over reconstruction included a central legal disagreement. Radicals contended that the Southern states were conquered territories, or had committed suicide, and thus could be governed by the victorious United States in any way it saw fit. The Constitution gives Congress the power to ensure that each state has a "republican form of government," the Radicals pointed out, and Congress had to do so for the "new" Southern states. (Thaddeus) Stevens, the most determined advocate of radical change, demanded that large Southern plantations be confiscated and distributed to the freedmen….
>
> Johnson, in contrast, embraced the principle that the states were sovereign entities joined in an indissoluble union. He held the metaphysical view that despite the acts of secession and four years of war, the Southern states never left the Union. "There is no such thing as reconstruction," he said six weeks after taking office. "These States have not gone out of the Union, therefor reconstruction is not necessary."[21]

By adopting the Lincolnian view of "indissoluble Union" of "sovereign" states, Johnson was reduced, like some sacred Rota, to maintaining fictions: either the States had never left the Union (in spite of four very bloody years to compel them back into it), or the marriage had never been consummated to begin with, and its appearance was a mere fiction.

Notwithstanding these deeper philosophical impedements, Johnson began his presidency with a record of statements that, initially at least, guaranteed his favor with the Radical Republicans. Ohio senator and President *pro tempore*

[21] David O. Stewart, *Impeached*, p. 18.

of the Senate, Benjamin Franklin Wade, advocated the hanging of a "baker's dozen" Confederate leaders for treason. Johnson objected, and stated that the number should be even more than that, a comment which endeared him to Wade, who actually stated he preferred the new president to Lincoln who had "too much of the milk of human kindness to deal with these damned rebels."[22] Johnson's initial attitude even brought him into conflict with his own General-in-Chief, Ulysses S. Grant, whose lenient terms of surrender to General Lee became a matter of honor for him and of contention with Johnson, who wanted to punish the Confederate military leaders. For Grant, Lee's army would never have surrendered had its soldiers and officers thought they would then be prosecuted for treason.[23]

2. Edwin Stanton Again, and the Refusal to Seat Southern Congressional Delegates

In addition to these philosophical and even metaphysical differences, there is one final factor that contributed to the conflict; after inheriting the remainder of Lincoln's second term in office, Johnson, in need of a secure foundation in the extreme political circumstances he now found himself, asked the entirety of Lincoln's cabinet to stay on. As Secretary of State Seward was still recovering from his

---

[22] David O. Stewart, *Impeached*, p. 16f.

[23] Lest it be forgotten, on the southern view, secession was an inherent and implicit right of states that were really and genuinely sovereign, and therefore, in the exercise of a right there could be no treason. It could be argued that the imposition of the idea of "indissoluble Union" was *ex post facto* and therefore legally questionable at the very least. Such basic arguments underscore much of the early pages of Jefferson Davis' memoir, *The Rise and Fall of the Confederate Government,* wherein he outlines the legal arguments and thinking of southerners prior to the secession.

injuries sustained in the assassination conspiracy against him and Lincoln on that terrible Good Friday of 1865, this meant that he was reliant upon the much more radically-inclined Secretary of War, Edwin Stanton.[24]

The situation soon exploded, and in a most peculiar manner. With the passage of the thirteenth amendment and the abolition of chattel slavery, as was seen, the result was that four million freed blacks were now counted as full persons, and state apportionment, which would be decided on that basis, now meant that the restored southern states would have 28 more congressmen and electoral college votes than they had in 1860 when they seceded! Needless to say, for "many Northern politicians, this outcome seemed completely outrageous."[25] Oddly, it was Johnson who seemingly rescued the Radical Republicans by insisting that the southern states, and not the general government, had the right to determine how freedmen were able to exercise that franchise.[26] Indeed, he had endorsed Stanton's "North Carolina" plan for the readmission of that state to the Union: he (the president) would appoint a governor for the state; that governor would in turn call a constitutional convention for the state, draft a constitution outlawing slavery and rescinding secession.[27]

In effect, what Johnson's approach meant—even if it was following a plan drafted by Stanton—was that the southern states, left to their own devices and with Johnson's apparent approval, were returning former Confederate leaders to Congress less than a year after the surrender of the last Confederate field armies. For Thaddeus Stevens, Benjamin Wade, Charles Sumner, Zachariah Chandler and other Republican leaders in Congress who called themselves the

---

[24] David O. Stewart, *Impeached,* p. 17.
[25] Ibid., p. 47.
[26] Ibid., p. 19.
[27] Ibid.

"Joint Committee of Fifteen" (its unofficial name) or "The Joint Congressional Committee on Reconstruction"(its official name), it was intolerable, and Thaddeus Stevens, Congressman from Pennsylvania and de facto leader of the group, proposed a simple plan to deal with it. Under the Constitution, each congressional house has the power to decide its members were properly elected and can be seated in the chamber. When the roll was called on Dec. 4, 1865, none of the returning southern congressmen's names were announced, and when they begged to be heard, they were ignored, because they were not seated members of the House of Representatives. A similar ploy was used in the Senate, and to reinforce the outcome, the Congress refused to pay any room and boarding expenses of the unseated southern members, forcing them to leave Washington.[28]

3. Johnson Vetoes the Freedmen's Bureau Bill, and the Joint Congressional Committee on Reconstruction, or "the Committee of Fifteen"

The next step on the road to the first impeachment crisis was Illinois congressman Lyman Trumbull's Freedmen's Bureau Bill. On its own, this bill was a modification of a compensated manumission policy, for it not only reversed the "black codes" of the readmitted southern states, it provided assistance on various legal matters to blacks trying to enforce contracts, own property, arms, or testifying in court. But Johnson who sent a blistering veto message to Congress, and in the aftermath of the refusal of that Congress to seat the southern delegations, the bill was yet another usurpation of state power by the general government, and a case of disenfranchising southern whites. Johnson had only half a point, for "the citizens of the Confederacy had not

[28] David O. Stewart, *Impeached*, p. 43.

voted for him any more than they voted for the congressmen and senators then seated in the Capitol."[29] By this point, the pots on both the executive and congressional burners were beginning to boil, and Johnson had the full measure of what he was dealing with in the Joint Committee of Fifteen, calling it "an irresponsible central directory" that was usurping "nearly all the powers of Congress" and concentrating its legislative powers "in the hands of the few."[30] By invoking the Directory and allusions to the "Committee of Public Safety" of the French Revolution, Johnson was, in effect, calling the Joint Committee of Fifteen and the wider Radical Republican faction a group of Jacobins.

In some respects, Johnson may not have been all that far off target with the assessment. Almost alone of the Radical Republicans of the North, Thaddeus Stevens was not afraid to befriend nor to be seen with black people. For others, the cause of freed blacks was more in the nature of an abstraction, useful for politics, but not for the day-to-day realities of life. In the case of Massachusetts Radical Republican Senator Charles Sumner, when someone told General-in-Chief Ulysses S. Grant that Sumner did not believe in the Bible, Grant retorted that it was because Sumner had not written it![31]

In drafting his veto message to Congress for his veto of the Freedmen's Bureau Act, Johnson had relied heavily on Ohio attorney Henry Stanberry, whom he nominated for the Supreme Court when a seat became vacant. Congress retaliated by not only eliminating the seat, but in the same legislation, eliminated the *next* seat when *it* became vacant, reducing the number of seats to seven, and preventing

---

[29] Ibid., p. 50

[30] David O. Stewart, *Impeached*, p. 51.

[31] Ibid., p. 37.

Johnson from making any nominations.[32] It was full scale lawfare, not by court *packing*, but court *reduction*.

> For this cantankerous group of Republicans to pull together, they would have to face a common foe of distressing proportions. In only seven months, Andrew Johnson had transformed himself into just such a figure. The Republicans also would need the leadership of someone with the political skills to pry Johnson's hands from the rudder of the government and then steer the nation in an entirely different direction. Only Thaddeus Stevens could perform that role.[33]

It was through the vehicle of the Committee of Fifteen that Congress not only sought to wrest control of Reconstruction out of the executive's hands, but, through the very same network of alliances and interests that the Committee represented, that the impeachments against Johnson would be mobilized.

4. Johnson's "Union" Party, the Elections of 1866, the Disastrous "Circle Tour," and the Beginning of the Tax and Tariff Reconstruction Racket

It is perhaps a measure of President Andrew Johnson's canny and crafty intelligence as a politician that he viewed the off-year elections of 1866 as an opportunity well-suited to launch a new political party, and remake the character of American politics, diverting it from the morally-confrontational sectional politics of the pre-war and wartime period of "Northern Republicans" vs. "Southern Democrats." Uncomfortable with identifying with the Republicans and

---

[32] Ibid., p. 54.

[33] David O. Stewart, *Impeached*, p. 40.

their radical wing, and yet as the lone Southern Democrat who had voted against secession, Johnson thought the time was right to transform Lincoln's 1864 expedient of the "Union" party, with its deliberate bi-partisan ticket of a Republican Presidential candidate including a Democratic Vice Presidential candidate, into a more permanent party, and thus he chose the 1866 elections as the year to formally launch the Union party, with himself as its head.[34]

The effort also demonstrated Johnson's shrewdness, for his call for a new political party was made to the members of his own cabinet whom—Republicans all—he had inherited from Lincoln. As he fully expected and counted upon, three of them—the postmaster general, the attorney general, and the secretary of the interior—resigned, permitting him to place his own loyalists at the heads of the agencies, and they in turn were able to fill the agencies with more Johnson loyalists.

In the center of Johnson's crosshairs was the collection of taxes. In that era, even though a small income tax had been approved in the Union for war-effort funding, most of the general government's income came from imposts and tariffs, and thus tax and customs houses in the ports, and particularly in New York, were highly sought offices of political patronage, and their use as rewards to loyal supporters was unparalleled since the officer-holder was afforded "plenty of opportunity for graft, both petty and grand."[35] Corruption was part of the system, and enabled it. By targeting the machinery of tax collection, Johnson was delivering to his loyalists all the "spoils of the Republican victory in 1864."[36] This factor, too, will play a huge role not only in the impeachments, but in the subsequent era of Republican rule.

---

[34] David O. Stewart, *Impeached*, p. 59.
[35] Ibid., p. 61.
[36] Ibid., p. 62.

When the "Union party" convention in Philadelphia was held in mid-August of 1866, the carefully planned symbolisms of delegates from Massachusetts linking arms with a delegate from South Carolina fell flat, for the old sectionalisms and party loyalties trumped any ability to hammer out a unifying platform. Johnson abandoned tradition once again, and decided to take his case directly and personally to the American people on a speaking tour, "the Swing around the Circle" or the so-called "Circle Tour" of 1866. With a very reluctant General-in-Chief Ulysses S. Grant, Admiral David Farragut, and Secretary of State William Seward in tow, the party steamed around the mid-Atlantic and mid-western States, from Philadelphia, to New York City, upstate New York, through the mid-west and Ohio Valley, to St. Louis, thence back to Washington.

Johnson, who could be deceptively calm and carefully calculating in private meetings, became a coarse and rough brawler when delivering speeches by torchlight to crowds, and his rhetoric on such occasions took on the flavor of coarse self-aggrandizement and glorification, and extreme vilification of his political enemies. Congress, the Committee of Fifteen and more particularly its de facto leader, Congressman Thaddeus Stevens in his rhetoric on the "Circle tour," was out to destroy the Union. So disruptive were the speeches that after just a few initial stops, staged appearances by opponents shouting questions and challenges were orchestrated in order to goad his rhetoric into "ever more strident pronouncements."[37]

So disastrous was the tour that many Republicans in the North feared that Johnson was attempting to launch another hot war. Ohio Senator John Sherman openly expressed this concern to his brother, General William Tecumseh Sherman, and Radical Republican George

[37] David O. Stewart, *Impeached*, pp. 67-68.

Boutwell of Massachusetts accused the President of conspiring to put southerners in exclusive charge of the general government. Adding fuel to the war-fever flames, Virginia's governor reactivated the state's militia, and requested arms from the federal army for the purpose, the army that was still under the command of Ulysses S. Grant, who, for quite understandable reasons, had profound misgivings about Virginians in arms. He and war Secretary Stanton drug their feet on supplying the arms, while Stanton warned his friends in Congress that both he and Grant were on their guard against an armed *coup d'etat* by the President. Grant even went so far as to write General Philip Sheridan to be on his guard against southern secret military societies and that he feared that Johnson might want to declare Congress "illegal, unconstitutional, and revolutionary" and that the military might have to protect the Union again.[38]

To make matters very much worse, Johnson and his new cabinet members also suspected the very same types of plots and conspiracies were being plotted against them by the radical Republicans in Congress and by the Northern States, organizing Union veterans for an armed march on Washington to unseat the President by force.[39]

5. Edwin Stanton Again, and Thaddeus Stevens

All of the detailed factors of the preceding pages in this chapter now combined to bring Johnson to the first impeachment crisis of his presidency, and that first crisis, in its turn, provided the basic template for the subsequent two.

Johnson could not have been ignorant nor unaware of the fact that the calling card left at his hotel by John Wilkes Booth on the day of his predecessor's assassination centered

---

[38] David O. Stewart, *Impeached*, pp. 69-70.

[39] Ibid., pp. 70-71.

him in the crosshairs of Stanton's attempt to investigate and punish all the alleged conspirators. Indeed, as will be seen subsequently in this chapter, there were powerful indicators that the Secretary of War was trying to tar him with a measure of responsibility and guilt in the event.[40] Nor could Stanton's connection to the Radical Republicans have passed his notice, for if there was one person and one agency in the Johnson administration to thwart its lenient reconstruction policies, it was Stanton and his Department of War, with its deep connections to organs in the northern media.[41] During the crisis that was about to unfold between him and the President, matters were not helped when Stanton made it clear that the nation "was in greater peril with Johnson in office than it ever had been during the Civil War."[42]

After the disastrous defeat of his "Union Party" in the November 1866 elections, 1867 began with a Congressional offensive to hedge in, limit, and ultimately shrink the power of the executive. Letters began to be received at midwestern newspapers calling for Johnson to be removed from office, and one may only suspect that some of these many letters may have been penned by a few individuals recruited for that purpose. We shall have more to say on this technique in our subsequent dealings with the "Impresario of Imposture," but suffice it to say, the idea of a nineteenth century version of an "ad-bot" penning false stories, letters, or comments on an editorial page did not begin with the social media of the twenty-first (or twenty-worst) century!

The Congressional assault was signaled by the attempt to admit two new—and Republican—states to the Union to make their advantage in Congress even more secure, and to

---

[40] David O. Stewart, *Impeached*, p. 65: Stewart states that Stanton regarded Johnson as "at least" a "guilty conspirator."

[41] Ibid., p. 64.

[42] Ibid., p. 66.

provide a bulwark against the eventual return of the southern states' delegations: Nebraska and Colorado. Nebraska made it past Johnson's veto; Colorado did not.

But Congress, and particularly Stanton, were not finished. Stanton invited Massachusetts representative George Boutwell to a confidential meeting at the War Department, where he proposed a typically byzantine and Stantonesque bit of legislation to Boutwell, who was to convey it to the powerful Thaddeus Stevens, who would bring it to the floor of the House. This was a law that would prevent Johnson from issuing military orders that did not go through the military chain of command, i.e., General Grant.

Stevens, for his part, put Stanton's dictated legislation into the military appropriations bill, thus presenting Johnson with the choice of vetoing the bill, and hence not funding the military, and losing massive political support in the north, or not vetoing the bill, and suffering a significant curtailment of his powers as commander-in-chief of the military. Unbeknownst to the President, when he himself asked Stanton for his advice on the bill during a cabinet meeting, he was asking the author of it what he should do! Stanton ambiguously responded that he would approve of whatever course of action Johnson would take.[43]

Congress, in the form of the powerful Pennsylvania Republican representative Thaddeus Stevens, was not yet done trying to hamstring the presidency, for with his allies Stevens had authored and steered a bill to the floor of the House called "The Tenure in Office Act," the act which formed the foundation, core, and principal impetus of all the impeachments against Johnson.[44] Under the terms of the legislation, the United States Senate "would have to concur in

---

[43] David O. Stewart, *Impeached,* p. 75.
[44] Ibid.

the firing of any executive official" whose appointment required Senate consent and confirmation in the first place.[45]

Again, David O. Stewart's summary of the bill, of the logic behind it, and of its effects and implications cannot be bested. Firstly, the legislation addressed an unresolved ambiguity of the original Philadelphia constitution of 1787, for while that document specified what appointees required Senate confirmation, it did *not* indicate who had the power to *remove* them. While the conventional wisdom as indicated in early statutes clearly signaled that it was within the executive power to remove such officials, Steven's legislation was, secondly, effectively arguing that it was within Congress's legislative power to alter the conditions and processes of the removal of officials.

But thirdly, the Stevens and his allies wanted the legislation to cover cabinet appointees, thus effectively arguing that a President could not remove a *cabinet* member without the advice and consent of the Senate, after all, if the advice and consent of the Senate had to be secured for an individual to *become* a cabinet member, the same should hold true for his dismissal. The clear intention of the extension of the measure to cabinet officials was to protect Stanton himself.[46] While many opposed this extension of the measure to cover cabinet officials, arguing that no President should be required "to retain a department head in whom he had no confidence,"[47] and even Stanton himself urged Johnson to veto the bill because it was an unconstitutional limitation of presidential powers, and even though it was designed to protect him from Johnson!

Nonetheless, the law passed over Johnson's veto, with what Stewart characterized as "a perverse result" that allowed

---

[45] David O. Stewart, *Impeached*, p. 76.

[46] Ibid., p. 76.

[47] Ibid.

the President to appoint officials, but not remove them without Senate approval, allowing Johnson's appointees to dig into the bureaucracy of the general government lick ticks![48]

Thaddeus Stevens was nothing else if not a schemer, for buried in the language of the Tenure in Office Act was a deliberately planted and ticking time bomb, because the sixth section of the act stated explicitly that any appointments or removals that *violated* the act were "high misdemeanors," a phrase that intentionally echoed the "high crimes and misdemeanors" phrase of the impeachment clause of the Philadelphia Constitution. With it, Stevens and the Radical Republicans in Congress were warning Johnson, if he tried to remove anyone (namely Stanton, but in reality anyone else the radicals wanted to retain bureaucratic power), he would be impeached.

Even this did not satisfy Stevens, for he pushed, and the rest of the Congress agreed and passed over the next months three acts of reconstruction, the net effects of which were to abolish Johnson's reconstructed state governments along with their "black codes," and restricting the ability of any whites with Confederate ties to participate in the process. In effect, this stage of "congress reconstruction" or "congressional reconstruction" was the exact opposite of what had obtained under Lincoln (toward the end of the war) and Johnson, for whereas these "presidential reconstruction" governments were proto-typical "Jim Crow" governments with white representation and a carefully controlled black franchise, the "congress reconstruction" was almost the exact opposite, with carefully disenfranchised whites, and a carefully cultivated and promoted black political class. And in all this, the legislation also reinforced the controlling and occupying role of the U.S. military in the conquered states.

---

[48] David O. Stewart, *Impeached*, p. 77.

a. The Fuse is Lit: Johnson, Stanton, and Grant

Whatever else he may have been, from coarse self-aggrandizing speechmaker, to self-made states' rights politician and "occasional heavy drinker," Andrew Johnson was not (according to the modern expression) a "lap poodle," and seldom if ever shrank from a fight, or allowed himself to be intimidated from embarking on a course of action he had determined to take.

Johnson's biggest opponents to his agenda were within his own administration: General and war hero Ulysses S. Grant, and Grant's immediate superior, the Secretary of War, Edwin Stanton. Johnson reasoned that Grant, who had already shown that he was capable of defying Johnson's orders regarding federal troops enforcing reconstruction, could be handled if he could get rid of Stanton.[49] Johnson waited for the Congress to adjourn for the summer, when its members were out of Washington to avoid the stifling summer heat and humidity, and then summoned Grant to a private meeting where he informed his General-in-Chief that he intended to demand Stanton's resignation and to dismiss General

---

[49] Grant's immediate subordinate, General Philip Sheridan, was in command of the "congress reconstruction" occupation zone that included the former Confederate states of "Kirby Smithdom," Arkansas, Louisiana, and Texas. Louisiana and Texas had reconstructed their state governments under Johnson's plan, and thus many former Confederates were elected to office and promptly passed laws and procedures making it difficult for newly freed blacks to exercise their rights. Sheridan responded by defying Johnson's reconstructed governments, and by enforcing Congress reconstruction and following Grant's (and presumably Stanton's) orders to disband the new governments, summarily dismissed several officials in Texas and Louisiana, and placed the latter under virtual marshal law until a radical Republican approved black leadership could take power. This time white riots ensued.

Sheridan. Grant, of whom one critic complained that he could "remain silent in several languages,"[50] returned to his office and composed a lengthy written reply to the President, pointing out that removing Stanton would violate the Tenure in Office Act. Johnson, however, had not played his last card. Summoning Grant once again to a private meeting, President Johnson informed his general that he planned to *suspend* Stanton from the exercise of his office until the Senate could reconvene in December, and confirm Stanton's dismissal. In the meantime, Johnson would appoint Grant to be the acting Secretary of War until the Senate could confirm his appointment.[51] At the same time, Johnson also removed Generals Philip Sheridan and Dan Sickles as military governors.

At this juncture it is also necessary to mention that Johnson's removal of Sheridan and Sickles was not only a calculated move against Congress Reconstruction, but that the dismissal of Sickles was a move calculated to be a direct message against Stanton himself, for prior to the War, Stanton had defended Sickles against a charge of murder by arguing—for the first time in American jurisprudence—that Sickles had been temporarily insane when he committed the deed!

b. The First Clue of a Deeper Agenda: Johnson, Grant, and "Kirby Smithdom"

With president Johnson's dismissal of General Sheridan as the military governor of the former states of the Confederacy's Trans-Mississippi Department, or "Kirby Smithdom" as it was nicknamed after the Confederate

---

[50] David O. Stewart, *Impeached*, p. 88.
[51] David O. Stewart, *Impeached*, pp. 94-96.

military governor of the department,[52] we have the first sign or clue that there may be a much deeper agenda at work, one involving that department, for as was seen in the previous volume of this study, *The Rialto in Richmond*, it was to this department that Confederate President Jefferson Davis, along with the archives, reserves, and official seals of the Confederacy, was trying to flee in a nineteenth century version of a "Continuity of Government" operation. Johnson's dismissal of Sheridan virtually eliminated all Union oversight of the very district which, in Davis' planning, was to form a rump Confederacy, for the Union army in Texas had no more than 5,000 men to patrol all of the Rio Grande, and to occupy the entire state![53] This fact alone underscores that the Confederacy shared a significant and open international border with a non-belligerent, and underscores that much of the Confederacy's foreign trade managed to elude the Union blockade via Mexico up to the end of the war. The threat of a "rump Confederacy" was thus a very real one.

This fact brings us to an event between Johnson and Grant that occurred in the background of the President's attempt to dismiss Stanton and replace him with Grant, for prior to this event, Johnson had pursued another tactic to break the Radicals' hold and representation within his administration *by ordering Grant on a diplomatic mission to Mexico and to Benito Juarez's government, which was in the process of overthrowing the French-backed Hapsburg Emperor of Mexico, Maximillian.* Grant declined this assignment, and was ordered, again, to accept the post, this time by Secretary of State William Seward, and again, Grant refused the assignment, stating that as a military officer, he

---

[52] Q.v. Joseph P. Farrell, *The Rialto in Richmond*, pp. 173-188.

[53] David O. Stewart, *Impeached*, p. 35.

could not be ordered on a civilian and diplomatic mission.[54] In Johnson's mind, this plan was intended to remove one of Stanton's key allies from the scene, and at the same time to accomplish two more objectives: ridding Mexico of a puppet regime beholden to a foreign power, and establishing contact with its new government.

As will be seen in a subsequent chapter, Mexico played a significant role not only in Jefferson Davis' Continuity of Government planning, but also in the little-known attempts to end the Civil War by some sort of negotiated peace. Its presence in President Andrew Johnson's reconstruction calculus is a sure and certain indicator that hidden and little-known geopolitical and financial agendas are playing out behind the scenes, as will be seen.

It is worth noting that President Johnson, like his Mexican counterpart, Benito Juarez, was a Freemason, of the higher Masonic degree of Knight Templar, so the possibility of a Masonic connection to these machinations cannot be ruled out. Grant himself, while not a Mason, *was* a member of the Odd Fellows Lodge, another American quasi-secret society with its own Masonic overtones.

---

[54] Ibid., p. 71.

President Andrew Johnson in his Masonic Knight Templar Degree Regalia

Whatever one might make of these possibilities, however, they ultimately pale beside the facts suggesting much deeper and more serious geopolifinancial players that will be explored in the second and third parts of this book.

c. The Second Clue of a Deeper Agenda: Lafayette Baker Implies a Johnson Connection to Jefferson Davis

There is a much more serious indicator, however, of "deep players" and "deep politics" playing out than just Johnson's geopolitical maneuvering vis-à-vis Grant and Mexico, events which in the light of hindsight appear to be "deep events." When Congress reconvened, the House Judiciary Committee, under the urging of Thaddeus Stevens and other Radical Republican members, began to take secret testimony in executive session against Andrew Johnson for the purposes of impeaching the president.

One of the individuals summoned to provide such testimony—no doubt at Stanton's urging—was his chief of police and intelligence, Colonel Lafayette Baker. Baker, well-known and celebrated as the man who had hunted down Lincoln's assassin John Wilkes Booth, testified to the committee that he had actually carried a communication from Johnson to then Confederate President Jefferson Davis. The only problem was, he—Baker—no longer possessed the communication, nor could he remember the date of the communication![55]

As if this were not enough to cast his entire testimony under a very dubious light, Baker went on to state that he had tried to prevent one Mrs. Lucy Cobb—a "disreputable woman"—from visiting the executive mansion because she had disclosed to Baker the President's "secret methods for communicating with 'his friends in the South'" and conducting a lively trade of selling Johnson's presidential pardons to southern leaders! "Having implicated Johnson in treason, bribery, and prostitution without producing evidence of any offense whatever, Baker retired."[56]

But this is not yet all of the second clue, for as the judiciary committee stumbled and fumbled about trying to concoct an impeachment case against Johnson, it "heard testimony that missing portions of John Wilkes Booth's personal diary might have implicated Johnson in the Lincoln assassination"![57] For the reader familiar with the predecessor volume of this study, *The Rialto in Richmond*, this will be seen and understood immediately as an all-but-certain indication of a deep and wide conspiracy involved in Mr.

---

[55] David O. Stewart, *Impeached*, p. 81.
[56] David O. Stewart, *Impeached*, p. 82.
[57] Ibid.

Lincoln's murder, for those missing pages of Booth's diary, as was explained in that volume, eventually *did* turn up, almost a century after the end of the war. They turned up in a set of chested drawers allegedly owned by the former Secretary of War, Edwin Stanton. As if that were not enough, the *transcript* of the missing pages implicated other players in the assassination, namely, the Radical Republican members of Lincoln's own administration and Congress, and *not* Andrew Johnson![58]

This leaves Baker's allegations of a direct and written correspondence from Johnson to Davis. As is evident from a reading of David O. Stewart's recent and excellent study of the Johnson impeachments, Stewart—and for that matter, most other investigators of the matter—have implied that Baker was simply concocting a story, and that there never was such a correspondence. The only written piece of evidence connecting Johnson to the Confederacy was the calling card that Booth left for Johnson at the latter's hotel in Washington on the day of the assassination of Lincoln. The idea of an actual written correspondence between the two ever existing seems highly unlikely…

… *unless* of course such a correspondence was *forged*, and at one time planted or circulated to implicate the President and sew general confusion in a still bitterly divided nation, the very sort of thing *agents provocateur* would do, the very sort of thing that fits the overall pattern of the Impresario of Imposture, as we shall see in a subsequent chapter.

In these circumstances, however, by June of 1866 the first impeachment attempt faltered and sputtered to an

[58] Q.v., Joseph P. Farrell, *The Rialto in Richmond*, pp. 137-172, particularly pp. 162-172 for the alleged transcript of the missing pages.

ignominious end in a vote of 5 to 4 against bringing any articles of impeachment against the President.[59]

d. The Third Clue of a Deeper Agenda: The Second Impeachment Attempt, The Connection to Canada's Confederates, and to the "Impresario of Imposture"

(1)Some Particulars about the "Congress Reconstruction" Acts of the Spring of 1867

Having escaped the first effort to impeach him, an effort that did not even make it out of the Judiciary Committee, Johnson, with his customary genius and flare, proceeded to create controversy and complication for himself and his administration yet again. By the spring of 1867 Congress once again attempted to assert total control over the process of Reconstruction by passing more acts, again over Johnson's veto. These acts stipulated

1) that five military districts would be created over the former states of the Confederacy;
2) that ten former states of the Confederacy excepting Tennessee must ratify the Fourteenth amendment and enfranchise all blacks;[60] and,
3) that the military had broad powers to interpret the laws, oversee elections, including the power to supersede and overturn orders of local and state governments, and to replace any elected official at the local and state level.[61]

---

[59] David O. Stewart, *Impeached*, p. 83.

[60] Stewart observes that this was an extremely hypocritical measure, for in 1867 blacks could only vote the five states of the North that were formally a part of the Union. Q.v. David O. Stewart, *Impeached*, p. 83f.

[61] Ibid.

As Stewart and many other commentators on "congress reconstruction" have noted, the real purpose of the legislation "was to establish state governments in the South that were controlled by the few Southern Republicans and Unionists and the many freed slaves."[62] Or to put it more plainly, the real and ultimate purpose was effectively to *dis*enfranchise southern whites and to exacerbate racial tensions. If indeed there was any potential and covert foreign involvement in creating this situation of racial division and tension, it could not have been better served, as the Southern reaction, both black and white, to the new laws was confusion as both "mingled at political meetings" trying to comprehend the new system. What was wanted were people willing to employ the statutes for the punishment (or plunder) of the South, black *or* white, and if one did *not* accept this agenda, then whether one was black or white, one was excluded from the new "plunderocracy." We have already noted that the Congress' first black member, Mississippi U.S. Senator Hiram Revels, was so disgusted by the whole thing that he would later write to President Grant to complain of it, and to resign from the Republican party with the complaint that reconstruction was sewing misery and racial tension, not resolving it. In 1867, however, it was for Southern Democrat Andrew Johnson to complain of the dangers of the approach in an interview where he stressed that the result of the legislation would be "a war of the races."[63]

---

[62] Ibid., p. 84.

[63] David O. Stewart, *Impeached*, p. 84. That both men proved to be correct to a large extent is manifest by a careful study of the economic results of reconstruction on the South's white and black poor. A book by "southern partisans" James Ronald and Walter Donald Kennedy titled *Punished with Poverty, the Suffering South* (Columbia, South Carolina: Shotwell Publishing, 2020) contains a valuable and truly heart-rending

In any case, as a result of his opposition to the new legislation, President Johnson requested his Attorney General, Henry Stanberry—the same person Congress prevented Johnson from nominating to the Supreme Court by reducing the number of seats on the court—to give a legal interpretation of the powers of the military in the new laws. Predictably, Stanberry gave a narrow interpretation to them, and equally predictably Secretary of War Stanton objected to it. When Johnson acted on Stanberry's opinion, yet a third Reconstruction Act was passed by the Congress, tightening the language regarding the military's power, and restoring the original extent of it.

Johnson vetoed it. Congress overrode the veto.

The House of Representatives began to consider resuming the impeachment hearings, and Thaddeus Stevens, from his powerful perch in the Judiciary Committee, when queried about the possible grounds for such an action, could point to the Reconstruction acts and to Johnson's attempts to undo their clear intention. Johnson had "unlawfully usurped" the "conquered *territory*" (the southern States) and, worse, had "attempted to raise up states therein." This, Stevens thundered with an irony that may have been lost on him, placed Johnson in the ranks of world class usurpers like Oliver Cromwell. As will be seen in a subsequent chapter, Stevens' rhetoric had departed that of Abraham Lincoln by a significant measure and distance, for Lincoln would insist, in his secret peace negotiations with Southern leaders in 1865, upon referring to "our one common country," of which the southern states were a part. In the absence of the "great Emancipator," the rhetoric had decayed to the point of reducing the southern states to "conquered territory" with all that concept and rhetoric implied: a subject population.

---

collection of photographs of the extreme conditions that white and black sharecropping families endured long into the twentieth century.

In the meantime, a new problem had presented itself to the "pro-impeachment" faction of Radical Republicans in the Congress, and this was Representative Stevens himself, or rather, his quickly declining health. Easily the strongest and most capable voice in the House for the impeachment, only Stevens possessed the political muscle and acumen to bring any resolutions to the floor to a vote, and only Stevens, ultimately, could bring any successful House vote to the Senate for trial, and with his declining health time was running out. Conversations with the northern press would reveal the old Stevens "fire," but this could be easily extinguished when he would lapse into incoherence, "leaving him," as *The Boston Post* put it, "more the appearance of a corpse then a living man."[64]

But corpse or not, Stevens managed to steer a new impeachment resolution through the Judiciary committee, which issued three reports on the proposed resolution, a "majority" report recommending the impeachment, a minority report by the Chairman of the Committee, James Wilson of Iowa, whom, as we shall see, was a powerful Republican voice that would argue against the measure on the floor of the full House when it came up for a vote, and a minority report by the two lone Democrats on the Judiciary committee (largely forgotten in the ensuing ruckus).[65] Thus, whatever the faults of the majority report—and there were many as will be seen momentarily—the Committee had finally managed to bring a resolution for impeachment to the full House.

But when the floor debate on the impeachment articles began, it was the chairman of the Judiciary Committee, James Wilson of Iowa, who led the charge against the measure, noting that there was no criminal charge that could be brought against Johnson. The impeachment was being used as a "vote

---

[64] David O. Stewart, *Impeached*, p. 103.

[65] Ibid.

of no confidence,"[66] and as such, Wilson argued in exchanges with Massachusetts representative George Boutwell, who favored impeachment, the process was being dangerously politicized to such an extent that if the precedent of impeachment without any underlying specific crime were established, it could return at some time in the future to afflict a Republican president.[67] The politicization of the process had, moreover, become even more apparent when some Radical Republicans called for the "suspension" of Johnson from the presidency and the appointment of an "acting president" (to be chosen by the Congress, of course) until the impeachment issue had been tried and resolved in the Senate.[68] Chairman Wilson, however, went further.

> Tracing the battle over Reconstruction, he denied that Johnson usurped Congress's powers, making the obvious point that Congress had overridden most of Johnson's vetoes. As for abuse of patronage powers, Wilson noted that Johnson's hirings and firings violated no laws; in fact, they followed the prevailing practices of the preceding fifty years. On pardons for Southerners, the restoration of Southern railroads, and other points, the Iowan countered that the president acted to achieve valid public purposes. Disagreement with the wisdom of a policy, he insisted, could not be the basis for impeachment.[69]

Lacking any specific impeachable crime, the floor vote in the House failed to approve the impeachment resolutions.

---

[66] Ibid., 112.
[67] Ibid., pp. 109-111.
[68] Ibid., p. 107.
[69] David O. Stewart, *Impeached*, p. 106.

(2) Representative James Ashley and the Impresario of Imposture: Charles A. Dunham's and the Canadian Confederate Connection's First Appearance

It was during this second impeachment attempt, however, that another episode occurred, and in it we have the first appearance of the Impresario of Imposture, and with him, the hints of much deeper players perhaps lurking in the background. As the House Judiciary Committee was still taking testimony from witnesses to formulate the impeachment resolution that would be brought to the floor for a vote, it took the testimony of congressman James Ashley of Ohio, himself a Radical Republican and an advocate of the impeachment, conviction, and removal of Johnson from office. David O. Stewart notes that Ashley, in his statements to the Judiciary Committee, "gave testimony that bordered on the delusional."[70] Working quietly with Secretary of War Stanton and his police-detective chief Lafayette Baker to tie Johnson to Jefferson Davis and the conspiracy to kill Lincoln, and to produce enough evidence to try Davis publicly (and not *in absentia* before a military tribunal),[71] Ashley sought out and obtained contact with one of the era's, and indeed, one of the entire nineteenth century's most accomplished grifters and con men, a con man, notes Stewart, "of many names": Charles A. Dunham, Sanford Conover, or James W. Wallace, to name but a few.[72]

It is Charles A. Dunham that I have been referring to in previous pages as "the Impresario of Imposture," and with his appearance here in the context of the impeachment efforts

---

[70] David O. Stewart, *Impeached*, p. 101.

[71] Carman Cumming, *Devil's Game: the Civil War Intrigues of Charles A. Dunham* (Urbana, Illinois: The University of Illinois Press, 2004, ISBN 978-0-252-07519-3), pp. 217-220.

[72] David O. Stewart, op. cit., p. 101.

against Johnson, that we have a potential indicator of deeper agendas and players. While this is not the time nor place to delve in detail into his many and varied exploits which will be done in a subsequent chapter, suffice it to say that with Dunham we are in the presence of a one-man hall of mirrors, and a man with clear connections to *both* sides of the War Between the States, who claimed contact both with Jefferson Davis *and* the Radical Republicans (including Stanton and Baker), *and* to the Confederate cell of operatives, spies, and cotton agents operating in Montreal, Canada. The labyrinth of aliases, forgeries, legends, schemes, scams, and frauds has been interpreted by most scholars who have taken the time to mention or examine his career as indicative of a "con man," as David O. Stewart has indeed understood him.

What has not been considered in the literature is that Dunham's pattern of impostures, aliases, forgeries, and frauds also perfectly fits the profile, not of a con man and grifter, but of an espionage agent and agent provocateur. This carries with it a profound and widespread implication, for *if that be the case, then the character and interpretation of every incident that he touches, including Andrew Johnson's impeachments, and all related events, changes profoundly.* They can no longer be considered to be disparate and unconnected, but must be connected at a profoundly deep level, the level of deep events and deep politics.

In this respect, pause and consider the *effect* of the Lincoln assassination. His 1864 "Union party" ticket with Andrew Johnson as a running mate was a clear political move calculated to appeal to southerners eventually restored to the Union. Had Lincoln lived, Johnson would have been an asset rather than a liability, and much of the drama surrounding Andrew Johnson may have been avoided. With his assassination, however, Johnson became the largest impediment to reunion: the country remained sectionally divided, with new racial tensions exacerbating the situation, and an impoverished South weakening what otherwise may have been a much more prosperous re-union. If one were a foreign power, or a *combination* of foreign powers wanting to see such an outcome, one could not have asked for a better situation. Thus, we shall have occasion to return to the impeachments of Andrew Johnson, and to this Impresario of Imposture, and the implications of his presence in the drama, much later in this book. Suffice it to note that my argument and thesis from here on out is that there are deep players and occulted foreign interests at work, and that the Impresario of Imposture is *not* a con man. Minimally, he *is* that, but the effect of his presence and activities is exactly the same as they would be if he were an espionage agent and *provocateur*, and that is how his activities must be interpreted.

4. The Third Impeachment and Trial
a. The Pattern of House Impeachment Votes and the Wider Context of the Binary Oppositions of Reconstruction

With this, we must return to Andrew Johnson and the *third* attempt to impeach him, an attempt that successfully brought him to a Senate trial, and to *a pattern of Senate votes suggesting precisely a connection to other agendas, to finance, and to probable foreign players.* This pattern of Senate voting must be viewed, in its turn, against the wider pattern of binary and dialectical opposition between Congress and the Executive thus far exposed in the first two impeachment attempts; the opposition of the Radical Republican Congress on the one hand, seeking to curb the executive power, punish and plunder the Southern states, defend the rights of newly emancipated black slaves and to proscribe and inhibit the southern white population's power, and on the other hand, of Andrew Johnson, trying to defend against the encroachments upon executive power and states' rights, and to pursue a more ameliorated policy vis-à-vis the southern states. While our concern in the coming pages is focused upon the political, financial, economic, and geopolitical implications of this pattern of Senate votes and the backdrop of the wider political dialectic in which they were cast, it should be noted that the racial component of this binary dialectic continued well into the twentieth century. One might even suggest that every instance in which it appears that a calm and peaceful resolution of the racial components of this binary political culture is immanent, some events or political pronouncements occur to exacerbate and raise them once again, but that is a case that must be argued on its own. Its possibility emerges, however, once one keeps the patterns and connections outlined in the remainder of this book in mind.[73]

b. Johnson, Grant, and Stanton: The Third Impeachment Crisis Breaks

Following his survival of the second impeachment effort and the good results for the Democrats in the 1867 elections, Johnson once again took the offensive against "Congress Reconstruction" by removing the military commanders for the occupation districts comprising Alabama, Florida, and Georgia, and Mississippi and Arkansas, generals John Pope and Edward Ord, respectively, and Philip Sheridan in Louisiana and Texas, replacing him with generals whom he

[73] David O. Stewart, *Impeached*, pp. 115-116 gives a very succinct and apt summary of this new racially-based dialectic and the mutual animosities that drove it against the backdrop of "Congress reconstruction" and the military occupation and force that backed it.

thought would administer their districts with less severity.[74] General W.S. Hancock swiftly countermanded the orders of his outgoing predecessor Sheridan in compliance with Johnson's wishes, but these orders were soon overridden by Grant, who, with Stanton's backing, continued to be too powerful an obstacle for Johnson to confront or remove.

Johnson had already "suspended" Stanton, yet the Secretary of War had refused to resign. At this juncture, Johnson faced a choice: he could comply with the Tenure in Office Act and request the Senate to confirm Stanton's dismissal, which the Radical Republican-controlled body would refuse to do, or he could attempt to "outflank" the Act by simply appointing a new secretary and asking for confirmation. In early January of 1868 Johnson decided to press the issue of the dismissal of Stanton, sending a report to the Senate outlining his disagreements with his War Secretary, specifically highlighting the fact that Stanton's reconstruction plans, drawn up while Lincoln was still alive and reflecting Lincoln's wishes, had been abandoned for the tenets of "Congress Reconstruction" once Lincoln was dead,[75] a fact that, again, can be interpreted in one of two ways: either (1) Stanton was simply drifting with the shifting winds of politics, or (2) the change of philosophy reflected Stanton's real commitments, underscoring his potential role as a member of the radical Republican conspiracy complicit in the assassination. In any case, Johnson's pleas for confirmation of Stanton's dismissal was not forthcoming and the third and final impeachment effort began.

Grant, who had been acting as interim Secretary of War until the confrontation between Johnson and Stanton could be resolved, acted quickly—and as it turned out, quite

---

[74] Ibid., p. 117. This is the same General Pope who lost the Second Battle of Bull Run/ Manassas junction to Lee in 1862.

[75] David O. Stewart, *Impeached,* p, 118.

craftily—to remove himself from the impending confrontation. Realizing that retaining control of the physical office of the Secretary of War would expose him to a ten thousand dollar fine under the terms of the Tenure in Office Act, the general, the day after the Senate decision, closed the office, gave the key to the door to his adjutant, and headed to his army headquarters office. There he composed a letter to Johnson indicating that Stanton had been restored to his office by the Senate, and that he, Grant, was thus no longer the interim and acting Secretary of War. Grant then attempted to avoid Johnson the rest of the day by never remaining in one place in Washington for very long.[76]

Johnson nonetheless was able to command the general's presence at a cabinet meeting, a crucial meeting on January 14, as it would turn out, and when he demanded an update on affairs in the War Department, Grant demurred, asserting that he could not do so because he was no longer the acting Secretary! Johnson dressed Grant down for not returning the physical control of the office—the key—to the executive, but rather for enabling Stanton to take physical possession of it again. Grant removed himself from the Cabinet meeting. Confronting Stanton, he advised the Secretary of War to resign, only to be meet with the well-known Stanton temper and invective, which Stanton could turn on and off when needed as a weapon. Grant then suggested to Johnson that the President simply *ignore* the Secretary, and order the army in turn to do the same, and accept orders only directing emanating from the White House. At this juncture, Johnson committed the mistake so many others had made, and underestimated Grant; while he agreed with Grant's proposed strategy for dealing with Stanton, he nonetheless did not issue the order, thinking that

---

[76] Ibid., pp. 119-120.

Grant and Stanton would resort to fighting amongst themselves.[77]

Grant, in response, decided to attempt to get Johnson "on the record," and to get his own impressions of the cabinet meeting on the record as well, and before Johnson could do so. On January 24, he wrote Johnson and requested that the President put his orders for the Army to ignore Stanton *n writing*. Johnson, equally cagily, did not respond. Grant then composed a second letter, and upped the ante considerably, first accusing Johnson of stating that he wanted to keep Stanton out of office, "whether or not that was permitted by the Tenure of Office Act."[78]

But that was not all.

Grant denied that Johnson's statements about the January 14th meeting of the Cabinet were accurate. "In short," says David O. Stewart of the affair, "after accusing Johnson of soliciting his help in violating the Tenure of Office Act, Grant called him a liar."[79]

The die was now cast, for Grant had thrown his support unhesitatingly and without any room to maneuver behind Stanton and the Radical Republican agenda for Reconstruction, and had left Andrew Johnson with no room to maneuver either. Stewart's summary of the situation cannot be bested:

> Johnson challenged his top general with a letter asserting facts that were "diametrically the reverse of your narration." He reported that every Cabinet member, "without exception," agreed with Johnson's version of the Cabinet meeting on January 14. Grant was not cowed. Unimpressed by the massed moral power of the president and his Cabinet.

---

[77] David O. Stewart, *Impeached*, p, 121.
[78] Ibid., p. 122.
[79] David O. Stewart, *Impeached*, p. 122.

> Grant replied that the "whole matter, from beginning to end, (was) an attempt to involve me in the resistance of the law, for which you hesitated to assume the responsibility in orders, and thus to destroy my character before the country."
>
> At this point, Congress demanded copies of the incendiary correspondence, which promptly appeared in newspapers across the land. The episode was fascinating and horrifying: the president and his military chief exchanging angry accusations of mendacity. Even some who disliked Johnson doubted Grant's version of events. Such doubts, it turned out, mattered little. The public was going to believe its hero general, not its president-by-accident.[80]

Whatever the truth of the matter may have been—and both men had surely stretched it—at the end of the day Grant had performed a nuanced and subtle calculation of the balance of political power between himself and the President, and had deftly used the disagreement to extricate himself from the situation, and pin Johnson into yet another battle with Congress, this time—with allegations on written record, and a public behind his own version of events—with a much more secure and substantial threat of impeachment and conviction. Additionally, Grant had also deftly and adroitly maneuvered *Stanton* out of the limelight. He was now merely an occasion for impeachment, and no longer a part of the equations of power politics.

Thus, for Thaddeus Stevens and the House radicals, both sides of the correspondence between the President and the General-in-Chief were damning: if the President's account was true, he was nevertheless implicating himself with the intention to bypass the clear dictates of Congress by attempting to bypass Stanton, and if the general's version was true, then again, the President was clearly trying to involve Grant in a conspiracy to violate the law. Either way, Stevens

[80] Ibid., pp. 122-123.

argued, there was a clear indication of high official misdemeanor.

And that was impeachable.

While the fires for impeachment were thus being lit once again in the House (with Thaddeus Stevens providing much of the fuel of combustible rhetoric), Johnson once again displayed his genius for trying to be subtle and nuanced and creating an even bigger mess for himself, for on February 21, 1868, Johnson undertook to have two letters composed, one dismissing Secretary Stanton, and the other appointing Adjutant General Lorenzo Thomas as interim Secretary of War. Unfortunately, Johnson had consulted absolutely no one in advance of the action; *none* of his Cabinet members and allies were notified, none of his Congressional allies were notified. The only ones who knew of it were Johnson, his aide who had actually drafted the two letters, and Adjutant General Thomas when he was summoned to the executive mansion and handed the orders. Thomas set off to deliver the orders personally to Stanton, and assume his office as interim Secretary of War.

Stanton, calculating his own political position, quickly surmised that he could afford a direct confrontation. After all, the Senate had only a month prior confirmed him in office, and in so short a time, nothing had significantly changed. Additionally, the Adjutant General had no reputation at all outside of Washington society, and hence was a non-entity without any political capital or weight. Stanton refused to leave the office, and immediately issued orders to the War Department staff to ignore Thomas.[81]

Meanwhile, Johnson executed yet another club-footed pirouette, and announced to the Senate via its fiery and

---

[81] The details of the affair were actually even much more convoluted than this summary can communicate. Q.v. David O. Stewart, *Impeached*, pp. 134-135.

Radical Republican reconstructionist president *pro tempore,* Benjamin Franklin Wade of Ohio, that he had dismissed Stanton. The result was a disorganized but immediate rush for yet a third round of impeachment. In the House a resolution for impeachment was quickly presented to Stevens' Reconstruction Committee, while Republican Senators, including Charles Sumner of Massachusetts, urged both Grant and Stanton to hold firm against the President.[82]

The seriousness of the situation is underscored by the fact that, as the rhetoric both for and against impeachment ratcheted up around the country, rumors of actual paramilitary support both for Congress and for the President spread swiftly around the country; to emphasize that the rumors were not mere puffery, actual pledges of support, with specific numbers of troops, were offered to both sides.[83]

The train in any case had left the station and there was no stopping it. Eventually, the House drafted and approved 11 articles of impeachment, articles that were, in effect, versions of one article,[84] namely, that the President had violated the Tenure of Office Act, and as such had committed a high misdemeanor, and should be impeached. The House approved of seven managers to present the articles to the Senate, and to try the prosecution's case before the Senate, and the Chief Justice, Salmon Chase, himself another Republican holdover from Lincoln's administration, and with presidential aspirations of his own. That the House meant business was revealed by the fact that its managers team included not only Thaddeus Stevens—part of the original Committee of Fifteen himself—but also the more moderate Republican chairman of the Judiciary Committee, Wilson of Iowa, and former general

---

[82] Ibid., p.135.

[83] Ibid., pp. 140-141.

[84] David O. Stewart, *Impeached*, pp. 159, 162.

Benjamin Butler, who would be one of the House's lead prosecutors.[85]

c. The Political Calculus and Voting Pattern in the Senate
(1) The Arguments of Johnson's Defense

Johnson's defense essentially elaborated three points: firstly, that the constitutional power of the Presidency was such that its office-holder could appoint and remove any member of his own Cabinet at will; secondly, that Congress had recognized this by passing laws recognizing this authority, and thirdly and finally, that the Tenure of Office Act did not extend to cases of Cabinet members who had been inherited from a previous administration, as Johnson had inherited Stanton. To deny Johnson the right to appoint his own Secretary of War was an illicit and unconstitutional circumscription of his executive power. Effectively, the defense was arguing that the Tenure in Office Act was unconstitutional.[86]

(2) Finances, and House Votes For and Against Impeachment

While the legal debates on the Senate floor about Johnson's conduct and the legitimacy, or lack thereof, of the Tenure of Office Act and its application to the special case of

---

[85] Ibid., pp. 149-150.

[86] David O. Stewart, *Impeached*, pp. 143f. Stewart argues that the Congress, by enacting such laws, is making it clear that the constitution does *not* grant such rights, otherwise such legislation would not even be needed. One might argue against *this* that perhaps Congress was merely clarifying the constitution, not establishing precedent for future restrictions of the appointment and dismissal powers of the executive. During the Senate debate, House Prosecutor Butler argued that Hamilton (who else?) had argued in *The Federalist* that the consent of the Senate was needed to remove as well as to appoint. (p, 195)

an inherited Cabinet minister from a previous administration are endless and fascinating, our purpose is not to review them here. We mention the defense strategy of Johnson's lawyers only to highlight that their defense was based on a political calculation of his support in the country at large, and hence, in the Senate. The numbers were daunting, but on closer examination, not so bad as they appeared on first glance. Stewart summarizes the calculus in the following fashion:

> Surveying the field before them, Johnson's team faced daunting challenges. The Republican majority in the Senate was overwhelming. Of the 54 Senators, only 9 were Democrats. The Democrats could be counted on to oppose impeachment even if they did not care for Johnson. Three Republican senators consistently voted for Johnson's policies and were solid for hm. That made 12 votes for the defense. To avoid conviction by a two-thirds majority, Johnson needed 19 votes, so he had to win over 7 more Republicans. That number—7 Republicans—would dominate impeachment strategies, press speculations, and backroom maneuvering.[87]

Yet, there were factors beyond mere numbers in this political calculus, and chief among them was the president *pro tempore* of the Senate itself, the "ripsnorting Radical"[88] Senator from Ohio, Benjamin Franklin Wade, who would succeed Johnson to the Presidency by the laws of that day, should Johnson be convicted.

The other factor was the Tenure of Office Act itself. Under its provisions, should Wade succeed to the presidency upon the conviction of Johnson, then any appointments *he* might make in the short year of Johnson's term (inherited from Lincoln!) remaining to him, would doubtless be

---

[87] David O. Stewart, *Impeached*, p. 164.

[88] Ibid., p. 166.

approved by his friends in the Senate which he just left. But under the terms of the Tenure in Office law, *that would mean whoever won the 1868 election would be saddled with Wade appointments*.[89] To some Republicans, particularly those of more moderate persuasion, the prospects looked much better—particularly for lucrative patronage appointments—under a President Ulysses S. Grant, than they did with a President Benjamin Wade.[90]

In mentioning the prospects of lucrative patronage appointments, we are chin-to-chin with the final factor in the political calculus, the geopolifinance one. Wade was a major supporter of very high tariffs on imported goods and in fact supported an immediate hike in tariffs on his assumption of office.[91] While in general the Republican party of the period supported the principle of tariff protections for industry—after all, it had been a Republican tariff that, in part, sparked the War Between the States in the first place—too high a tariff would result in falling trade, and falling trade meant firstly, falling revenues for the general government, and secondly, falling income from the tax collectors designated to collect them, for it must be remembered that under that system, appointment to customs and duties houses was a means of awarding patronage and benefices to political supporters, who could, and did, skim "fees" from taxes collected as their personal "bonus" for the efficient collection of taxes. A steep rise in tariffs, such as Wade favored, took direct aim at this system of patronage and largesse.

Additionally, Wade also favored a "cheap money" policy in addition to the high tariffs he advocated,[92] that is to say, Wade did *not* favor a post-war contraction of the money

[89] Ibid., pp. 222f.

[90] Ibid., p. 223.

[91] Ibid., p. 252.

[92] David O. Stewart, *Impeached,* p. 39.

supply by a so-called "sound money" policy of money backed by gold, but a continuation of the financing of projects through interest-free greenbacks.[93]

One must also entertain the strong possibility that behind this moderate Republican opposition to Wade there is foreign influence at work, exerting pressure to maintain current rates, or even lower them, making foreign goods cheaper to export to the U.S.A.

In any case, no evidence exists that Senator Wade made any promises of office in return for votes of conviction,[94] and this left both pro- and anti-conviction factions in a scramble to procure the remaining seven (for the anti-conviction faction) or eight (for the pro-conviction faction) votes. For the pro-conviction faction, they had little to offer votes for coniction other than Wade himself, and as was seen, he was not making any commitments other than high tariffs. The pro-conviction faction even considered seating the Congressional delegations from the Congress reconstruction governments of newly re-admitted and reconstructed states from the South which, with unionist and newly freed black votes, returned overwhelming Republican majorities in their delegations, some of whom were in Washington during the trial, waiting to be seated in Congress. Even for Thaddeus Stevens, this was too much, but it would have been the ultimate irony, for Johnson had insisted that Congress should and could take no legitimate action without the southern delegations being re-seated![95]

While Johnson himself eschewed the use of any bribery or other underhanded methods of securing the needed seven

[93] Wade also favored women's suffrage, eight hour work days, and roundly denounced Lincoln's lenient policies of Reconstruction in the 1864 elections. (p. 39)

[94] Ibid., *Impeached*, p. 272.

[95] David O. Stewart, *Impeached*, pp. 272f.

votes, a group of New Yorkers with connections to Secretary of State Seward gathered around publisher Thurlow Weed, worked behind the scenes to bribe moderate Republican votes to keep Johnson in office. The presence of this group, as will be seen, suggests other financial and geopolitical agendas that will become more apparent in later pages. Suffice it here to recall that John Wilkes Booth himself had financial connections with a shadowy group of "New York businessmen and financiers" who operated in conjunction with his own anti-Lincoln conspiracy, and who had in turn their own connections to the Radical Republicans. Thurlow Weed, it must be recalled, was mentioned by name in the alleged missing pages of Booth's diary.[96] Stewart's comment here is worth noting: "Taken together, the surviving evidence leaves the indelible impression that dark men undertook dark deeds to keep Andrew Johnson in office."[97] Indeed, for Stewart does not even mention the Booth diary and its explosive contents in reaching this conclusion.

In the end the Senate failed to convict Johnson on any article of impeachment by but one vote, and thus ended the stormy and accidental presidency of Tennessean Andrew Johnson. As indicated throughout this lengthy chapter however, there are patterns suggestive of the potential for hidden domestic and international players. These patterns include:

1) the widespread and general binary dialectical pattern of opposition of Congress and Presidency, a pattern which can be exacerbated and employed to political and financial gain;

---

[96] Q.V. the alleged transcript from Booth's missing diary pages, Joseph P. Farrell, *The Rialto in Richmond*, pp. 163-164.

[97] David O. Stewart, *Impeached*, p. 241.

2) a narrower binary dialectic between a "lenient" reconstruction policy toward the southern states, and a "punish and plunder" policy advocated by the Radical Reconstructionists that plundered the South; and, as the third impeachment attempt against Johnson revealed,
3) some of the same "deep players" as were alleged to be involved in the Lincoln assassination for political and financial gain are *again* involved in trying to maintain Andrew Johnson in office, to avoid a Wade presidency, an easy money "greenback" policy, and to promote a "sound money" agenda designed to contract the money supply.

With this last point in mind, we must now examine the revealing pattern of votes *for* and *against* impeachment in correlation with the postwar financial policy advocated by the votes in the impeachment trial.

When the full House of Representatives voted on the bill for impeachment at the end of 1867 and to bring the third impeachment to the trial in the Senate that we just reviewed, the pattern revealed the connections between Reconstruction and the financial matters, including what *types* of money were to be circulated, whether or not to expand or contract the money supply, and whether to suspend or resume specie payments; Michael les Benedict, in a rare and extremely valuable study of the Johnson impeachments in connection to the financial issues of the day, writes this:

> The pattern of the Republican vote on impeachment indicated the importance of the money question in determining representatives' positions. Voting records on the currency-expansion issue during the 40th Congress correlated with the vote on impeachment almost as well as

did voting records on Reconstruction issues during the second session of the 39th Congress, when Republicans had passed the Reconstruction Act.[98]

Dividing the 39th Congress House into (1) Ultra-radicals, (2) Radicals, (3) Radical Centrists, (4) Conservative Centrists, (5) Conservatives, and (6) Extreme—Conservatives, Benedict draws the following table of their votes for or against impeachment:

	Against Impeachment[99]	For Impeachment
Ultra-radicals		I(gnatius) Donnelly[100] (1 vote)
Radicals	F.C Beaman J.H. Driggs T.D. Eliot F.A. Pike P. Sawyer H. Van Aernam H.D. Washburn (7 votes)	S.M. Arnell J.M. Ashley G.S. Boutwell H.O.T. Bromwell S. Clarke A. Cobb E.R. Eckley A.C. Harding G.W. Julian W.D. Kelley J.W. McClurg I. Myers C. O'Niell H.E. Paine T(haddues) Stevens R.E. Trowbridge R.T. Van Horn H. Ward T. Williams S.F. Wilson (20 Votes)

[98] Michael Les Benedict, *The Impeachment and Trial of Andrew Johnson* (New York, W.W. Norton and Company, Inc., 1973 p. 81.

[99] Ibid., p. 82.

[100] Congressman Donnelly was the Minnesota representative who wrote the famous book on Atlantis.

The Rialto in Richmond, Reconstructed

Radical Centrists Radical Centrists	W.B. Allison B.C. Cook N.F. Dixon B. Eggleston C.T. Hulburd W.H. Koontz G.F. Miller J.K. Moorhead S. Perham R.P. Spalding C. Upson M. Welker J.F. Wilson (13 Botes)	G.W. Anderson J.M. Broomall R.W. Clarke S.N. Cullom w. Higby W. Lawrence B.F. Loan J. Lynch U. Mercur G.S. Orth G.W. Scofield W.B. Stokes (12 votes)
Conservative Centrists	D.R. Ashley J.F. Benjamin J.A. Bingham H.l. Dawes G.M. dodge C.D. Hubbard J.H. Katcham A.H. Laflin G.V. Lawrence J.M. Marvin T.A. Plants (9 votes)	H. Maynard H. Price (2 votes)
Conservatives	D.R. Ashley J.F. Benjamin J.A. Bingham H.l. Dawes G.M. Dodge C.D. Hubbard J.H. Ketcham A.H. Laflin G.V. Lawrence J.M. Marvin T.A. Plants (11 votes)	J.F. Farnsworth R.C. Schenck F. Thomas (3 votes)
Extreme Conservatives	I.R. Hawkins (1 vote)	

Now compare this table with the following table of votes for (1) expanding the money supply (through continued Greenback use), (2) Suspending the contraction of the money supply, and (3) contacting the money supply:

Position on currency question[101]	Against Impeachment	For Impeachment
Expansionists	J. Baker R.P. Buckland B.C. Cook B. Eggleston J.R. Hawkins, E.C. Ingersoll H.D. Washburn (7 votes)	H.P.T. Bromwell, B.F. Butler A. Cobb J. Coburn I(gnatius) Donnelly J.F. Farnsworth J.H. Gravely B.f. Hopkins M.C. Hunter W, Lawrence W. Loughbridge G.S. Orth J..P.C. Shanks A.F. Stevens W.B. Stokes (15 votes)
Suspensionists Suspensionists	W.B. Allison F.C. Beaman J.F. Benjamin J.A. Bingham G,M. Dodge J.H. Driggs T.W. Ferry B.M. Kitchen T.A. Plants D. Polsley R. Sawyer (12 votes)	G.W. Anderson R.W. Clarke S. Clarke S.M. Cullom E.R Eckley W. Higby N.B. Judd G.W. Julian B.F. Loan J.A. Logan J. Mullins C.A. Newcome D.A. Nunn H.E. Paine W.A. Pile

[101] Michael Les Benedict, *The Impeachment and Trial of Andrew Johnson*, p. 83

		R.C. Schenck R.E. Trowbridge R.T. Van Horn W. Williams (19 votes)
Contractionists Contractionists	O. Ames D.R. Ashley J.D. Baldwin N.P. Banks H.L. Dawes N.F. Dixon T.D. Eliot W.L. Fields J.A. Garfield[102] J.A. Griswold G.A. Halsey J. Hill C.D. Hubbard C.t. Hulburd J.H. Ketcham A.H. laflin G.V. Lawrence J.M. Marvin D. McCarthy J.,K. Moorhead S. Perham I.P. Poland R.P. Spalding H.H. Starkweather T.e. Stewart N. Taylor G. Twichell H. Van Aernam C. Van Wyck C.C. Washburn W.B. Washburn J.F. Wilson F.E. Woodbridge (33 votes)	G.S. Boutwell J.M. Bromall J.C. Churchill J. Covode U. Mercur H. Price G.W. Scofield H.Ward (8 votes)

[102] The future President.

Notice that, on the data of the *second* table, the contractionsist and suspensionists are *against* the impeachment of Johnson, and yet these very policies will prevail in the Grant administration which follows him. Notice also the presence of some radicals—such as George Washington Julian (G.W. Julian)—in the suspensionist column. Benedict summarizes it this way:

> A close look discloses that it was especially the contractionists whose votes on impeachment seem to have correlated to their fiscal positions. They divided 33 to 8 against impeaching the President, while Republicans favoring currency expansion or a suspension of contraction favored impeachment by much more modest margins. Even contractionists who had voted with the radicals or radical-centrists during the controversy over the Reconstruction Act opposed impeachment by an eight-to-five margin.[103]

This comparison is quite revealing, for it discloses that behind all the political and geopolitical patterns and potentialities of the Johnson presidency and impeachments, there are deep financial agendas at work, and these in their turn also point to deeper political and geopolitical potentialities. It is quite revealing that those voting to retain Johnson in office and against impeachment were advocates of the same monetary policies as being advocated by the New York financiers gathered around Thurlow Weed (and, if one allows the testimony of the missing Booth diary pages, Booth himself), and the very policies that Grant would follow. The radical reconstruction agenda of punish and plunder was fine, as long as it followed the contractionist agenda.

---

[103] Michael Les Benedict, *The Impeachment and Trial of Andrew Johnson*, p. 84.

There would be no President Benjamin F. Wade, nor high tariffs and cheap money expansionist agenda.

It would be Ulysses S. Grant, "sound money," and unparalleled prosperity for some classes and sections, and deflationary ruin for others.

To that part of the broader pattern suggesting deeper players, we now turn, but before we do, remember that we have now seen the following suggestive list of unusual events, and deeper players:

1) Ties to "Confederate Canada" via the Impresario of Imposture," Charles A. Dunham and the possibility of his being an *agent provocateur*, via various frauds and aliases;
2) The re-appearance of significant deep actors in the Booth conspiracy to assassinate Lincoln, including Benjamin F. Wade, Thurlow Weed, G.W. Julian, and, of course, Edwin Stanton;
3) A possible connection between Johnson's attempt to send Ulysses Grant to Mexico, and Jefferson Davis's continuity of government operation to flee to the Trans-Mississippi department to continue the war from a "rump Confederacy" via supplies through Mexico;
4) A potential Masonic connection between President Benito Juarez of Mexico and Mason Andrew Johnson (for whatever it may be worth); and,
5) A pattern of financial politics behind the Johnson impeachment, politics and policies bound to attract geopolitical interest for foreign powers potentially impacted by those policies.

With this in mind, we must now turn to arguably one of the most corrupt presidencies in American history, that of wartime hero Ulysses S. Grant.

The Eighteenth President of the United States, and Former General-in-Chief of all Union Forces, Ulysses S. Grant

3
Gold, Greenbacks, Grift, and Grant:
Republicans and the Racket(s) of Reconstruction

"The bullion basis of money—the view, in fact, that bullion was the only money—was... a secular religion. The split between gold monometallists and gold-silver bimetallists was consequently akin to a theological dispute."
Walter T. K. Nugent[1]

"Let the conqueror solve the problem of the nation's future. The South had a more intimate task to meet, an immediate one that engrossed every energy. That task was the personal one of salvaging from the general ruin the elements of livelihood itself."
Paul H. Buck[2]

His real name was Hiram Ulysses Grant. A mistake on the entrance rolls to West Point when he became a cadet there listed his name as "Ulysses S. Grant," and thus did his fellow cadets know him, using his first two initials as a symbol of the nation, of "Uncle Sam" himself. Thus by the nickname "Sam" was he known to his fellow cadets. Others had it that the "S" stood for "Simpson" and others, like the "S" in "Harry S. Truman," for nothing at all. But from West Point onward, he was never again Hiram Ulysses Grant. From that point forward he would always be

[1] Walter T.K. Nugent, *The Money Question During Reconstruction* (New York: W.W. Norton and Company, Inc.1967, No ISBN), p. 57.

[2] Paul H. Buck, *The Road to Reunion, 1865-1900*, p. 36.

Ulysses S. Grant. No one who knew anything about Grant's life before the War Between the States nor his less-than-stellar performance as a cadet at West Point could ever have predicted that he would rise to become the Chief General of the Union armies by the end of that war, much less President of the whole country, and arguably one of the most corrupt, at that.

Grant's career is, however, quite well-known, and there is no reason to rehearse it here again. However, viewed in the context of the binary oppositions that were manifest during the stormy Johnson administration – between Congress and the Executive, between radical Republicans, Moderates, and Democrats, and between blacks and whites – there are episodes and events in the Grant presidency that suggest that deeper forces, agendas, and players are on the field, exploiting these fissures as crises of opportunity for the geopolitical purpose of keeping the country divided and economically controlled while at the same time exploiting every opportunity for plunder and to recover losses from the Union and Confederate debt incurred by the war.

A. Congress Reconstruction Under Grant
1. Three Inextricably Intertwined Issues: The Repudiation of Secession, the Repudiation of Confederate Debt, and Reconstruction

Hindsight is always twenty-twenty, and that is nowhere truer than with Reconstruction. Had the enlightened voices in the South who had called for the end to slavery moved with more alacrity and proposed a system of compensated manumission, it may have been able to expand its power in Congress and to avoid those clashes with the North that led to the war in the first place. Conversely, had the radical abolitionists of the North also been willing to propose a compensated manumission with vigor, rather than to finance radical and murderous terrorists like John Brown, again the conflict might have been avoided. As it was, the policies of Reconstruction only exacerbated the racial tensions, which in turn cloaked many opportunities for fraud, graft, grift, money laundering, and these activities in *their* turn cloaked the plunder operation that was under way in the guise of "reconstruction."

Andrew Johnson's Reconstruction policies were essentially those of Lincoln: firstly, the average citizens and soldiers of the former Confederacy could apply for pardon and amnesty, and then be eligible for the restoration of all their property, with the exception of any slaves they might have held. Secondly, the various southern states—with the exceptions of Tennessee, Arkansas, and Louisiana - were to hold state conventions to create new state constitutions. These three states were exempted because they had already formed new state governments during the war which were recognized by Lincoln.[3]

Johnson had three requirements which these new state conventions had to meet: (1) They had to abolish chattel slavery; (2) they had to renounce secession; and most importantly for our purposes: (3) "*they must repudiate all Confederate debt.*"[4]

We must now pause and take note of what has occurred under Johnson's policy. First: had Mr. Lincoln lived to articulate these same policies—they were, fundamentally, his to begin with—he would have run afoul of the same political and financial realities as Johnson. This means, secondly, that if Mr. Lincoln's actual assassination was the

---

[3] Philip Leigh, *U.S. Grant's Failed Presidency*, p. 14f.
[4] Ibid., p. 15, emphasis added.

result of deeper financial and political intrigues removing him in order to enact policies that would enable the war's debt holders to recoup their investments, then it is probable that had he lived beyond the war's end, he would have been assassinated anyway. As it was, the plotters had to move quickly in the aftermath of Lee's surrender at Appomattox in order to be able to fix responsibility for the deed on the failed Confederacy and its leaders. Had they waited, other responsible parties may have been more likely to have been sought by the Northern press. With a southern Democrat in office—in office by assassination no less—the lenient policies could be blamed on him and his "southern loyalties," and more radical policies insisted upon.

This consideration now confronts us with the problem of secession, and the repudiation of the Confederacy's debts, for the two are tied together. The renunciation of secession in principle means that legally there is no heir at any *state* level to the debts incurred by their general agent at a *federal* level, the Confederate government itself, since the states that had established that government have legally ceased to exist under their original charter or constitution. Thus, for any holder of Confederate currency, bonds, bills of exchange, bills of credit, or any other such Confederate financial instrument, those carry no legal force. But for the holders of those instruments of Confederate debt—whether foreign or in the North itself(!) – this is an enormous loss and can only be recouped through (1) a lien upon southern labor lasting generations, or (2) actual confiscation and foreclosure on hard southern assets such as land, commodities, and so on. Thus, while these two principles are not often connected, they must be, for the renunciation of secession is an essential *legal* step in the refinancing of the accumulated debt, both Union and Confederate.

Or to put the whole conundrum with a kind of oxymoronic "blunt subtlety," the renunciation of secession almost required the pursuit of a much less lenient reconstruction policy if Confederate debt holders were not to face much more severe hardships, for it must also be recalled that even after the war, *substantial monies on Confederate accounts were still held in European banks. If there still existed legal entities that could post a prima facie claim on those assets—the original unreconstructed state members of the Confederacy—then those assets would have to be held in escrow until the funds could be claimed. Conversely if they had ceased to exist, the other claimants could step forward.*[5]

2. An Example of The Mess of Reconstruction: Arkansas

This brings us to the presidency and two administrations of Ulysses S. Grant, for shortly after Andrew Johnson narrowly avoided being removed from office in his Senate impeachment trial, the Radical Republicans were finally successful in imposing their agenda on the party by nominating, and electing, Grant to the presidency in 1868. The first step in the radical reconstruction policy was the de facto disenfranchise-ment of former Confederates, in effect, the disenfranchisement of the majority of the white population of the South. So long as the day-to-day administration of the amnesty policy remained in the hands of Republicans imported into the South for the purpose of administering it, the result was predictable: southern whites who had played any sort of role in the Confederacy were denied amnesty, or their amnesties were "slow-walked." The result was the same: a general disenfranchisement, while

[5] For the matter of money still in Confederate accounts in Europe after the end of the war, see my *The Rialto in Richmond*, pp. 252-255ff.

similarly, the newly emancipated slaves were not only voting, but promoted to political careers, in some cases without even being able to read or write.

In Arkansas the carpetbag governor Powell Clayton made the most egregious use of this "policy" by forming a state militia but prohibiting amnesty—and hence membership in the militia—to former Confederates. The militia thus became his own paramilitary enforcement arm for Reconstruction, while he used his powers to prohibit amnesty to the former Confederate white population, simultaneously promoting the state's minority black population. As a result, Powell's state militia soon became predominantly black, and the tensions between the two races predictably grew far beyond anything that had been the case prior to the war.[6] Additionally, Powell and his friends used their official positions to enrich themselves through the process of property tax liens, for as farms failed, they were repossessed, and sold at bargain prices to Powell's friends as rewards for their political and financial support.[7]

3. A More Trenchant Example of the Mess: Louisiana

Such corrupt practices daunted and hounded "Congress reconstruction" almost everywhere, but perhaps the best example of its practice under Grant occurred in

---

[6] Philip Leigh, *U.S. Grant's Failed Presidency*, pp. 101-102.

[7] Ibid., p. 103. The graft and corruption in Arkansas became so bad that at one point it led to the "Brooks-Baxter War," when competing candidates for governor's forces - both black and white on each side - openly clashed, with Federal occupation forces trying to keep them apart. Grant eventually intervened, making Baxter the the governor, until Grant himself then subsequently reversed his decision. Grant's about faces regarding the resolution of the "Brooks-Baxter War" eventually sealed the doom of the Republican party in the state for a century. (Q.v. Leigh, op. cit., p. 105)

Louisiana. There the carpetbag Republican governor, Henry Warmoth, decided *not* to run for re-election in 1872.

This did not prevent him from running afoul of the Grant political machine, however, for he and Grant had been less than friends because Warmouth, a soldier in Grant's army that had assaulted the Confederate fortress of Vicksburg in 1863, had openly criticized Grant's mishandling of that first – and failed – Union assault on the fortress. Grant, however, had his own powerful influence within Louisiana reconstruction politics, for his wife Julia's sister had married Kentuckian James F. Casey, who by dint of his connections, had been posted to be the chief customs and tariff collector at New Orleans in the year Grant took office, 1869. Under the law and standard practice of the time, and like all such tariff collectors, this gave him control of who would win the contracts to store exports and imports and to collect other fees. It was thus an enormously powerful and influential position to dole out political favors and patronage within Louisiana politics.[8]

This circumstance forced Henry Warmouth to reach out to the state's Democrats and to back their gubernatorial candidate, John McEnery, a former Confederate officer, and to back Grant's opponent in the national elections, Horace Greeley. Casey, of course, backed Grant and the Reconstructionist carpetbagger William Kellogg for governor.

In what can only be state election fraud on a Bidenesque scale, Warmouth had his *own* election board, which promptly certified McEnery as the winner of the gubernatorial election, (which he may have been because the Warmouth board actually held possession of the ballots). Enter the Bidenesque scale of fraud, for McEnery's opponent,

[8] Philip Leigh, *U.S. Grant's Failed Presidency*, p. 106.

Kellogg, also had *his* own election board, which promptly claimed it had 18,000 votes. Warmouth claimed, on the basis of his results, that he had won, and was scheduled to seat his legislature, when Kellogg persuaded federal Judge Edward Durell to arbitrarily rule on 6 December that Kellogg's board was the only legitimate Returning Board."[9]

The result of these machinations was that federal troops were called in to prevent—by force—Warmouth's legislature from being recognized and seated. Under the provisions of the 1870 Enforcement Act, "the act enabled the federal government to step in anytime a carpetbag regime complained that Southern whites had intimidated black voters."[10] In this instance, again in an example of corruption and fraud on a massive Bidenesque scale, Kellogg had *blank complaint affidavits printed* ***and signed*** *by federal officials, and then distributed by the thousands before the election, which forms could then be filled in with "complaints."* The result was that

> ...Louisiana's governance situation was intolerable. The state was left with two governors, two legislatures, and potentially two sets of tax collectors, each collecting for rival state governments. Since Kellogg had to resign as senator in order to become governor, and one of Louisiana's Kellogg-faction congressman (sic.) was elected "at-large," it fell to Congress to indirectly select the proper state government.

Even with the Republicans in control of the Congress, it was too much:

---

[9] Ibid., p. 107.

[10] Philip Leigh, *U.S. Grant's Failed Presidency*, p. 108.

> Washington's House of Representatives decided that the Kellogg regime was illegal and "not much better than a successful conspiracy." A Senate investigation concluded that the election had "so many frauds and forgeries as to make it doubtful what candidates received a majority of votes actually cast." Thus, Congress recommended new elections.[11]

President Ulysses S. Grant, however, was having none of it, insisting that the Congress should have chosen one of the two candidates, and made his preferences clear by relying on Judge Durell's decision "as a legal fig leaf to settle on Kellogg."[12] Grant rubbed more graft into the grift salt by reappointing his brother-in-law Casey to the tariff collections post in New Orleans *over* a congressional inquiry had found Casey responsible for misconduct and corruption in office.[13]

The result of Grant's decision was a complete fiasco, for "Governor" Kellogg "governed" from New Orleans, supported by his reconstruction "state militia" and the local federal garrison, while the rural areas of the rest of the state was run by pro-McEnery factions. Kellogg, in an effort to bridge the gap, made promises to appoint McEnery supporters to various local parish offices in Grant parish, in return for their support. But his own supporters in the same parish complained, and Kellogg broke his promise to the McEnery supporters and appointed his own people to the local parish offices. McEnery's supporters determined to take the government buildings at the parish seat by force, and two weeks of intermittent violence finally led to the first casualty, a freed black man. More confrontations followed. With

---

[11] Ibid., p. 109.
[12] Philip Leigh, *U.S. Grant's Failed Presidency*, p. 109.
[13] Ibid., p. 109.

"Governor" Kellogg failing to intervene, many of McEnery's supporters suspected that Kellogg was hoping for racial violence to break out in order to enable him to call for federal help and support. Once this was gained, he could extend his government to the rural parishes of Louisiana removed from the environs of New Orleans.

Instead, Kellogg inadvertently made things even worse by deciding to send the commander of his militia to the parish to bring the two sides to peace. The trouble was, the commander of the militia was none other than former Confederate General James Longstreet, one of Robert A. Lee's most capable corps commanders. Longstreet, however, was also a prewar friend of President Grant, and even related to him,[14] and thus was viewed by many people in the post-bellum South as "untrustworthy" at best and "treasonous and treacherous" at worst.

Needless to say, this effort, too, failed, and the pro-Kellogg forces, largely black, barricaded themselves in the Grant parish government building, while the pro-McEnery forces, largely white, occupied the exterior. Violence ensued, the building was burned, many blacks were shot trying to escape the flames, many were captured and then subsequently shot in cold blood.[15] The result of this bloodshed resulted with all sides learning, and doubling-down on, the wrong lessons: for the Louisiana whites, it demonstrated the weak foundations of the Reconstructionist government of Kellogg, who could only rely on federal bayonets to retain power. For the Louisiana blacks, when Grant's Republican-controlled Supreme Court was unable to return a modicum of justice against those who had massacred the blacks in the confrontation in Grant parish, the lesson was that neither the

---

[14] Philip Leigh, *U.S. Grant's Failed Presidency*, p. 115.

[15] Ibid., p. 112

party nor the federal government were, in the final analysis, really genuinely interested in their plight. And for the Reconstructionists in the form of Kellogg, it led to the passage in 1874 of even more stringent and complete control of the election boards certifying results of state votes, virtually guaranteeing future Republican-Reconstructionist victories in state elections.[16] And in states like Louisiana with large black populations approaching, or even in some cases an actual, majority, it fueled the inevitable white resentments at disenfranchisement as their own amnesty was slow-walked, and "black rule" was imposed by bayonet. The "white leagues" were the inevitable reaction.

In any case, the tense situation in Louisiana reached the zenith when General Philip Sheridan was dispatched to New Orleans to enforce Kellogg's government. Sheridan recommended that Southerners *suspected* of resisting any carpetbag government should be subject to *military* regulation and jurisdiction. With this, Grant's heavy-handedness and obvious patronage of the financial arrangements in Louisiana were too much, even for a Congress controlled by his own party, and the media and legislators in such Republican strongholds as Massachusetts, New York, and Ohio began to wonder aloud, and in print, that if the military could be used to select and enforce his favored office-holders in Louisiana, how long would it be before similar measures were used outside the South?[17]

---

[16] Ibid., p. 115.

[17] Philip Leigh, *The Failed Presidency of U.S. Grant,* p. 117. Mention has already been made of U.S. Senator Hiram Revels of Mississippi's disappointment with, and abandonment of, the Republican party after similar—though not as dramatic—episodes in Mississippi. Revels applauded the 1875 election victory of the state's Democrats over his own party's (very corrupt) carpetbag governor, Adelbert Ames, as a victory over "corruption, theft, and embezzlement." (p. 122.) Apparently

B. Money, Debt, Bullion, and Greenbacks
1. The Background to the Coinage and Credit Acts

Shortly after the end of the war, New York *Tribune* owner and publisher Horace Greeley, Grant's principal opponent in the 1872 elections, made a comment about the character of the man who would become the eighteenth President of the United States of America; it was a statement that could have served as a summary of the principal financial and economic focus and corruption of his two administrations. Greeley quipped acidly that Grant spent his spare time conjugating the verb "to receive" in "all its moods and tenses, but always in the first person singular."[18] If Andrew Johnson's stormy presidency exposed the cultural and political dialectics that created opportunities for the "deep players" to exploit, and if it also exposed connections to some of those players—the "Impresario of Imposture" for example—then the two Grant administrations expose, in the full light of day, the financial, political, and geopolitical agendas at work, and who they were designed either to destroy, or benefit. It is not an exaggeration to say that Grant's two administrations would lay the foundations of

---

Revels was not persuaded by Ames' rhetoric that "the true purpose of Southern whites was to restore the Confederacy as a separate nation and put the black man in a state of serfdom."(p. 123). Or perhaps Revels had concluded that reconstruction carpetbag whites had their *own* version of serfdom. Grant had pulled his support from the Mississippi governor because Ohio Republicans had warned him that continuing with Louisiana-style reconstruction enforcement might cost Ohio Republicans in their own state's elections. "Thus, the President," writes Philip Leigh, "abandoned Mississippi's mostly black Republicans in favor of the mostly white Ohio Republicans."(p. 123)

[18] Philip Leigh, *U.S. Grant's Failed Presidency*, p. 8.

American "geopolifinance"[19] until the very outbreak of World War One and the "progressivism" of Woodrow Wilson. On this view, America's intervention in World War One may have been about something deeply hidden in a rarely noticed or commented upon event after the end of Grant's political life: his meting with a prominent European statesman.

In any case, the culture of graft, grift, frauds, and corruptions that became almost synonymous with Grant's two administrations began during the war itself, and for a very fundamental reason: cotton. If there was one commodity in the world besides food that was a commodity essential to human life itself, it was clothing, and in that era, there were really only two sources for clothing: wool, or cotton.

The North had the food, and the South had the cotton. It was a situation that compelled the emergence of a covert black market trade between the two sections that were ostensibly at war with each other. That trade thrived as early as 1862, particularly along the Mississippi-Missouri-Ohio river system, and hence in the very military district where Ulysses S. Grant began his illustrious Civil War career. This trade was fully known to both Presidents during the war, and as will be seen in a subsequent chapter, both men approved of

[19] In minting the term "geopolifinance" I thus mean to convey not only the notions of deep politics, deep states, and deep events in the senses expounded by Professor Peter Dale Scott in his numerous books on the subjects, but also to indicate that these often play out in a peculiarly tight combination and synthesis of international finance and geopolitics. I mean also to convey the notion that in this synthesis, the political and financial components are equally influential on the other in a kind of "feedback loop." Thus, at any given moment, the political component might dominate the synthesis to such an extent that the financial and economic component makes no sense, or *vice versa.*

it from the sheer financial necessity of financing their respective war efforts.[20]

2. The Public Credit Act, the Resumption Act, The Railroads Acts, the Homestead Act, and Union Sovereign Bonds Underwriter and Financier Jay Cooke

As was seen in the previous chapter, the cultural, financial, and political project of Reconstruction that the Radical Republicans advocated could not really begin so long as Southern Democrat Andrew Johnson was determined to fulfill Lincoln's Reconstruction legacy, at least, as far as he understood it. The radical agenda could not move forward until Johnson was removed, a task that consumed most of the time of his short four years in office, and most of the political energy and capital of both sides. More importantly, if there *were* deeper players waiting for a final outcome of that dispute in order to recoup their losses from bad investments during the war, then they, too, like their Radical Republican counterparts, would have to wait until Johnson was no longer in the picture.

It is thus with the incoming administration of Ulysses S. Grant, eighteenth president of the United States of America, that the full slate of "reconstruction" policies, including financial, currency, debt, and credit acts seemingly

---

[20] In a very telling explication of this necessity, Leigh comments that in 1860, federal spending in the *entire* Union prior to the southern secession had been about $80,000,000. By the end of the war, in *the North alone*, this had ballooned 1600% to more than 1.3 *billion* dollars. Cotton which began the war at ten cents per pound, ended around one dollar and ninety cents per pound, a nearly 20 times increase.(Q.v. Philip Leigh, *U.S. Grant's Failed Presidency*, p. 32). Leigh might have added that the situation is even worse when one throws in the Confederacy's accumulated war debt of approximately $990,000,000.00

far removed from "reconstruction" itself, are enacted. In these acts, we may discern the lineaments of deeper players and agendas.

For the sake of understanding that these acts are related to the plunder and reassignment of hard assets, we may divide them into two classes: acts having to do with hard assets, such as land, and railroads, and acts having to do with liquid financial instruments such as bonds, greenbacks, currency, and credit. In viewing things "whole" in this fashion, it should be noted that some of these acts were enacted over half a decade *before* Grant took office, and some were passed and signed into law by him during his two administrations. Viewing things whole in this fashion exhibits both the underlying consistency of the *policy*, but also the nature of the deeper players, and is a profound indicator as to their proper identification.

a. Acts Having to do with Hard Assets:
(1) The Railroad Acts:
Transcontinental and Transglobal Railroads, and the Real Reasons for Seward's Folly

Prior to the War Between the States, the sectional party strife between North and South drove much of the debate over the admission of new territories and states to the Union, as each side jealously guarded its congressional representation from being overwhelmed by the other: if too many free states were admitted, it would curtail the congressional power of the South. If too many slave states were admitted, or if southerners moved to territories and took slaves with them, it would mean an increase in Southern congressional power over the North. The strife was exacerbated by the fact that the industrializing North favored protective tariffs to allow its nascent industry to grow, while the commodities-and-export driven South favored free trade and very low tariffs. Add *railroads* on a trans-continental scale to the mixture, and it becomes a very unstable explosive, waiting like nitroglycerine for the slightest jiggle to detonate it. The transcontinental railroad issue became particularly volatile. Jefferson Davis himself, during his tenure as U.S. Secretary of War during the administration of President Franklin Pierce, explored various routes for a transcontinental railroad to California along a predictably southern route, a route more or less eventually followed when the Southern Pacific railroad was finally born after the war.

The southern secession, however, provided the Union Congress with the perfect opportunity to create the technological infrastructure that would bind the nation together in a "more perfect union" when it passed and President Lincoln signed the Railway Act of July 1, 1862. By the terms of the act, the Union Pacific and Central Pacific railroad companies, hitherto largely paper companies, were provided government subsidies.

The act was cleverly conceived, after all, Lincoln himself was a "railroad lawyer" when elected to the Presidency. Under the terms of the act, the government would issue bonds to the railroads which in turn could sell them to investors. The government would guarantee the principal and interest on the bonds. But the bonds in turn were issued on the collateral of the public lands of the West. These lands, in their turn, became a part of the subsidy to the railroads, as they were granted a 400 feet wide right-of-way along the rail route. To each side of this right-of-way, the public lands were blocked off in a five-square mile checkerboard pattern, with alternating squares to be *given* to the railroads for each mile of track that was laid. The alternation was to ensure that public lands adjacent to the railroad blocks would grow in value, and invite people to settle and develop the land and resources in conjunction with the Homestead Act, also passed by the Union Congress during the legislative opportunity caused by the southern secession. The bonds granted thus depended on the miles of track laid, and was calculated on the basis of the *type* of terrain that the mile of track traversed. The rates were $16,000 per mile in relatively flat terrain, $32,000 in rougher terrain, and $48,000 in very hilly and mountainous terrain. With the 1864 Railway Act, these subsidies were dramatically increased, with the "checker-board" pattern land grants being doubled to ten square miles, *including* all mineral rights on the land. Additionally, the railroads were allowed to issue their own company bonds.[21] The actions of the Union Congress are again illustrative of the differences of attitude reflected in the currencies and war objectives of the two sections,[22] the Union was engaged in an offensive war to crush the Confederacy and re-incorporate its territories, resources, and population into the Union. Similarly, it pursed an aggressive infrastructure development project in the vast western part of the continent. The Confederacy, conversely, was engaged in a defensive struggle for survival, and undertook no similar congressional measures with its western territories. The closest it came, as was seen in *The Rialto in Richmond*, was President Davis' instructions to General Kirby Smith for the development and administration of the Trans-Mississippi Department.[23]

Needless to say, all these subsidies created the beginnings of the "lobbyist-and-special-interest" culture that so infects American politics to this day. Thus, behind well-

[21] Philip Leigh, *U.S. Grant's Failed Presidency*, pp. 36-37.
[22] Q.v. my *The Rialto in Richmond*, p. 198ff.
[23] Ibid., pp. 173-187.

known "Reconstructionists" there was often a railroad subsidy. For example, Philip Leigh writes that when the railroad act of 1864

> ...was under consideration, one Union Pacific lobbyist distributed $250,000 in bonds among influence peddlers. For example, twenty thousand dollars went to Charles Sherman for "professional services." He was the eldest brother of Union Major General William T. Sherman and Ohio Senator John Sherman....[24]

Pennsylvania Congressman Thaddeus Stevens, whom we encountered in the previous chapter as a principal actor in the efforts to throw Andrew Johnson out of the presidency, required that the railroad acts explicitly state that all iron for rails and other infrastructure and machinery of the railroads be of the highest quality and manufactured in America. Not for nothing was Stevens an advocate of high tariffs and a harsh reconstruction policy, for he also owned an iron foundry in Pennsylvania.[25] These examples suffice to show that, far from being disconnected policies, reconstruction and the railroad subsidies often coalesced in the same individuals.

(2) The 1862 Homestead Act, the Other Half of the Railroad Bills

The other half of the Railroad Act of 1862 was the Homestead act of the same year. It is important to note how the southern secession actually aided and played into the agenda of the northern industrialists:

---

[24] Leigh, op. cit., p. 37.
[25] Philip Leigh, *U.S. Grant's Failed Presidency*, p. 38.

> The federal Congress, freed by secession from stubborn Southern conservatism, passed a series of laws representing a spirit of economic activism and nationalization that was never again to be dissipated. Among these laws were the Homestead Act of 1862, giving away parcels of the public domain to persons who would settle on and cultivate them; the Pacific Railway Acts of 1862 and 1864, by which the federal government...subsidized by money and land grants the construction of a railroad across the North American continent...[26]

In other words, if the railroads were to have something to *transport* in the vast empty reaches of the American west, there would have to be people in that region producing, and they would not move there unless given an incentive—land—to do so. The Homestead Act was thus the other half to the checkerboard land grants given to the railroads, for the lands given to homesteaders were from the parts of the checkerboard that remained "public," i.e., government, lands. One cannot understand the Railroad Acts without the Homestead Act, nor *vice versa*, as they belong together. Additionally, as the War Between the States itself proved, railroads were a crucial means not only of moving goods and people quickly, efficiently, and in vast quantities cheaply, they were now a crucial means of the strategic projection of military power, as they could move vast quantities of troops, weaponry, and supplies to great distances, as the Confederate General Joseph Johnston demonstrated in the first major battle of the War Between the States at First Manassas. If the states of the far West and Pacific coast were to be fully integrated into the nation economically, politically, culturally,

---

[26] Walter T. K. Nugent, *The Money Question During Reconstruction*, p. 23.

and militarily, then a railroad and local population were needed.[27]

There is a final point to be addressed in connection to the foregoing arrangements, and that is, how was the profitability of the railroad companies to be maintained to the satisfaction of investors during the construction phases of the railroad? The answer was simple and ingenious: the shareholders of the railroads created construction companies affiliated with the railroads that could charge whatever costs were needed to make the construction itself profitable.[28]

(3) "Geopolifinance": The Railroad Acts, Trans-Global Railroads, the Real Reasons for Seward's Folly, and a Special Cameo Appearance by Tsar Alexander II

It is with the Railroad Acts and the Homestead Act that one also is able to see the deeper agendas and players of "geopolifinance" entering the scene. Here we must dramatically expand the "geopolifinancial" context in which the Grant administrations were operating in order to see the international deep players at work during and after the War Between the States. It is worth noting that the other great transcontinental railroad project of the nineteenth century, the Russian Trans-Siberian railroad connecting European Russia to the far eastern Russian outpost of the Pacific, Vladivostok, was undertaken for very similar national security, geopolitical, cultural, and economic reasons, though the project was much more vast in length and scope, and the

---

[27] *McCarthy, Marshall, and the Other International: Roosevelt, Trotsky, Stalin, and America's Progressivist Deep State* (Lulu Books, 2020), pp. 114-119.

[28] Philip Leigh, *U.S. Grant's Failed Presidency*, p. 38f.

development of resource rich Siberia took much longer. To some extent this development was inhibited and arrested by Soviet collectivization, and its effect of once again ending the upward economic mobility of its recently-emancipated serfs, and again tying them to the lands they were working, or forcibly resettling them. This process was temporarily ended in a minor fashion, as I noted in my book *McCarthy, Marshall, and the Other International: Roosevelt, Trotsky, Stalin, and America's Progressivist Deep State*. There I pointed out that Soviet Marshal Mikhail Tuchachevsky had defied Stalin's collectivization policy, and had enacted a kind of small-scale Russian version of the Homestead act by giving plots of land and farm animals in the Khabarovsk region (north of Vladivistok) in far eastern Siberia to some displaced Kulaks in return for their military service, creating a cadre of military units loyal to the Marshal known as the Khabarovsk lot. This was one of the reasons that finally forced Stalin to liquidate the Marshal in his purges of the party and military in the 1930s.

This mention of the Trans-Siberian railroad connection may seem to be stretching a point until one remembers some little known and little remembered "geopolifinancial" facts, for the Trans-Siberian Railroad received the benefit of the experience of Lincoln's engineering and surveying overseer, General Grenville Dodge, who advised the Russian engineers on their massive railroad building project.[29] *Prior* to the War Between the States, Tsar Nicholas I had hired the American engineer George Washington Whistler to supervise the building of Russia's first long-distance railroad from Moscow to St. Petersburg.[30]

---

[29] Matthew Ehret, Cynthia Chung, *The Clash of the Two Americas*, vol. 1, *The Unfinished Symphony* (Canadian Patriot Press, 2021, p. 149.

[30] Ibid.

For the sea-based trade of the British Empire, the emergence of railroads (and later, of course, aircraft) spelled a massive threat to British international political and financial hegemony, to the extent that the late nineteenth and early twentieth century geopolitical theorist, Sir Halford Makinder, predicted that the entire Eurasian land mass could be bound together by this new technological infrastructure, and that infrastructure and the supply lines it enabled would not be able to be challenged and interdicted by British sea power.[31] As a result of his theorizing, he maintained that whoever controlled the European heartland—that area of Eastern Europe roughly encompassing the modern-day Ukraine, Byelorussia (Belarus), the Baltic states, and Eastern Poland—would be the power able to dominate the entire Eurasian continent and thence the world, by the creation of an enormous interconnected infrastructure of economic development. That meant, effectively, that either Russia, or Germany, would dominate. Consequently, the principal aim of British "geopolifinance" should be the prevention of the emergence of any Russo-German alliance. But another possibility was never mentioned in Makinder's public works on geopolitics, and that was the possibility of a rail connection between the American continents and the Eurasian landmass via a railroad connection either over the Bering Strait between Siberia and Alaska via a bridge, or under it, via a tunnel.

In 1867 Massachusetts Radical Republican Senator Charles Sumner defended the purchase of Alaska from Russia by Secretary of State William Seward—Seward's Folly—by making reference to what one of the real purposes of the purchase was all about, namely, stitching the Eurasian and

---

[31] For the continued influence of Mackinder's ideas, see my *Hess and the Penguins*.

American landmasses together in a Russo-American hegemony, and utterly by-passing the western European powers: "To unite the East of Asia with the West of America is the aspiration of commerce now.... Of course, whatever helps this result is an advantage. The Pacific Railroad is such an advantage; for, though running westward, it will be, when completed, a new highway to the East."[32] Colorado's first governor and former Lincoln bodyguard, William Gilpin, maintained that the proper development of Alaska and Siberia depended on a direct railroad link between the continents,[33] and these were no mere abstract dreams, for in 1906, the *New York Times* reported

> The Czar of Russia[34] has issued an order authorizing the American syndicate, represented by Baron Loicq de Lobel, to begin work on the Trans-Siberian-Alaska railroad project. The plan is to build a railroad from Siberia to Alaska by bridging and tunneling the Bering Strait. It is said that the enterprise will be capitalized at from $250 to $300 million and that the money centers of Russia, France, and the United States will be asked to take bonds.[35]

It should be noted that Britain took a dim measure of Russia's far eastern ambitions, and not only helped mid-wife Japan into a first class world power by huge transferences of naval technology, enabling Japan to build its enormously powerful fleet, but that it used Japan in the Russo-Japanese War to wrest Manchuria from Russian control, thus wresting from

---

[32] Matthew Ehret and Cynthia Chung, *The Unfinished Symphony*, volume II p. 139.

[33] Ibid., pp. 140-141.

[34] Nicholas II.

[35] Ehret and Chung, op. cit., p. 141, citing *The New York Times*, "London by Rail," March 27, 1906.

Russian control the portion of the Trans-Siberian railroad that traversed that province of China to Vladivostok, and requiring the Russians to build another route around the province along the Russian side of the border. The Trans-Siberian-Alaskan railroad project was thus delayed. The peace between Russia and Japan, arbitrated by Teddy Roosevelt, meant that the United State's and Russia's railroad project was now confronted by a new geopolitical factor with the power and technology to interdict such a rail link: Japan.

These "geopolifinancial" considerations thus help to illuminate their similar operations earlier during the century, *during* the War Between the States and its immediate aftermath during the Reconstruction period. For example, during the war Robert Cecil, Lord Salisbury and one of the most influential British politicians of the time, spelled out these British imperial geopoliciancial interests in Parliament with a rare and explicit clarity:

> The Northern States of American never can be our sure friends because we are rivals, rivals politically, rivals commercially... With the Southern States, the case is entirely reversed. The population are an agricultural people. They furnish the raw material of our industry, and they consume the products which we manufacture from it. With them, every interest must lead us to cultivate friendly relations, and when the war began they at once recurred to England as their natural ally.[36]

No less than Tsar Alexander the II himself, the *other* Great 19th century Emancipator of slaves, in an interview given to the American banker Wharton Barker in 1879, was even more

---

[36] Matthew Ehret and Cynthia Chung, *The Unfinished Symphony*, p. 146.

candid, and in doing so, made it clear how dangerously close the big two European powers were to military intervention on the side of the Confederacy:

Tsar Alexander II Romanov, 1818-1881,
Reigning, 1855-1881,
The Other Great Emancipator of the 19th Century

> In the Autumn of 1862, the governments of France and Great Britain proposed to Russia, in a formal but not in an official way, the joint recognition by European powers of the independence of the Confederate States of America. My immediate answer was, *'I will not cooperate in such action; and I will not acquiesce. On the contrary, I shall accept the recognition of the independence of the Confederate States by France and Great Britain as a casus (sic) belli for Russia.* And in order that the governments of France and Great Britain may understand that this is no idle threat, I will send a Pacific fleet to San Francisco and an Atlantic fleet to New York.
>
> ...All this I did because of love for my own dear Russia, rather than for love of the American Republic. I acted thus *because I understood that Russia would have a more serious task to perform if the American Republic, with advanced industrial development were broken up and Great Britain should be left in control of most branches of modern industrial development.*[37]

With such geopolifinancial interests at stake with the development of trans-continental railroad infrastructure, it should come as no surprise that these same interests were in play in the development of the various legislative measures of the post bellum federal Congresses regarding currency, war debt, national credit, and finance.

(4) Jay Cooke, Bond Underwriter for the Union, for the Northern Pacific Railroad, his Financial Collapse, and His Link to "the Secret Six"

[37] Tsar Alexander II, cited in *The Independent*, March 24, 1904, emphasis added; Matthew Ehret and Cynthia Chung, *The Unfinished Symphony*, pp. 147-148.

The Philadelphia brokerage firm of Jay Cooke was the Shearson-Lehman, the Kuhn-Loeb, the Dillon Reed, and the Chase Manhattan of the day. From the northern routes for a transcontinental railroad to civil wars, if there was a colossally large project to finance, he was at the center of it.

Jay Cooke, the Philadelphia financier and bond underwriter who helped finance the Union's war effort

If there was one single financial mastermind behind the twin 1862 Homestead and Railroad Acts, it was most probably Jay Cooke, for the *effect* of the Railroad act is well-known, but the passage of the Homestead Act in that same year was pure geopolifinancial calculation, for ipso facto, the Southern population—both black and white—was excluded. At the strokes of Lincoln's pen signing the bill, all the ante bellum political maneuvers and "compromises" between the sections over whether southerners could, or could not, settle the western territories with, or without, their black slaves in tow was settled; the vast expanse of the North American west would be settled by "good, industrious, northerners." Thanks to Reconstruction, the southern population, both black and white, would be even further confined to the old South by the system of debt peonage known as sharecropping. Financiers like Cooke, underwriting the bonds for the North's war effort *and* the bonds for the transcontinental railroads (like Cooke's own "Northern Pacific"), had the most to gain. Cooke was also quite predictably in favor of high tariffs, gold-backed money, and Ulysses S. Grant,[38] a constellation of interests that suggests a strong geopolifinancial aptitude on Cooke's part.[39]

When the war ended, Cooke sought to replace his lucrative underwriting of the North's sovereign securities with the bonds for the Northern Pacific railroad which by 1870, though chartered by the Railroad Act of 1864, had not built a mile of track to fulfill its charter to connect Lake Superior with the Puget Sound. After buying the moribund Northern Pacific for bargain prices, Cooke then capitalized his new railroad by raising approximately one hundred

---

[38] Philip Leigh, *U.S. Grant's Failed Presidency*, p. 90.

[39] One might go so far as to suggest that the deflationary monetary results brought about by the Resumption act of 1873, and the squeeze it placed on farmers in the South and western plains states was designed as yet another component of the Railroad-Homestead strategies to drive populations into the lands of the west.

million dollars selling stock in the railroad to people like Grant's Vice President, Schuyler Colfax, newspaper publisher Horace Greeley, or radical abolitionist preacher and pre-war abolitionist financier, Henry Ward Beecher.[40] Beecher was one of the ante bellum radical abolitionists who were part of the New England secularized Calvinist-Unitarian financiers known as the "Secret Six" who, among other things, funded the murderous rampages of John Brown in Kansas and elsewhere.

Radical Abolitionist New England preacher Henry Ward Beecher, a stockholder in Jay Cooke's Northern Pacific Railroad

[40] Philip Leigh, *U.S. Grant's Failed Presidency*, pp. 125-126.

New York Tribune Owner and Publisher Horace Greeley, Stockholder in Jay Cooke's Northern Pacific Railroad

There was, however, a soft and vulnerable underbelly to all this sudden railroad expansion, and Cooke's Northern Pacific was about to expose it. It will be recalled that, in order to maintain profitability during the period of the construction and early operation of the transcontinental railroads, the railroad companies—in particular the Central and Union Pacific Railroads—had started their own subsidiary construction companies, which *could* and did generate profits for their companies to offset the losses of the parent railroad company. The idea, in fact, came from France, a country that was engaged in its own rapid railroad network expansion. The French construction company, Credit Mobiler, became a major foreign investor in the Union Pacific's own construction company. In other words, just as there was a geopolifinancial motivation for the expansion of railroads, there was to some extent a countervailing geopolifinancial motivation for the dramatic *overbuilding* of the network, which potentially could bring dreams of a transglobal network crashing down, delaying if not altogether ending it.

So long as Cooke could continue to sell bonds and stock, he could continue to build his railroad. But if the money supply *suddenly and dramatically contracted*, the market for these securities would evaporate, and with it, so would the completion of the Northern Pacific Railroad, and Jay Cooke.

This is exactly what happened under the effects of the various other financial acts undertaken or being contemplated and debated in the press and Congress, and by Grant's administrations. By the summer of 1873 Cooke's railroad tracks had reached Bismarck, North Dakota,[41] but that same year Congress had also passed the "Coinage Act," otherwise more popularly known as "the Crime of '73." As will be seen momentarily, the effect of this and other acts was a dramatic shrinkage of the money supply and a vicious and ruinous deflationary cycle. The effect on Cooke was almost immediate.

Breakfasting privately with President Grant on September 18, 1873 at his estate outside Philadelphia, Cooke informed Grant of the inevitable: that noon Jay Cooke and

[41] Philip Leigh, *U.S. Grant's Failed Presidency*, p. 126.

Company ceased operations, and closed its doors once and for all. With that event, Philadelphia ceased to be the financial capital of the country, as its competitor New York City took over the role. The wider effects, however, were to ripplc throughout the over-built railroad industry and the New York Stock Exchange. Author and researcher Philip Leigh, whose exposition we have followed in this chapter, puts the whole collapse with an aptness and precision that can hardly be bettered:

> Cooke's failure initiated a panic and then a depression. The total bonded indebtedness of the railroad industry was over $2.2 billion. That was equal to the entire debt of the federal government, which had been inflated by massive deficit spending during the Civil War. Huge blocks of railroad securities were quickly put on the market, but there were few buyers. Price declines of 50% were common among the leading rail stocks. Brokers called customers for more securities margin but too many did not have enough case of liquid collateral to meet the calls. Their brokers failed. The New York Stock Exchange closed for ten days, amplifying the panic.
>
> .... Cooke's failure was a tocsin(sic) for five ensuing years of depression. Twenty-five railroads defaulted on their debts during the first few months following the Cooke collapse. Seventy-one more followed in 1874 and another twenty-five in 1875. By 1876 almost half of America's railroads were in receivership.
>
> Railroads had overbuilt. There wasn't enough traffic to support the available capacity.... By the end of 1876 the industry had defaulted on more than $800 million in debt.[42]

---

[42] Philip Leigh, *U.S. Grant's Failed Presidency*, p. 127.

It is as if, desiring the collapse of the American railroad growth—and of its long-term transglobal plans—other interests had decided upon a dramatic contraction of the money supply.

But there was a final victim of the Jay Cooke collapse, one not often mentioned, although here too the work of Philip Leigh is indispensible. Reconstruction, for all its many faults, had not been undertaken in a complete financial vacuum, for there *was* an attempt to provide some economic compensation and financial assistance to the manumitted slaves, if not, of course, to their former owners. In March of 1865, before Lincoln's assassination, the northern Congress had created the Freedman's Savings Bank, along with the Freedman's Bureau. The bank was open to deposits from freed and former slaves only. The goal was to have a bank, run by former slaves, into which savings could be deposited and, hopefully, grown to the point that they were able to purchase their own farms. While this fell far short of the Russian manumission of the serfs, and far short of the 1862 Homestead Act, by1870 the bank was initially relatively successful, having spread "thirty-four branches in seventeen states as well as the District of Columbia. It was," notes Leigh, "one of America's first multistate banks." Additionally, most of its branches were under direct black management.[43]

This situation was not to last, as the bank's trustees—mostly white, Republican, and supporters of President Grant—moved the headquarters of the bank from New York City to Washington during the period that the modern District of Columbia was being urged as a unified territorial government by a Washington City alderman. When this movement succeeded, President Grant named Henry Cooke,

---

[43] Philip Leigh, *U.S. Grant's Failed Presidency*, p. 132.

brother of the banker Jay Cooke, to be the new governor of the newly created "District of Columbia," probably in return for his brother's financial support of his 1872 presidential campaign. Having gained from the Congress permission for the bank to engage in commercial loans, the bank's loans quickly came under the influence of the Cooke interests to such an extent that the Freedman's Bank lent directly to Cooke, *on the collateral of Northern Pacific Bonds*.[44]

The reader can guess the rest of this sad story: when the Northern Pacific Railroad failed, dragging down Jay Cooke and Company with it, the Freedman's bank also collapsed, sucked under in the vortex of Cooke's collapse.

(5) Gold: More Background to the Coinage and Resumption Acts, Railroads, and Reservations

There is yet another complex context behind the various currency, coinage, and financial acts that accompanied the railroad acts, the Homestead Act, and Reconstruction, and this was the American Indian, and particularly, the tribes of the northern plains Dakota territory. These tribes, unlike the "Five Civilized Tribes" of the Indian Territory of the Confederacy in what is now modern-day Oklahoma, were not agricultural tribes, nor did they, like some of their Oklahoma counterparts, have any written language nor any real "government." They were, for all intents and purposes, still "hunter-gatherers." There were, of course, exceptions to this generalization, but the point of the generalization is made to underscore the attitude of President Grant's administrations to them. In short, Grant believed that the terms of all treaties with any tribe had to be honored, *but*

[44] Philip Leigh, *U.S. Grant's Failed Presidency*, p. 134.

he also believed that the federal government simply could not pretend that "the tribes were sovereign nations capable of enforcing treaty terms on all of their members."[45] What may have been true for the Iroquois or the Cherokee, for example, was not necessarily true of the Sioux, and vice versa.

For Grant, the problem was sparked precisely by the expansion of transcontinental railroads... through lands already recognized by the federal government, by treaties, as belonging to various tribes. With the Resumption Act, it became even more necessary than ever before to find, secure, and develop sources of gold and silver, since these bullions formed the basis of "sound circulating currency" by the thinking of that day.

When gold, massive amounts of it, was discovered in the Black Hills of what would become South Dakota and its famous Homestake Gold Mine,[46] the clash between "the Great White Father" and the Dakota tribesmen became a foregone conclusion. Grant needed the land and its gold for the railroads and the money. And the tribes had the land and the gold in abundance, for under the terms of the Treaty of

---

[45] Ibid., p. 141.

[46] Having grown up in South Dakota during the final decades of the Homestake mine's operation, the author is very familiar with the enormous size of the mine, which ceased final operations only in the early 2000s. There is still much gold in the area, it is just too costly to mine, but one can still occasionally find flakes and small nuggets in nearby Spearfish creek. The mine itself, located in Lead, South Dakota (pronounced like the verb "to lead" not like the metal), literally "right over the hill" from Deadwood, has an enormous open pit still visible as a tourist site today, while the mine shafts themselves penetrate to a depth of approximately 8,000 feet, over a mile. Leigh notes that one of the original owners of Homestake Gold Mine was George Hearst, father of William Randolph Hearst. (p. 146) During its operation, the mine produced over one billion dollars' worth of gold, based on the then contemporary prices.

Fort Laramie, the lands west of the Missouri River in the Dakotas belonged to the Sioux and Crow tribes.[47]

When a military expedition was sent by Grant into the Black Hills under General George Armstrong Custer to investigate the rumors of gold, an expedition with included Grant's first son, gold was indeed discovered in amounts suggesting much larger deposits. Word soon was spread, and another gold rush was on.[48] By late 1874 and early 1875, with the depression caused both by Jay Cooke's collapse and by the various Coinage, Credit, and Resumption acts in full swing, President Grant finally decided that, treaty or no treaty, the Black Hills had to become direct federal territory and the Sioux reservation territory west of the Missouri severely trimmed.

At this juncture, Chief Red Cloud and other tribal chiefs actually travelled to Washington, D.C. to meet directly with President Grant. It was an unfortunate summit meeting. Red Cloud and the other chiefs reminded "the Great White Father" that under the existing treaty, the lands were theirs, in perpetuity. Grant responded by confronting the chiefs with the two grim realities of their situation. Under the terms of the same treaty, the federal government's obligation to provision the tribes with rations of food had expired. He continued to do so only because of his "kind feelings toward the tribes."[49] The second problem, Grant informed them, was that he had no control over the people flooding into the Black Hills to prospect for gold. At this point, Grant terminated the summit meeting by stating that the tribes must cede the Black Hills or the federal rations would be jeopardized.

---

[47] Philip Leigh, *U.S. Grant's Failed Presidency*, p. 143.

[48] Ibid., pp. 145-146.

[49] Ibid., p. 146.

Red Cloud and the other chiefs departed the city and returned to their lands, followed by an official commission from Grant authorized to negotiate the purchase of the Black Hills from the chiefs, who demanded more than the commission had been authorized for the purchase. The commissioners returned to Washington, D.C. with an astonishing and barbaric recommendation: terminate the rations, and starve the Sioux into submission and buy the Black Hills at a price to be determined by the federal Congress![50]

Grant, however, had his own even more devious and devilish solution. Under the terms of the 1868 Treaty of Fort Laramie, not only were the lands of the Dakota territory west of the Missouri River to belong to the Sioux, but those lands in what is now eastern Montana and Wyoming were to be open to the tribes to hunt bison for as long as there was bison to hunt. Also under the terms of that same treaty, if a *legal* (note the qualifier!) 3/4ths of the Sioux population agreed to a cession of territory, meaning effectively, the adult males of the tribes *on the reservation and not hunting in the Wyoming and Montana regions outside the reservation*, then the territory was ceded.[51]

A report was concocted by a Bureau of Indian Affairs inspector that the Indian hunters in the Wyoming and Montana "hunting grounds" had committed various violations of the Treaty and other acts of violence. These tribal villages were informed that they must return to their reservation by the end of January, 1876, or be "declared hostile." Various U.S. Army provocations occurred against various villages in the hunting territory, including attempts to capture tribal horses and ponies, leaving them unable to hunt. The final

[50] Philip Leigh, *U.S. Grant's Failed Presidency*, p. 146.
[51] Ibid., pp. 146-147.

campaign was, of course, the famous massacre of the 7th Cavalry under George Armstrong Custer at the Battle of the Little Big Horn. It was a short-lived victory, for now Grant had his various false flags and a *casus belli*. Sending a new commission led by George Manypenny to negotiate the sale of the Black Hills *only with the Sioux who had remained on the reservation*, when these objected that they could not do so without the 3/4ths consent of all adult males including those in the hunting territories, the response, and the pressure, was swift. *Those* tribal members were now "hostile" and no longer legal participants of the tribe. Besides, the commissioners argued, the old treaty had been abrogated the moment the U.S. Army had been attacked at the Little Big Horn. (If this sounds rather similar to the "logic" of Reconstruction regarding the southern states, that's because it's almost identical.) One final turn of the thumbscrew was applied when some commissioners implied that either the new treaty be signed, or the entire Sioux nation would be moved to Oklahoma (violating *those* tribes' rights!), and thus lose their rations, and be required to lose their firearms and horses (since, of course, they were no longer needed for hunting!).[52]

Congress approved Manypenny's treaty in February 1877,[53] and though Grant was by that time out of office, the monetary and coinage policies of his administrations were still in force, and the Union had a new and rich vein of gold to mine.

C. Gold, Coinage, Credit, and Resumption:
1. The Acts and the Deflation

---

[52] Philip Leigh, *U.S. Grant's Failed Presidency*, p. 149.
[53] Ibid.

Having examined all the complex contexts and implications of the policies we have alluded to throughout the *previous* chapter and the previous sections of *this* chapter, we are in a position to comprehend the acts directly bearing on them, and to see with clarity the indicators of deeply hidden players and their deep states, motivations, and agendas.

The problem may be simply put: the creation by the Union North during the War Between the States of a fiat currency that was debt free, and legislating by law that it was legal tender, meant that there were basically three forms of money in circulation: (1) specie, in the form of gold and silver coins, or paper certificates redeemable in specie; (2) paper notes circulated against bonds, i.e., an interest-bearing monetized debt; and (3) the Lincoln greenbacks, the fiat interest-free money. But while this enormous expansion of liquidity enabled the war to be financed, it was also done against a wider backdrop that all money must, in principle, be backed by, and convertible to, specie, which itself could be used in transaction. But there was simply not enough bullion in the treasury to redeem all the greenbacks.[54] In the thinking of the day, in order to restore convertibility, one had either to expand the bullion supply for the specie, or contract the amount of certificates and financial instruments circulating on its basis.

a. The Coinage Act of 1873, or "the Crime of '73"

[54]Philip Leigh, *U.S. Grant's Failed Presidency*, p. 155.

The Coinage Act of 1873, one year into Ulysses S. Grant's second administration, was, on its surface, simplicity itself, for it simply *"dropped* the standard 412 ½-grain silver dollar from the list of American coins."[55] One of the key movers of the bill, Ohio U.S. Senator John Sherman, brother of Union General William Tecumseh Sherman (who, it will be recalled, issued plunder orders to his army as it cut a fiery swath through Georgia)[56] had sponsored similar measures earlier in the north.

But much more importantly, Senator Sherman was part of an international movement dedicated to the establishment of a world currency standard based upon a monometallic, or gold, standard:

> … (In) January 1868, Senator John Sherman introduced a bill to make the gold dollar the sole standard monetary unit of the United States *at a weight conforming to twenty-five gold French francs.* Before that, in (the) spring of 1867, Sherman and others were instrumental in bringing the Paris International Monetary Conference to declare for universal gold monometallism.[57]

This raises the inevitable possibility that not only is there an international component of geopolifinance exerting an influence on domestic American financial polity and polity (as there self-evidently is from the foregoing quotation), but that this influence *may* ***possibly*** have played some role in the plunder policy of Sherman's brother, William Tecumseh, as the latter's army was plundering its way through Georgia.

---

[55] Walter T.K. Nugent, *The Money Question During Reconstruction*, p. 67.

[56] Q.v. my *The Rialto in Richmond,* pp. 28-30.

[57] Ibid., emphasis added.

What was it possibly doing with all the gold and silver plate it may have collected? Whether or not this is the case, it is intriguing to note that *Senator* Sherman's international monetary connections also may have extended to Great Britain's famous Baring Brothers' Bank, for Sherman was formally introduced to that bank's head by a letter from a Congressman prior to the Senator's departure from the U.S.A. to attend the Paris monetary conference. Barings, in turn, was known in its heyday as "the Sixth Great Power," with an international power and influence rivaling the Rothschild banking interest, and, incidentally, it was Barings Bank that was the British underwriter of the *French* bonds floated by Napoleon Bonaparte to enable the U.S.A. to buy the Louisiana Purchase when England and France were at war with each other! Wheels within wheels!

In any case, while silver had not been circulating as money for some time, prior to the Coinage Act of 1873, it still remained a legal tender and a currency. It was its *rarity* as a specie metal more than its relatively inferior value to gold that removed it from circulation. But that was about to change—dramatically so, as will be seen—and already there were monetary experts in Germany, England, and the United States who were predicting to their treasuries, and in contradiction to the prevailing ideology of what may be called "gold buggery," that silver was poised to "make a comeback."[58]

The popular and populist reaction to the Coinage Act of 1873 was responsible for giving it the name by which it went down in the history books, "the Crime of '73," for as far as the poor farmers of the American West were concerned,

---

[58] Walter T.K. Nugent, *The Money Question During Reconstruction*, p. 67.

they joined their poorer comrades, the sharecroppers of the "reconstructing" South in designating it

> … a monumental fraud upon the people, committed *by a conspiracy of legistlators and financiers, English and European bond-holding interests, to make sure that their investments would be paid in gold*, (when they) sent Ernest Seyd to America in 1872 with £100,000 to smooth the way of silver demonetization through a venal Congress… it had fastened a repressive, deflationary gold standard on the helpless masses in the interests of a corrupt few.[59]

In other words, there was *international pressure for a monometallic gold standard*, while *domestically*, in America, there was both the legal and Constitutional precedent for a bi-metallic gold-and-silver standard.[60]

This produced a tremendous financial pressure in two ways: firstly, it contracted the potential supply of money by excluding, by law, what had previously, by law, been recognized constitutional money. This, in itself, resulted in a contraction of the money supply. The result of *this*, in turn, was a deflationary spiral (exacerbated by the Cooke collapse) that particularly affected the farmers (whose good were presumably to have moved on Cooke's, and other's, railroads!). Farmers would have to take out loans for the

---

[59] Ibid., p. 65, emphasis added.

[60] For the ancientness and persistence of the gold vs. silver systems and monies and banking based upon them see my *Babylon's Banksters: The Alchemy of Deep Physics, High Finance, and Ancient Religion* (Port Townsend, Washington: Feral House, 2010 (ISBN 978-1-93259-579-6)), particularly pp. 187-207, and my *Financial Vipers of Venice: Alchemical Money, Magical Physics, and Banking in the Middle Ages and Renaissance* (Port Townsend, Washington: Feral House, 2010 (ISBN 978-1-93623-973-3)), particularly pp. 93-191.

seeds to plant their crops. When the crops matured and the loans came due, if the farmers profited, the loans could be repaid. But in a deflationary cycle, when the supply of money is dwindling proportionally as its value is increasing, this meant that farmers would have to repay their loans, not only the interest but the principle, with money that had gained in value during the period of the loan. In effect, the deflation was itself a second form on interest on the money leant. Small wonder that in 1893 William Jennings Bryan, voicing the frustrations of the South and West, complained of the "cross of gold."

For most Americans of the Reconstruction period, as the effects of the policies began to spread from the South, thence to the west, and finally to the "west" of the Northern Union states like Ohio, Indiana, Michigan and Illinois, it eventually became clear that "the quiet, recondite financial legislation of the Reconstruction period had revealed itself shamelessly for what it really was: conspiratorial robbery by class against mass. And it had been purposeful."[61] Such was not, of course, the interpretation of those advocates of the monometallic gold standard, among them, George Boutwell, Treasury Secretary in 1873 when the act was passed. For Boutwell and the advocates of "gold buggery" the contrasts could not have been clear nor their own principled positioned more misunderstood, far from being perpetrators of a crime who had "refinanced the Civil War debt in such a way as to fasten an immense burden on future tax-paying generations, and at the same time had redefined the country's monetary standard so as to induce severe deflation," they turned out, on the contrary,

---

[61] Walter T.K. Nugent, *The Money Question During Reconstruction*, p. 27.

> ...to be the embattled guardians of the public honor and credit, striving to keep American finance on a respectable level among civilized nations. Conversely, the toiling masses, the farmers and laborers, the producers upon whose pure hearts and brawny shoulders the future of the country depended, were really trying to pull a gigantic confidence trick by which they would pay their own and the country's creditors in the debased and fraudulent currency of free silver.[62]

Lest it be forgotten, George Boutwell was a Radical Republican Abolitionist, and one of the chief proponents of the impeachment of President Andrew Johnson.[63]

The proponents of "bi-metallism," or rather, that silver should be re-monetized as legal money, were vociferous in

---

[62] Ibid., p. 19.

[63] Nugent also makes the very trenchant observation that the United States was trying to resolve *cultural* issues on the basis of a cosmology and philosophy of money and currency. His conclusion, however, that "the whole issue, the money question itself, now seems so tinny that a present-day audience has to marvel at how the whole post-Civil War generation could ever have let themselves become so fascinated with it," seems to do an injustice to both sides, for both sides understood what the modern does not, that one's understanding of currency and money is part of a wider cosmological and even physics view: is the system open, or closed? On this view, the gold-and-silver 'bi-metallists" were in effect and by analogy arguing that the system is open; and the gold-buggery supporters were arguing that the system was closed. Or, if one prefer to view the debate from the standpoint of my "topological metaphor of the medium" and its "primary and first differentiation," the bi-metallists are arguing that ever more differentiations increases the amount of information in the cosmological system, while the monometallists are arguing that the primary differentiation results in *fractions* of the whole, each new differentiation only reducing the size of the fractions. One multiplies the pies, and the other, the slices of one pie.

their denunciations of foreign influence at work behind the acts, and as was to be expected, blamed foreign financiers such as the Rothschilds for being behind the Coinage Act and its deleterious effects.[64] They were *not* without a basis in fact for doing so, for it will be recalled that the British Rothschild financial affairs magazine, *The Economist*, had abruptly and massively reversed its position on the Confederate Cotton Erlanger loan of 1863, from first denouncing its speculatory and risky nature, to promoting it heavily. It will be recalled that the terms of the loan were onerous in terms of the interest payments on the bonds due either in cotton or specie, which meant, gold.[65]

b. The Specie Resumption Act of 1875

An important point must now be explicitly stated, lest it go unnoticed by the reader, and lead to misunderstandings of what has preceded in this book, and what now succeeds: the real reconstruction is not just of the South. *Southern reconstruction is but one, and the most visible, effect of a whole collection of legislation and policies designed to reconstruct the entire system of American finance,* and to dramatically contract the money supply that had resulted from massive Civil War debt back to a scale where the circulating financial instruments could be safely converted to specie payments. In effect, the effort being mounted was to "walk back" and "reverse" the courses of action that had been undertaken by the federal (Union) government to finance the war. For the Union, these five courses of action, brought about by the war in its very earliest stages when the sheer

[64] Ibid., p.16.

[65] See my *The Rialto in Richmond*, pp. 241-256f.

scale of what was financially required became apparent (to *both* sides!) were for the Union, the following:

(1) an immediate suspension of specie payments on demand presentation of banknotes at a bank, for the specie reserves were too small to support the massive finance for the war effort, and what specie there as *did* exist was needed to support international trade;
(2) Higher taxes were needed, beyond the revenues that tariffs would support, and thus the Union quickly introduced the country's first income tax as a wartime measure (an indicator that permanent income taxes are to support war economies);
(3) The Treasury was authorized to issue bonds to raise even more money and thus to massively enlarge the national debt;
(4) A new system of "nationally chartered" banks was established and authorized to sell bonds against gold deposits, as a means of raising further money, and gold bullion reserves; and finally,
(5) When even these measures proved inadequate to the sheer scale of the military operations to be sustained, the Congress authorized the creation of a fiat, interest-free currency, the Lincoln "greenbacks."[66]

While the observation that the post-bellum monetary and fiscal legislation and policies were attempts to walk back or reverse these measures is my own, but the point is that if one wishes to view this effort from the standpoint of my

[66] Walter T.K. Nugent, *The Money Question During Reconstruction*, pp. 24-25.

"topological metaphor of the medium," what is being attempted is to reverse the effects of lower order derivatives and to return to a state of the "pie" where there are fewer fractional slices. The difficulty that was neither then nor now acknowledged is that once information of any sort is added to a system, its effects always remain. Nugent puts it this way:

> The questions that concerned people long after the Civil War, much longer than Reconstruction policy itself ,were the stubborn by-products of the financial emergency of the early war years that were to vex the country for more than a generation.... Any return to normalcy in the area of national finance would have to involve an accommodation between long-standing pre-war practice and principles, and the new realities that stemmed from the war emergency.[67]

Notice that what is *missing* in all these observations is a *lot* of missing money: the ***Confederate** debt, and **its** creditors*.

It is precisely this *last* point of missing money, Confederate debt, and *its* creditors, not to mention the *Union* debt and *its* creditors, many of whom are foreign in both cases, that lies behind the next Act that led to such a disastrous deflation (and to the "railroad overbuilding" prior to it that was based on the wartime spending).

The roots of the Specie Payment Resumption Act of 1875 is made clear by the title of the bill: it authorized the resumption of the convertibility of circulating paper certificates for specie money; in effect, its purpose was to allow gold specie to be exchanged for the presentation of greenbacks. Again, it is to be noted that it is *gold* that is being referred to, because silver had ceased to be a circulating

[67] Walter T.K. Nugent, *The Money Question During Reconstruction*, p. 26.

form of specie due to its *scarcity*. It had to be carefully done, for if it was not, the country would soon run out of foreign exchange "because the government was obligated to pay its creditors (many of them foreign), and private businessmen their foreign creditors, in gold."[68]

The Public Credit Act of 1869, shortly after Grant took office, was the first step to the Resumption act six years later, for it stipulated "that the faith of the United States is solemnly pledged to the payment in coin or its equivalent of all the obligations of the United States" with the exception of debts that were authorized to be paid in "lawful money" that was other than silver or gold.[69]

Two important factors enabled the Resumption Act, factors that began to enter the calculus of financial and economic thinking at that time: (1) bank concentration, or the local "mass" of money, and (2) the local *velocity* of money.[70] As most banks at the time of the passage of the Resumption Act and the scheduled resumption of specie payments (January 2, 1879) were located in the northeast of the country, this factor meant that specie resumptions would likewise be concentrated in that area, and thus the convertibility of greenbacks to specie could be safely resumed (1) because some greenbacks had been deliberately removed from circulation already (and some, as I hypothesized in *The Rialto in Richmond*, deliberately moved into covert financing of secret projects), and (2) because one had only to ensure adequate specie concentrations in areas were convertibility was likely to be demanded by creditors, i.e., the northeast.

---

[68] Ibid., p. 27.

[69] Walter T.K. Nugent, *The Money Question During Reconstruction*, p. 30.

[70] F=MV.

With this in view, it is crucial and vital that the reader notice what has happened as a result of the Resumption Act, for

(1) the greenback, which was originally a debt-free legal tender *not* accompanied by convertibility, has now, by legal decree, *become convertible*; and thus, and even more extraordinarily *and suggestively*,

(2) *the greenback has become by an extraordinary and little-noticed sleight of hand, exactly the* ***same*** *type of currency as issued by the Confederacy, as something "payable to the bearer" upon a certain length of time after the conclusion of the war!*[71]

This is strongly suggestive prima facie *evidence that either the victorious Union had covertly and secretly decided to assume responsibility for the Confederacy's debts, or that it had been* ***secretly pressured*** *to do so and had secretly acquiesced.*

There is a final point to be noted about the Specie Resumption Act, and that is that it was rammed through the Congress by the Republicans after the Democratic victories in the off-year 1874 elections.[72] The Democrats, oddly, were not in favor of resumption but allowing the continued circulation of greenbacks as an expedient against further contraction of the money supply during the deflation affecting the country.

---

[71] Q.v. my *The Rialto in Richmond*, pp. 205-215. The failure to prosecute Davis for treason is, in my estimation, another clue that this is the case, for *legally*, as Davis pointed out in his *The Rise and Fall of the Confederate Government*, the Southern states were entirely within their legal right to secede, regardless of their reconstruction foreswearing of the possibility at the point of Union bayonets: after all, a contract signed under duress in law is no contract.

[72] Philip Leigh, *U.S. Grant's Failed Presidency*, p. 161.

As will be seen in the next section, the foreign pressure and influence to create an international gold standard currency system was enormously influential art that time.

Here, again, President Grant entered the picture with a novel interpretation of a particular feature in the Resumption Act. As an enticement to advocates of a softer money policy, and in order to win their support for the bill, a provision had been included that would allow the new "national banks" to issue banknotes against bonds, provided that circulating greenbacks be *reduced* by 80% of any such new banknotes issued. But was that "80%" stipulation *net*, or, as President Grant interpreted it, *gross?* In other words, if $100 million dollars of new banknotes were created and circulated, while $50 million of old banknotes were retired from circulation, then that meant that $40 million dollars' worth of circulating greenbacks also had to be retired for a net increase of a modest $10 million dollars of circulating paper.

But if the law meant *gross* circulation, then the 80% reduction of circulating greenbacks would have to be $80 million dollars to correspond with the gross issue of $100 million dollars' worth of new banknotes. Grant and his party were thus interpreting the law in a much more deflationary way than the "soft money" advocates were, for their primary concern was to reduce the amount of circulating greenbacks as much a possible prior to the resumption of specie payments in 1879.[73]

. 2. The Hidden Players: The Nineteenth Century Quest for a Global Currency based on Gold

---

[73] Philip Leigh, *U.S. Grant's Failed Presidency*, p. 162,

As was hinted earlier, there was an international pressure at work during this period, in which the Republican leaders of the Union and in which Grant's administrations and personal power networks were involved. That movement was the world's first public push for a global currency system, based on gold, a cautionary tale for the present time. Given that the Union, and perhaps equally if not more importantly, the Confederacy had foreign creditors, this meant that the post bellum money, credit, and debt policies of the federal government, and indeed, the whole process of Reconstruction was of immense geopolitical importance and interest, for whatever decisions were made, they would have "international repercussions—in the international bond market, in net trade and payments balances, and in the attitude of foreign parties to someone else's monetary standard."[74]

The War Between the States changed everything, and brought the problem of "geopolifinance" to the forefront of discussions of monetary policy within the councils of world power politics in Europe and America that even the Napoleonic Wars had not, for the "potentially chaotic diversity of monetary standards worked reasonably well as long as there were no massive changes in the relative world supplies of refined gold and silver, and as long as the economies (and economic crises) of various countries were relatively independent."[75] The War Between the States changed all of that, for as even as the single the example of the Erlanger Confederate Cotton loan demonstrated, while

---

[74] Walter T.K. Nugent, *The Money Question During Reconstruction*, p. 39.

[75] Ibid., p. 40.

gold alone was "very hard to get away from in international payments systems," it could not, on its own, "do the job."[76]

A step, however, in the right direction was made to coordinate the values of currencies on the basis of gold, a step predictably advocated by the French Emperor, Napoleon Bonaparte III, who, like his famous predecessor, tried to organize political institutions along the most rational lines possible.[77] Napolean III's reasoning was simple and straightforward: because the French currency system was a decimal system, and the franc in turn was based on "integral multiples of the gram and meter" and the meter, in its turn supposedly a decimal fraction of the "eternal circumference of the earth itself," it was proposed to unify a system of weights, measures, and most importantly, currency, on this system. Different systems inhibited trade and commerce.[78] Interestingly enough, this means that France itself, like the pre-bellum USA, and the British pound *sterling*, was a "bi-metallic" nation, at the time under discussion in the immediate years after the War Between the States, the French advocates of "gold buggery" held the upper hand, and had even succeeded by treaty arrangements with the Papal States, Greece, Romania, Belgium, Italy, and Switzerland to unify the coinages of the countries by the expedient of valuing them in reference to the franc.[79]

---

[76] Ibid.,

[77] While avoiding the Jacobin excesses of "rationality" of course!

[78] Walter T.K. Nugent, *The Money Question During Reconstruction*, p. 42.

[79] Ibid., p. 43. For those paying attention, this is the first European "snake" system of currency "unification," based on the franc and the subsequent late 20th century version would be based on the German mark. It should be pointed out that there is no similar mechanism that I know of in this arrangement to the later German snake system, where in the Bundesbank would step in to keep other currencies

Notably, William Gladstone, a holder of Erlanger bonds, supported the idea of currency unification through definitions of currency along a unified system of weights and measures,[80] and Bismarck endorsed the idea, since he had adroitly used "gold buggery" monometallism to unify the German states—many of which were on silver standards—under Prussian hegemony.[81]

In the United States, the idea of using the basis of the franc for an international system of fixed exchange rates exercised some considerable influence during the final year of the Johnson Administration, and commanded "the loyalties and energies of Sherman,[82] Ruggles, Seward,[83] McCulloch,[84] and certain others." Sherman and McCulloch had actually composed a bill based on the French principles redefining the nature of American coinage.[85] Viewed in the context of everything else presented in the previous chapter and in this chapter, it is difficult to avoid the conclusion that a concerted effort was being mounted to do an end run around American financial sovereignty, to hamstring it to a European gold monometallism, and thus to recoup losses to European creditors to the belligerents of the War Between the States.

There was just one fly in the ointment of gold buggery: silver was just about to make a comeback… big time…

---

within that system from exceeding certain exchange limits vis-à-vis the Deutschmark.

[80] Ibid., p. 46.

[81] Walter T.K. Nugent, *The Money Question During Reconstruction*, p. 44.

[82] The Ohio U.S. Senator and brother of General William Tecunseh Sherman.

[83] William Seward, Secretary of State

[84] McCulloch, Secretary of the Treasury under Johnson.

[85] Nugent, op. cit., p. 73.

3. Silver Comes Back: The Discovery of the Comstock Lode(s)

As all of this was transpiring, there was a discovery in Nevada territory during the last year of the War Between the States that proved to be a rich vein, or rather, veins, of silver that became known as the Comstock Lode. In spite of its name, which gives the impression of one large vein, the Comstock Lode was rather a few very large veins. This was known in the Johnson Administration as his treasury secretary McCulloch had ordered that a close eye be kept on developments. Major strikes were made in 1866 and again in 1870, but in 1873, the year that Ulysses S. Grant entered office, the mother lode of the Comstock Lode was discovered to be worth a quarter of a *billion* dollars, an amount, interestingly enough for our story, that was worth more than fifty percent of the face value of all "outstanding greenback issue of the United States."[86]

The significance of the Comstock Lode and its enormous valuation means nothing less than that the whole process of the Credit, Coinage, and Resumption Acts was undertaken with the deliberate knowledge that a non-deflationary solution to specie resumption could have been made, a policy that would have enormously benefitted the post bellum reconstruction. The decision to avoid the continued silver monetization was thus, and could only be,

---

[86] Walter T.K. Nugent, *The Money Question During Reconstruction*, pp. 37-38. Interestingly enough, a German baron, Ferdinand Baron von Richthofen(!), had studied the Comstock Lode(s) and concluded that the veins would *widen* as one went deeper, rather than narrow.(p. 35) The question of why a German baron with *that* last name should be wandering around the barren wastes of Nevada studying a silver lode raises its own "Bosleyesque" questions about financing secret airship projects. Q.v. *The Rialto in Richmond*, pp. 270-280.

made by those intending only to enrich themselves, and, if the foreign interests implied thus far be any indicator, also made by those intent on avoiding the geopolifinancial implications of railroads, and particularly of direct rail links between the American continents and Eurasia. The emerging potentials of a Russo-American trading bloc had to be avoided at all costs.

D. Grant's Post-Office World Tour: What was the Purpose of the Meeting Between President Ulysses S. Grant and...?

While much more could be said about the election of 1876, Grant's questionable role in some of the political shenanigans that propelled fellow Republican Rutherford B. Hayes into office, much of it relevant to the discussion thus far, I believe an adequate enough template has been established from which the reader may view those events on his own. But one more very strange thing must be examined from the standpoint of this template.

When Ulysses S. Grant left office in 1877, he undertook a twenty-eight months' long circumnavigation of the globe, traveling first to Europe, thence through Asia and returning to San Francisco, to return to New Jersey by the transcontinental railroad that had been finished ten years earlier. During his travels, he met the Japanese Emperor…

…and while in Berlin, he met Imperial German Reichs Chancellor Otto von Bismarck.

One may, of course, assume that the two politicians exchanged pleasantries about being heads of government, and in a way, the two had much in common on that score, for both had presided over political, and financial, unifications of their respective countries, both of which had histories of quarrelsome "states." Both had fought wars to do so.

But perhaps there was another reason altogether. Perhaps on this occasion the *Eisenkanzler* enlightened Mr. Grant about the real reasons for the financial difficulties his country had gone through during his two administrations, and who was behind them, and perhaps it may be from this conversation that those apocryphal remarks of Bismarck about the American Civil War, and Lincoln's assassination being orchestrated by the high financial powers of Europe originated. Perhaps it was an anecdote Grant later shared with his wife and family, and the story percolated through the cobblestoned back alleys of European gossip until it was published by a Frenchman in the 1920s.[87] Or perhaps it originated from the Elanger loan bond holders themselves. We perhaps will never know.

Or, perhaps, Grant was there to report to Bismarck on the progress of the covert "airship" research that the Germans were sponsoring in America.[88]

Personally, I doubt very much that they merely exchanged pleasantries. Ulysses S. Grant and Otto von Bismarck having a friendly conversation about their grand children over tea and cigars!?

Ausgeschlossen!

What now seems evident is that the Serpents of the City had, perhaps, coiled and struck, and in a most subtle and nuanced way.

We have now dug down through the first and most obvious layer of players and agendas, but before we can look for the telltale signs of slithering Serpents of the City, or the footprints of their cousins, the Weasels of Wall Street, we must pause for an intermission, and take stock.

---

[87] Q.v. my *Rialto in Richmond*, pp. 233-240f.
[88] Ibid., pp. 270-281ff.

4
Intermission:
Taking Stock

"The development of the money question during Reconstruction is an interesting problem in historical motivation, because it was at once naively simple and darkly mystifying."
Walter T.K. Nugent[1]

BEFORE WE CAN PROCEED TO DIG DOWN BENEATH this surface layer of suggestive activity and policies to the deeper veins of agendas and players, we must pause for a brief "intermission" to take stock of the implications and potentialities thus far explored, lest by dint of the surfeit of information presented, or by dint of the lack of an explicit statement of them, they be missed or ignored. These are summarized and itemized as succinctly as possible in the following inventory and preçis:

1) While Lincoln's and the Republicans' decision to choose Southern Democrat and former Tennessee U.S. Senator Andrew Johnson as his 1864 running mate may have been shrewd politics necessary to their victory in the elections that year, the calculation also was likely a profound temptation to the Radical factions within the Republican Party, dissatisfied as they were with Lincoln's lenient proposals for the post bellum South, to risk the

---

[1] Walter T. K. Nugent, *The Money Question During Reconstruction*, p. 52.

murder of the President in order to inaugurate a harsher policy.

2) Initially, while Johnson seemed to be on the side of the Radicals in his announcements that the Confederate leadership should face legal consequences for their treason, the initial brace of support for Johnson evaporated when it became clear that he opposed the Radical plans for southern "reconstruction."

3) The political calculus that the Radicals employed in accepting Johnson as Lincoln's Vice Presidential running mate was revealed during the impeachment efforts to remove him from office, as the pro-impeachment forces of the Republican party repeatedly stated to the northern press—still controlled by Johnson's Secretary of War Edwin Stanton—that Johnson held the presidency only accidentally and by dint of an assassin's bullet.

4) Thus, the *assassination of President Lincoln and the impeachment efforts against President Johnson should be viewed as two parts of one complex strategic plan, for the possibility must be entertained that in choosing to rid themselves of Lincoln, the plotters knew that in order to press their agenda, they would have to remove Johnson from office, using his party affiliation as a Southern Democrat against him.* Having assassinated one President, the next could hardly be assassinated without raising suspicion, but impeachment lay open as the means to do so without raising suspicion. The means was contrived to hamstring Johnson through a variety of acts, including the Tenure in Office Act, and the various machinations both Johnson and his opponents showed in the

attempt to replace Stanton as Secretary of War and curb his, and the Radicals' influence over southern reconstruction and the military jurisdiction over it.

5) At a deeper level, the oppositions and splits within the post bellum Union provided a wide and rich field in which *agents provocateur* could operate, if any were in the field. These fissures became evident when the voting records and positions of Senators and Congressmen during Johnson's Senate trial on the third and final House impeachment indictment were compared to their votes on key financial and currency matters. While no such *agents provocateur* were covered in the examination of the Johnson impeachment efforts, mention was made of the "Impresario of Imposture," Charles A. Dunham, who will be treated later in this book.
6) When turning to the two Administrations of the 18th President of the United States, Ulysses S. Grant, the indicators of a deep geopolifinancial interest becomes much more visible. The deliberate demonetization of silver during the currency, credit, coinage, and resumption acts that characterize and mark his administrations, when the vast extent of the Comstock Lode(s) discoveries were fully known, means that silver was *deliberately* removed as a potential means of the resumption of specie exchanges for circulating greenbacks in a deliberate pursuit of deflation. In seeking a monometallic gold standard, the geopolifinancial background is exposed in three ways:
   a) Firstly, by the presence at that time of a movement in Europe and the United States to define their

money on the basis of gold coins, which were fixed in value relative to the French franc. This movement, as was seen, was supported by Republican Radicals such as Senator Sherman of Ohio, brother of Union General W.T. Sherman, close friend of Ulysses Grant.

b) Secondly, by the fact that the *effect* of the Resumption Act entirely changed the character of the Lincoln greenback from a fiat currency designated legal tender without any backing, to a currency exchangeable at par for specie, in effect, reducing it to the same character as the *Confederate* currency, and suggesting that resumption, coupled with reconstruction, was the means for holders of Confederate debt to recoup their investments and losses; and finally,

c) Thirdly, by the fact that Grant literally contrived various false flag operations and other deceits to create a *casus belli* with the Sioux Indians in order to seize the rich gold vein of the Homestake lode in the Black Hills of the Dakota territory.

The effect of these policies—including the demonetization of silver in spite of an abundance of cheap silver—created a deflationary crisis that spilled over to effect farmers, and played a role in the collapse of the railroads. As farmers had to take out loans for seeds to plant their crops, these loans had to be repaid with scarcer dollars that had increased in value. As this increasingly affected the farmers, the economic contraction hit the over-built railroads, as farmers were moving less goods on the railroads, and fewer people had the money to travel on them. The collapse of Jay

Cooke and Company in Philadelphia signaled the end of the railroad boom.

7) Railroads played their own part in the wider geopoli-financial calculus as well, for when looking into the future, one discerns grand "transglobal" railroad projects being advanced by leaders both in the USA and in Imperial Russia to connect the American continents with Eurasia via rail links through the Bering Strait, a project advocated by Tsar Nicholas II himself. As was seen, Britain stepped into the picture to raise Japan to world power status by transfers of British naval technology to that country, thus creating an interdiction threat between Russia and the United States and to their Bering Strait Plans. It should be stressed in this context that the United States, in the person of Theodore Roosevelt, was the arbiter of peace negotiations ending the Russo-Japanese War. As a result of the war, Japan gained the Russian territorial concession in Manchuria, and the Russian Trans-Siberian Railroad, which had gone through Manchuria, had to be rebuilt around Manchuria to re-establish the railroad link to Vladivostok.
8) With this backdrop of the future in mind, it was then argued that the other part of the assault on the potential to execute this transglobal railroad project consisted in the advocacy for the monometallic gold standard, and the deliberate contraction of the money supply, and the collapse of the railroad-building boom.
9) Finally, President Grant's twenty-eight month circumnavigation of the world, and especially his meeting with Imperial German Chancellor Otto von Bismarck, strongly suggest agendas in play that may have had something to do with all of this, and more

> besides: the Prusso-German sponsorship of exotic airship technology development in North America, a development that, coincidentally, or perhaps, not so coincidentally, ended up in Texas, in the Confederacy's old "Trans-Mississippi department.

To sum all these points together, one could not wish for a set of geopolifinancial circumstances more tailor made for certain parties to exploit, parties with an interest in *preventing* any Russo-American "railroad rapprochement," parties interested in *preventing* any German-American technological end-run around its control of the sea lanes, parties interested in recouping investment losses from bad investments in the Confederacy, parties interested in preventing any further experimentation along the lines of the Lincoln greenback, and turning the greenback itself into a variation of the type of currency used by the Confederacy.

There was, in short, a vast and deep geopolifinancial context and agenda in which the War Between the States was fought. The question now becomes, what domestic and international footprints did that context and agenda leave during the war?

There were two principal events that manifested those footprints. One we have encountered already in *The Rialto in Richmond*, and the other, an almost forgotten and little understood attempt between Abraham Lincoln and Jefferson Davis to negotiate a peace to end the war. For those willing to look at the geopolifinancial ground beneath these two events, the muddy footprints in the trail are all too clear. To that one already-encountered event, and to the other all-but-forgotten event, we now turn.

Part Two: The Second, Deeper, Layer: The Disastrous Raid, The Foiled Peace Conference, and Murdered Mercy

"How were the troopers supposed to find Jefferson Davis and the other targets of the plot? Dahlgren was familiar with Richmond, but most of the men were not."
—Duane Schultz,
The Dahlgren Affair, p. 252.

"Several Confederate armies more or less worthy of the name were still in the field, most notably what was left of General Johnston's in North Carolina, another in Texas, a third in Alabama."
—James B. Conroy,
Our One Common Country: Abraham Lincoln and the Hampton Roads Peace Conference of 1865, p. 275.

"'In the greatest effort of his life,' Varina (Davis) said, 'he failed from the predominance of some of his 'noble qualities... his courage, integrity, and devotion to duty...'"
—James B. Conroy,
Our One Common Country, p. 294.

Union Colonel Ulric Dahlgren (top)
Leader of the Infamous Dahlgren Raid on the Confederate Capitol, Richmond, in 1864, below in his uniform as a captain.

5
A RAID ON RICHMOND RIDDLED WITH RIDDLES:
COLONEL ULRIC DAHLGREN'S DESPERATE RAID AND ITS LINGERING QUESTIONS

"I had felt much the same unwillingness, having been intimate with (Dahlgren's) parents. Once Commodore Dahlgren had brought the fair-haired boy to show me how pretty he looked in his black velvet suit and Vandyke collar, and I could not reconcile the two Ulrics."
Confederate First Lady Varina Howell Davis[1]

PERHAPS NO ONE EPITOMIZES THE PROFOUND SADNESS of the War Between the States better than Union Colonel Ulric Dahlgren, whose handsome visage the reader may see on the facing page. His father, was, of course, Union Rear Admiral John Dahlgren, whose method of making heavy naval ordnance even lent the family surname to the cannons. His uncle was a Confederate general. And as the epigraph which begins this chapter notes, Ulric had been proudly displayed by his father to the future Confederate First Lady, Varina Howell Davis, for the Dahlgren and Davis families had been friends before the war when Jefferson had served as U.S. Secretary of War under President Franklin Pierce. As a young officer in the Union Army during that terrible war, he distinguished himself in several major battles

---

[1] Varina Howell Davis, quoted in Duane Schultz, *The Dahlgren Affair: Terror and Conspiracy in the Civil War* (New York: W.W. Norton and Company: 1999, ISBN 978-0-393-31986-5), p. 239.

in the Army of the Potomac, including the Second Manassas, Fredricksburg, Chancellorsville, and Gettysburg. He quickly rose to the rank of Colonel by the tender age of twenty-one, when he was chosen in early 1864 to lead the infamous raid on Richmond that also bears his name, the Dahlgren Raid.[2]

Union Rear Admiral John Dahlgren, Father of Colonel Ulric Dahlgren, standing next to one of the "Dahlgren" naval guns named after him[3]

---

[2] Q.v. my *Rialto in Richmond*, pp. 25-27ff.

[3] Admiral Dahlgren's younger brother, Charles Gustavus Ulrich Dahlgren had been, at one time, an officer of the Second Bank of the United States at Natchez, Mississippi, and a brigadier general in the Mississippi militia before a dispute with Jefferson Davis over the disposition and command of the Mississippi militia

The story of the raid is simple enough. While his immediate superior, Brigadier General Judson Kilpatrick was to lead a cavalry raid of approximately 3,500 troops to Richmond, and free the Union prisoners of war in the Libby Prison; during this raid, however, the young Colonel Dahlgren was to lead a much smaller party to the government district of the Confederate capitol, burn the government buildings, and then, according to the written orders that were found on the unfortunate colonel's dead body after the Confederate forces defeated the raid, kill Davis and the Confederate federal cabinet. These captured orders were conveyed to President Davis while he was meeting with his Secretary of State, Judah Benjamin, by none other than General Fitzhugh Lee, nephew of the famous commanding general of the Army of Northern Virginia. Davis' reaction, when he read the orders, was to laugh, and turn to Benjamin, and say "This means you, Mr. Benjamin."[4]

This is as far as I pursued the matter in *The Rialto in Richmond*, for the very simple reason that while the story of the event is simple, the questions and implications surrounding it, when one drills into it, are not. In fact, it is with the Dahlgren Raid that we see very clear and deep footprints of other hidden actors at work, actors in turn who have their own even more deeply hidden influences and motivations.

Here we must pause to take note of something else that affects the methodology of this book, the methodology

---

ended his army career. Both Dahlgren brothers were the sons of the Swedish merchant and consul Bernhard Ulrik Dahlgren.

[4] Duane Schultz, *The Dahlgren Affair: Terror and Conspiracy in the Civil War* (New York: W.W. Norton and Company, 1998 [ISBN 978-0-393-31986-5]), p. 153.

implied in the first chapter: the scholarship of some of the personages and events we shall examine often has, quite literally, only one publicly and easily available source. These studies are thus indispensable not only for the little-known details they provide, but for the fact that they raise important questions and implications, and equally as often, *fail* to raise the important questions and implications regarding the real or potential connections of their studies to other studies covering *other* subjects, events, and personages of the war. Or to put this point differently, when these recent studies *do* speculate, they tend not to go far enough, and they still tend to view things in a disconnected rather than a synthetic manner.

This is the case with the Dahlgren Raid, for there is only one easily and publicly available source that studies it, and that has the advantage of at least beginning the process of asking some very deep questions with deep implications, questions and implications that moreover imply that the Dahlgren Raid was a "deep event" of the deep politics of a deep state (or deep states!) in the full senses of those terms.[5] That source is Duane Schultz's *The Dahlgren Affair: Terror and Conspiracy in the Civil War*. Our focus in this chapter will *not* be on the details of the Dahlgren Raid, which details the reader can read by obtaining Schultz's work. Rather, our focus will be upon the details that are important both to the questions he raises and to those he does not.

---

[5] Deep politics, deep events, and deep states are the terms used by Professor (emeritus) Peter Dale Scott in his various studies of contemporary events such as the assassinations of the Kennedy's. By employing his terms in connection to this and other events of the war such as the flight of Jefferson Davis as a continuity of government operation, I mean to show that the historiography of the war will remain inadequate until such examinations and speculations are entertained.

A. Dahlgren Details Indicative of a Deep State Event
1. The Raid Takes Shape: General Kilpatrick and Lincoln

As noted in the previous pages, at the beginning of 1864 the political future of Abraham Lincoln was in doubt to the extent that the President himself entertained doubts about winning that year's elections and being returned to office for a second term. Lincoln desperately needed a clear and decisive Union victory in the fields of arms to buoy his chances, and thus far, his generals' best victories had still not been decisive.

This is the political context for the daring raid to free Union prisoners of war from the belly of the beast, the Confederate capitol itself. The commanding officer for the raid, Brigadier cavalry general Judson Kilpatrick, as noted, was selected for the job. Kilpatrick's brigade was part of the corps command of Major General George Gordon Meade, the victor of Gettysburg, a detail that will become important as our examination of the deep questions and implications proceeds. Kilpatrick brought the idea for the raid to the attention of President Lincoln in a personal meeting with him on the morning of February 12, 1864. Lincoln approved the raid, provided it was understood that its principal objective was the freeing of the Union prisoners of war in the Libby prison. Lincoln did *not* ask for any further details of plans of the raid, leaving it to General Kilpatrick to work these out *directly* with the Department of War.[6]

Notice two things.

Firstly, we do not know how much detail Kilpatrick communicated to Lincoln about the Dahlgren aspect of the

---

[6] Duane Schultz, *The Dahlgren Affair*, pp. 74, 77.

raid, or if he even discussed it at all. Lincoln merely authorizes the raid, and instructs Kilpatrick to coordinate directly with the Department of War, and that meant, of course, *Secretary of War Edwin Stanton once again is at the center of a question-able "deep event."* As we shall see near the very end of this chapter, however, Lincoln may not have been entirely in the dark about the real and hidden purpose of this raid, namely, the murder of Jefferson Davis and his cabinet. If he had his suspicions on this score, his behavior in not wanting to discuss any further details other than the freeing of Union prisoners is condign to it; Lincoln withdrew himself from involvement in any deeper planning. *If* this reading is correct—and again, we shall present a detail at the end of this chapter that clearly suggests that it is—then this also indicates that Lincoln had his own suspicions about his Secretary of War and the interests and agendas he represented.

Secondly, *notice now that the all aspects of the raid are being coordinated by a special chain of command, one in which General Kilpatrick is coordinating directly with the Secretary of War, Stanton, and altogether bypassing his corps commander, Major General Meade.* At this juncture, it is important to note that Colonel Dahlgren himself had received his first officer's commission directly from Lincoln and Stanton themselves,[7] and thus the special chain of command may have included him from the outset of planning the raid.

One final player must be mentioned, for it is yet more indication that the Raid with its "off-the-books" chain of command was a covert operation. This is the presence of Brigadier General Benjamin Butler. Butler had coordinated the placement of various spies in the Confederate capitol, and

---

[7] Duane Schultz, *The Dahlgren Affair*, p. 95.

was thus responsible for relaying their messages to Stanton.[8] It would be General Butler who would coordinate telegraph reports to Stanton during the actual conduct of the operation.[9] This is the same General Butler who, as a Congressman for the Commonwealth of Massachusetts, would be one of the House Managers, and indeed, one of the chief prosecutors, during the Senate impeachment trial of Andrew Johnson for trying to fire Stanton!

2. Ulric Dahlgren: The Logical Choice for a Covert Operation

Now we must pause again and take careful note of the implications of the epigraph that began this chapter: Varina Howell Davis, like her husband the Confederate President, had known the Dahlgrens before the war; the admiral had brought his son to show him off to her. Her response, upon learning of the raid, was disbelief that the Ulric she knew could be responsible for such a raid, with such a grizzly objective. On the other side of this network of personal contacts, Ulric had received his first commissions from the President and Stanton. *Thus, if there was a logical choice of personnel to lead such a covert decapitation raid that could, with reasonable confidence, approach the Confederate President with any chance of success, it would have to be a former family friend, someone whom Davis had known for some time. Someone, in other words, like Ulric Dahlgren.* Davis's laughter on learning of the objective of the raid may thus have been along the lines of expressing a similar shock and disbelief as his wife had when learning of the raid. In any

---

[8] Duane Schultz, *The Dahlgren Affair*, pp. 52-54.

[9] Duane Schultz, *The Dahlgren Affair*, p. 149.

case, Dahlgren's selection is the clearest indicator that the entire raid was a covert operation of the highest order, and that the *ostensible* purpose of the raid, to liberate Union prisoners, was to cloak a deeply hidden objective: the murder of Davis and his cabinet.

B. The Richmond Examiner's *Report on the Raid*

As noted in the previous companion volume to the present study, *The Rialto in Richmond,* the Southern press was quick to print the story of the raid, and to publish the alleged written orders and remarks to his troops that Colonel Dahlgren had composed and delivered prior to the commencement of the operation. The *Richmond Examiner* published Dahlgren's written address to his troops:

> HEADQUARTERS
> Third Division Cavalry Corps
> ________, 186___
> Officers and Men:
>
> You have been selected from brigades and regiments as a picked command to attempt a desperate undertaking—an undertaking which, if successful, will write your names on the hearts of your countrymen in letters that can never be erased, and which will cause the prayers of our fellow-soldiers now confined in loathsome prisons to follow you and yours wherever you may go. We hope to release the prisoners from Belle Island first, and having seen them fairly started, we will cross the James River into Richmond, destroying the bridges after us and *exhorting the released prisoners to destroy and burn the hateful city; and do not allow the rebel leader Davis and his traitorous crew to escape.*
>
> The prisoners must render great assistance, as you cannot leave your ranks too far of become too much

> scattered, or you will be lost. Do not allow any personal gain to lead you off, which would only bring you to an ignominious death at the hands of citizens. Keep well together and obey orders strictly and all will be well; but on no account scatter too far, for in union there is strength. With strict obedience to orders and fearlessness in the execution you will be sure to succeed.
>
> You will join the main force on the other side of the city, or perhaps meet them inside. Many of you may fall; but if there is any man here not willing to sacrifice his life in such a great and glorious undertaking, or who does not feel capable of meeting the enemy in such a desperate fight as will follow, let him step out, and he may go hence to the arms of his sweetheart and read of the braves who swept through the city of Richmond.
>
> We want no man who cannot feel sure of success in such a holy cause. We will have a desperate fight, but stand up to it when it comes and all will be well. Ask the blessing of the Almighty and do not fear the enemy.
>
> U. Dahlgren,
> Colonel, Commanding[10]

The other papers found on Colonel Dahlgren's body after the failure of the raid included orders given to one of his officers, some "general instructions" and an itinerary of the raid, and a few "notes in a memorandum book." Most importantly, all of these items were explicit and clear that President Davis "and his cabinet must be killed on the spot."[11] In other words, it was a classic de-capitation strike; with the Confederate leadership gone, the Confederate field armies might have dissolved in the field and collapsed. It was a bold, and dangerous, gamble.

---

[10] Duane Schultz, *The Dahlgren Affair*, pp. 156-157.
[11] Ibid., p. 157.

At this precise juncture, Schultz's own assessments—and loyalties—surface to raise the issue of deeper politics, and a potential for a false flag operation *conducted by the Confederacy itself and blamed on the Union*; Schlutz writes:

> A March 5 editorial in the *Richmond Inquirer* challenged Southerners to consider the significance of the Dahlgren papers for the Confederacy's future conduct of the war:
>
>> "Soldiers, read these papers and weigh well their purpose and design. Will not these documents take off the rosewater sentimental mode of making... campaigns? Should our army again go into the enemy's country, will not these papers relieve them from their restraints of chivalry that would be proper with a civilized enemy, but which only brings upon them the contempt of our savage foe? Decidedly, we think that these Dahlgren papers will destroy, during the rest of the war, all rosewater chivalry, and that Confederate armies will make war afar and upon the rules selected by the enemy."[12]

Drawing his own set of hypothesized implications connections from this observation, Schultz continues in the following vein, drawing a connection to Confederate terror campaigns in New England, and drawing the conclusion that the whole raid may have been a Confederate false flag that used the raid as a crisis of opportunity:

> For the South, the nature of warfare changed forever. Gone was the gentility and idealism of the past. "The Papers taken from the slain young colonel convinced Davis that Lincoln and Stanton had approved a new level of warfare –

---

[12] Duane Schultz, *The Dahlgren Affair*, p. 157.

> including arson, pillage, and assassination." The result would be total war, carried directly to the people of the Union, as Dahlgren had tried to carry that terrible fate to the people of Richmond. If Federal leaders were prepared to loose murder and rapine on the citizens of the South, then the South was free to respond in mind.
>
> *For Davis and the other Confederate leaders, how better to respond than with the program of terror, arson, and murder proposed by Captain Thomas Hines—his Northwest conspiracy—to carry the fight to the faraway cities of the Union?* Any scruples they had professed earlier about initiating such a plan were overruled when Dahlgren's plot was exposed. ***The Confederate government could not have had a better justification for sanctioning this type of warfare than if it had written the Dahlgren papers itself.***[13]

The Captain Hines program of murder and terror that Schultz is referring to in the previous quotation is that campaign of cross-border incursions, robberies, and arson that the Confederate secret service cell in Montreal, Canada, had engaged upon in the summer and autumn of 1864.

It was this cell that Jefferson Davis authorized be expanded after, *and in response to*, the Dahlgren Raid, as was pointed out in *The Rialto in Richmond.*[14] However, it will be recalled that Davis authorized this expansion for the express purpose of a base from which to stage operations designed to sway the state elections of Indiana, Kentucky, and Maryland against Lincoln in the upcoming 1864 elections. A campaign of terror was not on his mind, nor was such a campaign apparently on his mind when he laughed at the news of the

---

[13] Duane Schultz, *The Dahlgren Affair,* pp. 157-158, italicized and boldface emphases added by me.

[14] Q.v. my *Rialto in Richmond,* pp. 26-27.

raid. Davis' reaction to the raid is more one of amusement, or even of amused disgust, than it is one indicative of vengeance and an eye-for-an-eye mentality.

For Schultz, in other words, the Dahlgren raid serves to rationalize the Confederate terror campaign in New England—most notably the notorious St. Alban's raid into Vermont by Confederate secret service forces in Canada—and to connect them directly to Jefferson Davis himself. While this is, indeed, a possible and plausible interpretation of the state of existing evidence and Schultz is to be commended for elaborating this implication of the raid. Davis' initial response to the news of the raid, however, is a small indicator of problems with that view.

What Schultz does *not* consider is the possibility that there may be an entirely *different* and deeper player on the field than either the Union *or* the Confederacy, one with a vested interest in seeing the war continue. Indeed, Schultz himself mentions yet another circumstance drawing his interpretation into more doubt, for Davis had discussed the raid "for many hours" with his cabinet, most of whom were in favor of executing all, or at least some, of the prisoners captured from the raid. Davis, however, did *not* agree, and decided to ask General Lee what should be done with the prisoners.[15]

This, in my personal opinion, was most likely shrewd politics on Davis' part. Possibly because of his family's friendship with the Dahlgrens prior to the war President Davis may have had personal difficulties accepting that raid at face value. Perhaps he suspected that neither Ulric, nor even Lincoln could be personally involved in such an affair, and perhaps he suspected Stanton or other Union "deep players"

---

[15] Duane Schultz, *The Dahlgren Affair*, p. 159.

of being involved, perhaps even with a view to forcing the Confederacy to resort to its own terror campaign which the Union press could then exploit just as the Southern press was exploiting the raid. Perhaps, too, the idea of a terror campaign was just not within the character of someone like Davis to contemplate sanctioning. But one factor of the political calculus *was* crystal clear to Davis during that cabinet meeting: the majority of his cabinet, including his own Secretary of War, John Seddon, wanted to execute Union prisoners from the raid for acts against citizens and contrary to the laws of war. Davis thus cleverly appealed to the one authority—especially in military matters and the laws of warfare that he knew had the political cachet to offset his cabinet, and whom he knew would hold a similar position to his own - Lieutenant General Robert E. Lee, overall commander of the forces that had defeated the raid in the first place.

With these thoughts in place, we have at last arrived at...

C. The Central Question of the Dahlgren Raid: Were the Orders Discovered on Dahlgren's Body Authentic?
1. Southern Belief and the Case for Authenticity, & Northern Disbelief and the Case Against Authenticity

In his classic one volume study of the Dahlgren Raid, scholar Duane Schutlz observes that the Raid had transformed the dashing young Union cavalry officer from a heroic figure of idealistic youth, into "Ulric the Hun." When, towards the end of the war in the early weeks of 1865, Francis Blair, scion of the powerful Blair family of Maryland undertook his peace mission for the Union to Confederate President Jefferson Davis—an episode we shall examine in the next chapter—he noted to Davis' wife, Varina Howell Davis, that he, like many in the North, had great difficulty believing that the young Colonel could have any part in such a dastardly enterprise. It was, indeed, this very meeting between the Confederate First Lady and the informal Union peace representative that prompted Mrs. Davis to make the observation that she, too, could not reconcile the image of the little boy Ulric, whom her father had proudly presented to her, with the mature commander of the raid as depicted in the Southern press.[16]

These vignettes highlight what is really a glaring problem with the whole narrative of the Dahlgren raid, and to his great credit, Duane Schultz finally exposed the problem.

> Francis Blair was not alone in being reluctant to accept that Ulric Dahlgren had turned into Ulric the Hun. Virtually no Northerner who had known the young Dahlgren believed he had written the papers that now bore his name. Indeed, public opinion in the North was unwilling to accept the fact that *any* Union officer could have contemplated so reprehensible an act as the assassination of Jefferson Davis and the members of his Cabinet. And even if some officer secretly harbored such a repugnant desire, he would never have put it in writing or left proof of it behind.
>
> The Dahlgren papers had to be forgeries; so held the people of the Union. Admiral Dahlgren had testified to that, and if he did not recognize his own son's handwriting, who would? As far as the Union was concerned, the Dahlgren papers were obvious lies and forgeries designed to discredit the reputation of a fine young man and, by extension, the whole of the United States.
>
> The people of the South believed just as fervently that the Dahlgren papers were genuine. The barbaric Yankees would stop at nothing to win the war, even planning to

[16] Duane Schultz, *The Dahlgren Affair*, p. 239.

> murder Confederate leaders in their beds. Admiral Dahlgren was not being honest when he denounced the papers as fraudulent. What father would not lie to protect the honor of his son? Not that Yankees knew anything about true honor.
>
> Besides, what reason would Confederate leaders have for forging such documents, Southerners asked—*unaware of the plans for the Northwest conspiracy.* Why would they claim that the Yankees were out to kill them? The South had nothing to gain. Therefore, the Dahlgren papers had to be genuine, not fabricated or tampered with in any way.
>
> Arguments raged between North and South and continue to the present day. Long after Appomattox, long after the monuments and memorials grew stained and pitted with age, long after the last old soldier died, the disagreement endures.[17]

Note that Schultz's predispositions regarding the implications of the affair are again clearly in evidence: it triggered the Confederacy's response of mounting its own "terror operations" across the Canadian border into the "northwest" i.e., the Great Lakes region and the "northwest" of Michigan, Ohio, and the Buffalo-Niagara region of New York, not to mention the Confederate raids into New England in 1864. What Schultz does *not* contemplate is that the whole affair, at its deepest level, may not have been a Union decapitation strike, nor a Confederate false flag operation, at all, but perhaps a much deeper operation designed to look like both—and neither—at one and the same time, and to inflame the passions and divisions even more, *even to the point of keeping the embers of the conflict with all of its sectional, class, and race divisions going long after the war.*

---

[17] Duane Schultz, *The Dahlgren Affair*, p. 240, emphasis added.

2. The Dahlgren Papers and the Assassination of Abraham Lincoln

As was seen already, the operation *was* designed and initiated as a covert operation to recover Union prisoners of war, and perhaps even initially designed with that operation as the *cover* operation for a deeper plan to decapitate the Confederate government, for the whole chain of command bypassed the commanding officers in the field—Meade, and ultimately *Meade's* superior, Grant himself—and placed the operational officers in command, Kilpatrick and Ulric Dahlgren himself, *directly under the command of Secretary of War Edwin Stanton, via a Union spymaster, Benjamin Butler.* And because of *Butler's* involvement, one *must* assume that Lafayette Baker, Stanton's overall intelligence and security chief, and his chief telegraph communications and cipher officer, Major Thomas Eckert, were also involved. *Thus, all the major Union deep players in the Lincoln assassination were also intimately involved in the chain of command of the Dahlgren Raid.*[18] *It is the persistence of personnel and of their interests and networked connections as a stable feature over time and in the context of several deep events—the assassination of Abraham Lincoln, the impeachments of Andrew Johnson, and so on—that indicates the presence of a deep state successfully pursuing its interests despite the vicissitudes of changing surface circumstances.*

3. The Dahlgren Papers and the Continuity of Government Flight of Jefferson Davis

---

[18] Q.v. my *Rialto in Richmond*, pp. 75-135.

Nowhere is this more in evidence than in the fact that *no one* possesses the original versions of the Dahlgren papers. The reason? *They were an integral and central component in the archival papers that Jefferson Davis took with him in his Continuity of Government operation when he and his government fled Richmond in the spring of 1865:*

> One problem facing contemporary researchers is that the Dahlgren papers available for examination are copies. The original papers allegedly removed from Dahlgren's corpse have been missing since 1865. The historian James Hall has provided a detailed account of the custody of the papers.
>
> When Confederate leaders evacuated Richmond on April 2, 1865, the original Dahlgren papers went with them, part of eighty-one boxes of records from the adjutant general's and inspector general's offices.
>
> The boxes were deposited in Charlotte, North Carolina, when Davis and the other government leaders fled further south. The Confederate adjutant general Sam Cooper, to whom the papers had been entrusted after Jefferson Davis saw them following the Dahlgren raid, hoped to preserve all the records. He realized that they would provide historians with invaluable documentation.
>
> Cooper advised the Confederate general Joe Johnston, the ranking military officer in North Carolina, of the records' whereabouts. After surrendering, Johnston notified the Union general John Schofield, who arranged for the eighty-one cartons to be shipped to Washington, D.C.
>
> ...
>
> ***In November 1865, seven months after the Confederate material arrived in Washington, Secretary of War Stanton directed (Dr. Francis Lieber in the office of the Union adjutant general) to locate and turn over the Dahlgren papers to him. This was done on December 1,***

> ***1865 – and there the visible trail of the Dahlgren papers ends. No record of them exists beyond that day.***[19]

In other words, just like the eighteen missing pages of John Wilkes Booth's diary, and the rest of his diary, the trail of the original Dahlgren papers comes to an absolute stop and dead end in *exactly* the same place: in the office of the Union's Secretary of War Edwin Stanton himself.

This raises two possibilities. Firstly, it explains why Stanton was so reluctant to accept General Sherman's negotiation of the surrender of General Johnston's armies, for as was seen in the previous volume of this study, *The Rialto in Richmond*, Stanton, upon learning of Sherman's negotiated surrender, quickly overrode the decision and attempted to block any further military negotiations of surrenders of Confederate field armies, and ordered Sherman to resume hostilities against Johnston and his troops! A possible reason for the abrupt reversal of a surrender both generals had negotiated in good faith has now presented itself: Stanton wanted, for whatever reason, to ensure he had possession of Dahlgren's original orders. This means, secondly, that just like the alleged missing pages of Booth's diary surfaced when an antique cabinet that once supposedly was owned by Stanton was sold at auction, and discovered to contain the eighteen missing pages of the diary (along with some grizzly memorabilia of the hanged Lincoln assassination conspirators), the original Dahlgren papers might yet surface in some rediscovered Stanton family memorabilia.

But why would Stanton have sought to gain possession of the original Dahlgren papers?

---

[19] Duance Schultz, *The Dahlgren Affair*, p. 241, bold and italicized emphases added by me.

Again, the precedent of the missing pages of the Booth diary supply the reason, for the diary's missing pages clearly and explicitly named Stanton and other members of the Radical Republican abolitionist cabal as being implicated in the deeper layers of plotting behind Lincoln's assassination. By parity of reasoning, this suggests the original Dahlgren papers may somehow have incriminated Stanton himself as the origin of the orders to decapitate the Confederate leadership. Indeed, as we shall also discover, there is evidence—*known to Mr. Lincoln*—that a plot to *kidnap* the Confederate leadership might have met with some success, and as far as de-capitation operations were concerned, kidnapping was as effective a measure as outright assassination. In some respects, it had more to commend it, for a kidnapped leadership could conceivably have placed a duress on the remaining government of the Confederacy that dead and assassinated leaders would not. These considerations also open the possibility that, far from incriminating Stanton, *the Union Secretary of War may rather have increasingly come to suspect that he was being masterfully set-up by an elaborate tapestry of incriminating documents whose origin he had no control over, or, at best, may only have come to suspect. In either case—guilty involvement or framed patsy—he had motivation to recover the documents and spirit them away from any public scrutiny.*

It is thus *also* possible that, somewhere between Lincoln's knowledge of a *kidnapping* plot and the actual Dahlgren raid, the same operational plan was modified from kidnapping to assassination, *following the exact same pattern as obtained in the case of Lincoln's assassination itself, which was changed from a kidnapping to an assassination plot, using the same "infrastructure."* The *modus operandi* is exactly the same, and this in turn suggests that, just like

Booth's assassination conspiracy, the Dahlgren raid *was itself a penetrated operation; it was, like Booth's conspiracy, an op within an op.*

With these observations in hand, a closer look at the contents of the the extant copies is in necessary because these, as Schultz observes, constitute a basis upon which "to pursue the question of the authorship and authenticity of the Dahlgren papers."[20] In his orders to his subordinate, Captain Mitchell—remembering always that these are the *copies* of the original and hence, may *not* have been the original orders —Colonel Dahlgren explicitly stated that once over the bridges of the James River and into the government quarter of Richmond, the bridges were to be burned, the city destroyed, and "Jeff. Davis and cabinet killed" adding that "pioneers will go along with combustible material"[21], presumably to ensure that all this will happen, and implying that Davis and his cabinet were to be burned to death. In the general orders as published on April 1, 1864 in *The Richmond Examiner*, the order ends, again, with "Jeff. Davis and Cabinet must be killed on the spot," as was seen.

Schultz states that, "Several witnesses testified that the papers as published in the Richmond newspapers were the same ones removed from Dahlgren's body. These witnesses include the soldiers who first saw the papers, as well as others in the chain of command who forwarded the documents to Jefferson Davis."[22] A further problem was encountered when, in 1996, a document purportedly quoted General George Custer has having related that Dahlgren told him that the secret purpose of the raid was not to capture, but rather, to kill Davis and his cabinet, and that Custer informed Dahlgren that

[20] Duane Schultz, *The Dahlgren Affair*, p. 242,

[21] Duane Schultz, *The Dahlgren Affair,* pp. 242-243.

[22] Ibid., p. 245.

he did not think the purpose was moral and right.[23] The problem with this discovery is that there is no evidence that Dahlgren and Custer ever even met before the raid, nor why Dahlgren would inform Custer of the raid's true purpose when he did not even inform his second in command.[24]

While these are certainly facts counter-indicating the authenticity of the "kill" orders, there are two very credible witnesses in favor of its authenticity, none other than General Fitzhugh Lee, nephew of the famous general and the officer who delivered the papers to Davis while he was conferring with his Secretary of State, Judah Benjamin, but Benjamin himself attested to their authenticity, *adding that "the photographic copy leaves no room for doubt upon this point.*"[25]

So, in yet another irony resembling the saga of the missing Booth diary pages, there existed, at one time, and according to the Confederate Secretary of State, photographic copies of the papers, doubtless made by the Confederacy after they fell into its possession, and doubtless on the orders of Davis, or Benjamin, or both, just like there were photographs of the missing Booth diary pages.[26] And like those photographs, after this one cameo appearance on stage, these plates disappear utterly, never to be heard from, *or mentioned*, ever again. One may safely assume, however, that these photographic plates were part of the Dahlgren papers "dossier" that travelled in the Confederate archives with Jefferson Davis in his Continuity of Government flight from Richmond a year later.

---

[23] Ibid., p. 248.

[24] Ibid.

[25] Duane Schultz, *The Dahlgren Affair*, p. 247.

[26] Q.v. my *Rialto in Richmond*, pp. 146-170.

At this juncture, even some on the Union side had begun to think the Dahlgren papers were authentic. Union Captain John McEntee revealed to Union General Marsena Patrick that he thought the papers alleged to have been found on Colonel Dahlgren's body said exactly what the Southern press said they said, because, McEntee related, they agreed with what Colonel Dahlgren had told him personally.[27] But arguing against this view is the fact, as Schultz points out, that of the hundreds of men who rode with Colonel Dahlgren on the fateful and doomed raid, none of the others ever publicly suggested that the papers were authentic.[28]

But if there were Union soldiers and officers ready to believe in the papers' authenticity, there were also Union officers, like Captain Mitchell and a member of Colonel Dahlgren's command, who stated flatly and explicitly that he knew that "it was not Colonel Dahlgren's intention to kill Jeff. Davis, *in case he could be captured,"*[29] a statement that implies the original plot may have just been to kidnap the Confederate leadership. Dahlgren's commanding officer, Judson Kilpatrick also denied that any such plans or orders to kill Davis and his Cabinet existed. Another member of Dahlgren's raiding party, captured and held prisoner until after the war, stated:

> The colonel's instructions were, that if we were successful in entering the city, to *take no life except in combat,* to keep all prisoners safely guarded, but to *treat them with respect*, liberate all Union prisoners, destroy the public buildings

---

[27] Schultz, op. cit., p. 247.

[28] Duane Schultz, *The Dahlgren Affair*, p. 247.

[29] Ibid., p.250.

> and government stores, and leave the city by way of the Peninsula.[30]

These sentiments were echoed by Confederate prisoners captured by Dahlgren's party prior to its own capture, in turn, by Confederate forces. These prisoners, upon liberation by their own forces, reported that that had been well-treated by Dahlgren's men, and never heard "nothing during the four days (of their captivity) from Dahlgren, his officers or men, of the 'hellish design' later attributed to him."[31] So just as there were Union believers in the authenticity of the "hellish design" of the Dahlgren papers, there were Confederate *disbelievers* in it, which disbelief may have included the Confederate President and First Lady themselves, as was seen.

In an extremely important and apt summary of the dilemma, Schultz observes the following points about the whole affair:

> Strong evidence indicates, then, *that if there was a plan to murder Confederate leaders, Dahlgren's men had not been told about it.* Also, even if they all (except, supposedly, Captain McEntee) were lying to protect themselves and their slain leader—if they really had been told their mission included assassination—then Dahlgren omitted one vital piece of information from his address, instructions, and memorandum book.
>
> How were the troopers supposed to find Jefferson Davis and the other targets of the plot? Dahlgren was familiar with Richmond, but most of the men were not. How were the soldiers, fighting through the streets of the rebel capital, expected to locate the homes and offices of the various officials? There is no indication of these alleged targets.

---

[30] Ibid., p. 251.

[31] Ibid.

> Another unanswered question involves the retaining of the Dahlgren papers. If the papers were genuine—if Dahlgren intended to kill the Confederacy's civilian leaders in Richmond—why would he, an experienced military officer, keep such incriminating evidence on his person for two days and forty miles after he knew the raid had failed? There was no possibility of accomplishing the mission by then. Surely Dahlgren would have foreseen the damage any such papers would have done to his good name, and the embarrassment to his country if he were captured or killed. He had demonstrated in his career coolness under fire and the ability to think and plan ahead. It seems unlikely he would have kept such damning documents during the retreat.[32]

Before we are able to speculate on what all this means, there is one more extremely relevant fact that must be mentioned: in the initial reports of the action that finally killed Colonel Dahlgren and ended the raid, the Confederate officers reporting on the event *made no mention of the Dahlgren papers*, "some of the most important and incriminating documents of the war."[33]

We must now assemble what we have discovered:

1) When Colonel Dahlgren's raid was finally eliminated, the initial reports of the action makes no mention of the incriminating documents and their diabolical orders to execute the Confederate leadership;
2) The Plan *may* have originated as a simple kidnapping plot, but even then, there is still no mention of the

---

[32] Duane Schultz, *The Dahlgren Affair*, pp. 251-252.
[33] Ibid., p. 253.

papers in the initial after-action reports of the Confederate officers that had defeated the raid;[34]

3) The plan had a special chain of command ending directly in Union Secretary of War Edwin Stanton, who eventually took possession of the original missing pages of Booth's diary, and of the originals of the Dahlgren papers;
4) These originals may have included photographs of the documents that were mentioned by Confederate Secretary of State, Judah Benjamin. These photographs travelled with the Confederate archives along with Davis and his Cabinet in the Continuity of Government flight operation, and eventually ended up in Stanton's hands. These photographs would have allowed a comparison of the handwriting of Colonel Dahlgren on the alleged orders with other samples of his known and authentic handwriting, which in turn would have allowed the authentication, or repudiation, of the legitimacy of the orders.

At this juncture, we need to pause once again to take note of the speculation that Schultz advances as an explanation for all these dilemmas and discrepancies; "Let us," he writes,

> deal with the timing of the Northwest conspiracy. Tom Hines had presented his plan to Jefferson Davis in January,

---

[34] Schultz notes that in the report of Colonel Beale to General Fitzhugh Lee, he mentioned only "sundry papers taken from the body of Colonel Dahlgren," and no mention of their allegedly explosive contents, yet another indicator that the explosive papers emerged at a point in the narrative *after* the Confederate action that defeated the raid.

> *but the president could not bring himself to implement it.* He was sensitive to public opinion both in Europe and in the South. *The Confederacy could not be seen as the first party to carry a war of terror to civilians.*
>
> Was it coincidence that Hines was recalled to Richmond within days of Dahlgren's death? Or had Confederate leaders planned the event ever since learning that the Union was preparing to mount a raid on Richmond? In January (1864), the raid was known throughout the social circles of Washington—"all Willards [Hotel] talks of it"—and Dahlgren heard of it then.
>
> *With the efficient Confederate spy network in place in Washington, the fact that a raid of some kind was in the offing had to be known in Richmond long before any Yankees departed Brandy Station. Dahlgren's death and the securing of his general orders, along with blank sheets of "Headquarters Third Division" stationary, provided the opportunity for the South to fabricate a set of orders that would demonstrate that the North had been the first side to resort to a new, barbaric style of warfare.*
>
> *With a discreet clerk to handwrite a new set of orders and instructions, the so-called Dahlgren papers could easily have been based on Dahlgren's actual orders. It had to be made to appear that the plan was dastardly—release the vengeful Union prisoners on Richmond's helpless civilians, torch the hateful city, kill the president and his Cabinet—to justify the launching of the Northwest conspiracy.*[35]

And thus does Schultz argue for a Confederate "false flag of opportunity" operation.

But there are two significant difficulties to this otherwise plausible speculation, namely and firstly, that the

---

[35] Duane Schultz, *The Dahlgren Affair*, pp. 254-255, emphasis added.

purpose of Captain Hines' recall to Richmond may *not have been* for the purpose of the Northwest conspiracy at all, and secondly, the geopolitical calculus that induced Davis *not* to approve of such plans had not changed all that substantially even in the aftermath of the raid. The Confederacy still had much more to lose than to gain from such an operation.

Which leaves a third possibility, one not examined by Schultz (or anyone else for that matter) in his otherwise critical study of the raid: *the very circumstances and possibilities that enable a* ***Confederate*** *forgery of the orders, could also argue for a Union* ***or "Someone Else's"*** *forgery of the orders, which were planted on the body, or replaced with the original papers somewhere in the chain of custody between their "discovery" on the body and their presentation to President Davis by General Fitzhugh Lee. These considerations would necessitate a small cadre of men planted in Dahlgren's unit for this purpose, or a network of spies in the Confederacy to carry it out after the raid and able to intervene in the chain of custody. It implies, in short, an extensive and devious spy network such as Stanton and Lafayette Baker commanded.*

Further, this third possibility implies, and indeed necessitates, an expert in the forgery of *handwriting*, and able to mimic not only the handwriting itself, but the style of diction of the purported author, and such expertise could not just be summoned—neither in Richmond nor in Washington—at the snap of the fingers. Additionally, this third possibility implies something else yet again, namely, that the forgery plan may have been a part of the original plot of the raid, even before it set out, and unbeknownst to Lincoln, Kilpatrick, or Dahlgren himself. Thus, whoever was to execute this component of the plan had to be someone capable of bridging *both sides of the lines, with contacts on both sides to enable the planting of the forged papers on Dahlgren or in some other place, as circumstances required.* In other words, once one admits the possibility of a penetrated "op within an op", and an even deeper third level of player(s), the conclusion inevitably follows that someone, somewhere, *wanted* the raid to fail. In this, while Schultz's research and even his speculations are to be praised for raising possibilities, the fact that he is unwilling to consider any deeper or alternative possibilities and speculations of deeper Union *or third party* involvement, the reluctance to pursue the questions of why both the Booth missing diary pages and the missing Dahlgren originals (and the Confederate photographs) end up in Stanton's hands, or the possible presence of even deeper players and layers as is indicated by the Canadian connection, is clearly tendentious and a methodological flaw, for the War Between the States, as is now evident from all the foregoing discussion, did not take place in a geopolifinancial vacuum, but was intricately and subtly connected to other massive and deep currents on the world stage.

D. The Curious Picture of Colonel Dahlgren and...

Nowhere is that wider geopolifinancial context and those very deep players and agendas perhaps more clearly indicated than in a curious picture which Schultz includes on page 161 of his book without any further comment, and readers of *The Rialto in Richmond*, and of this book, will instantly perceive its huge and vital importance.

Sometimes, a picture, rather than a thousand words, is the best way to end a chapter:

Colonel Ulric Dahlgren, Standing on the left. Seated, on the ground, are Major Ludlow, Lieutenant Colonel Dickenson (of General Hooker's staff), and seated on the extreme right, is Lieutenant Rosencranz. The Man kneeling in the middle and holding paper, is the German Count (Graf) von Zeppelin.

Francis Blair,
Lincoln's Informal Peace Delegate to Richmond, 1865

6

Blair's Breathtaking Business: Geopolitics and the 1865 Hampton Roads Peace Conference

"Davis...handed Blair a letter, written and dated the day before, after their first meeting. He addressed it to Blair but intended it for Lincoln, avoiding direct communication between the two heads of state just as Lincoln had done.... As Davis well knew, the last two words were fatal."
James B. Conroy[1]

Francis P. Blair had a brilliant, off beat, idea, an idea so brilliant, and so offbeat, so absurd and out-of-the-box, that it might just work, provided he could motivate the right people and, with their support, persuade President Abraham Lincoln to at least consider it, and reach out to his opposite number in Richmond. Then, Blair would have to travel to the Confederate capital, and sell the idea to Jefferson Davis. Both men would be hard sells, he knew. For Lincoln it would be a hard sell because all the geopolifinancial high cards were in his hands, and he was not about to give them up. For Davis, it would be a hard sell because of his almost mulishly stubborn devotion to principle and duty: Southern blood had been shed in the cause of its independence, and he was not about to betray that trust. Nevertheless in Blair's mind, the attempt had to be made. The chance for peace, and for an end to the bloodletting, no matter

[1] James B. Conroy, *Our One Common Country: Abraham Lincoln and the Hampton Roads Peace Conference of 1865* (Guilford, Connecticut: Lyons Press, 2014, ISBN 978-0-7627-7807-2), p. 89.

how great or slim, was worth it, and that fond hope was the ultimate basis of his brilliant idea.

A. The Geopolifinancial Context of Blair's Brilliant Idea

For Blair, the political calculus also presented certain encouragements. For one thing, he could count on Mr. Lincoln's Secretary of State to be open to the idea. After all, Seward had been friends with the Confederate President before the war, and regarded Mr. Davis as "a splendid embodiment of manhood,"[2] the epitome of a well-educated, well-spoken Southern gentleman. For another thing, in spite of a vast preponderance of supply, weapons, and men, the South fought on, and decisive victories eluded the Union armies. The southern armies, for all their lack of numbers, supply, and modern armaments, were outfighting those of the North. And at the beginning of 1864, Ulysses S. Grant's Wilderness campaign was still in the future (and even that, according to the grizzly post bellum quip, would mean that Grant had lost an entire army in order to save the nation); at

---

[2] James B. Conroy, *Our One Common Country: Abraham Lincoln and the Hampton Roads Peace Conference of 1865* (Guilford, Connecticut: 2014 [ISBN978-0-7627-7807-2]), p. 2. Conroy notes that the friendship between the Davises and the New Yorker, who would run against Lincoln for the Republican party presidential nomination only to lose and become a member of Lincoln's cabinet, was deep. Mentioning an episode recorded by Varina Howell Davis herself, Seward attended upon the future Confederate president for an hour every day when the latter lay suffering from an eye infection that threatened to burst his eye. He also intervened to prevent a duel between Davis and the "future Jacobin Senator, Zachariah Chandler of Michigan." (p. 17). Chandler would become Lincoln's campaign manager in 1860, and later President Grant's Secretary of the Interior overseeing, among other things, that Administration's policy toward the Indian tribes of the upper plains.

the beginning of 1864, the Confederacy fought on, the Union was weary, and according to the Confederate constitution, Davis, unlike Lincoln, still had two years left on his six year term in office; Lincoln on the other hand was up for re-election that year, and even Lincoln himself increasingly viewed his chances as slim, unless some great victory came to Union arms. To put matters with what is perhaps too much of a contemporary gloss, Lincoln was running afoul of what many presidents after him would encounter: the unwillingness of Americans to fight for very long in causes that appear to have no clear nor decisive end, and even then, those most willing to enlist in the military and fight came from… the South.

Mr. Lincoln had other difficulties, not the least within his own party, as we have seen in this and the previous volume, *The Rialto in Richmond.* For one thing, in 1864 the Radical Republicans—whom many of the more moderate wing of the party had already begun to refer to by the nickname of "Jacobins"—had, through their chief congressional champion, Senator Benjamin Wade of Ohio, managed to ram through the Congress what amounted to the first "Congress Reconstruction" bill, a measure that argued that the Southern states had "committed suicide" and that they be treated as conquered territories, and not be readmitted to Congress. Lincoln, to the outrage of the "Jacobins," had pocket-vetoed the bill.[3] The reader has encountered Senator Wade before, for this is the same Benjamin Wade mentioned in the missing pages of the diary of John Wilkes Booth as having been a prominent mover in the Lincoln assassination,[4] and the same Benjamin Wade that waited in the wings to assume the Presidency on conviction of Andrew Johnson in the latter's impeachment trial. What made matters very much

---

[3] James B. Conroy, *Our One Common Country*, pp. 9-10.

[4] Q.v. my *Rialto in Richmond*, pp. 146-172.

worse for Lincoln and the moderates, the President himself had begun to "flirt" with the idea of peace conferences, an idea pushed by the powerful publisher of the *New York Daily Tribune*, Horace Greeley.[5] By July of 1864, with General Grant's "appalling losses" in the Wilderness campaign a matter of record, Greeley moderated his views and called publicly for Lincoln to negotiate an end to the war, pointing out that his contacts with the large and well-known Confederate cell in Montreal had conveyed the Confederacy's sincere desire for an end to the war.

1. Lincoln's Disastrous Blunder: The "To Whom It May Concern" Letter of July, 1864

Mr. Lincoln attempted to head off Greeley's pro-peace forces by drafting a letter "To Whom it May Concern," to be delivered to the Confederate Canadian cell. In it, Lincoln stated that he would be open to receive any envoy that would accept "the integrity of the whole Union," i.e., the idea that the Union was an "indissoluble, once in, never out" sort of Roman Catholic marriage, a suicide pact, and that whatever envoy would also agree to the abolition of slavery, and be accompanied by an authority "that can control the armies now at war with the United States."[6] James B. Conroy, whose study of the peace negotiations and Blair's "brilliant idea" forms the principal source of material for this chapter, observes that this last provision was a clever way on Lincoln's part to avoid recognized the legitimacy of the Confederate government, while at the same time inviting a potential *coup d'etat* to overthrow it.[7]

---

[5] James B. Conroy, op. cit., p. 11.

[6] James B. Conroy, *Our One Common Country*, pp. 12-13.

[7] Ibid., p. 13.

Unfortunately, Mr. Lincoln's cleverness backfired dramatically when the Confederate Canadian cell forwarded it to Richmond, where Davis' government quickly published it in the Confederate press. In my opinion, the decision to do so was most likely urged by the wily Confederate Secretary of State, Judah Benjamin, for the resulting publicity was typical of the sort of calculation and subtlety of which Mr. Benjamin was capable, for Conroy observes that "Overnight, negotiation became anathema in the South, and Lincoln's stock plunged in the North. Democrats who were willing to die for the Union refused to die for the slaves. On the other side of the aisle, the Jacobins exploded, set off by the very idea of negotiations, let alone by liberal terms."[8]

2. Davis' Turn to Blunder: His Reply to the 1864 Methodist Attempt for a Peace Negotiation

Another attempt was made to initiate peace talks when Colonel Jacques, a Methodist minister who had donned the blue to fight for the Union, asked for, and received Lincoln's permission to travel through the lines to the Confederate capital for an attempt to engage Jefferson Davis in peace talks. This given, Colonel Jacques utilized contacts on the Confederate side of the lines, and was able to make his way to Richmond, where he was indeed able to meet with Davis. Insisting that the South could not possibly win the war, and insisting that slavery was dead, Colonel Jacques then inquired "how a Christian peace might be obtained."

Davis' response is worth noting, for it is indicative that the realities about slavery were perhaps sinking in, for in answer to Colonel Jacques' inquiry, the Confederate President responded:

---

[8] Ibid.

> "In a very simple way," Davis said. "Withdraw your armies from our territory and peace will come of itself." Mr. Lincoln's terms were "*very* generous," but the South had no need of his amnesty. "Amnesty, sir, applies to criminals." *Nor was it fighting for slavery.* "We are fighting for independence, and that, or extermination, we *will* have." Showing Gilmore and Jacques the door, Davis suggested they might "say to Mr. Lincoln that I shall at any time be pleased to receive proposals for peace on the basis of our independence. It will be useless to approach me with any other."[9]

This time it was Davis who blundered, for in a return of the favor, the Northern press published *his* reply to Lincoln's overture, revealing that the South, too, was unwilling to compromise.

3. Francis Preston Blair's 1861 Peace Proposal to Lincoln and Other Matters

So what was Francis Preston Blair's brilliant idea? A native of slave-holding Maryland, Blair was perpetually straddling the fence between the ante bellum battles on slave-states versus free states, and all the territorial land grabs and battles that surrounded them. It was Blair who had aided President Andrew Jackson in heading off the nullification crisis of 1832 and who had helped Jackson win the seemingly endless contests with Southern statesman John C. Calhoun.[10] His "brilliant idea" stemmed from a long ancestry in trying to straddle the fence with compromises that satisfied all but the most intransigent, and avoid getting splinters in the uncomfortable place that often accompanies fence-straddling.

---

[9] James B. Conroy, *Our One Common Country*, p. 13.
[10] Ibis.., p. 20.

In 1861, for example, he proposed to President Lincoln an ambitious plan not only to free the slaves, but to use them as colonists and leverage in America's expanding "manifest destiny," sending them to Meso-America as colonists and a geopolitical foothold in the region.

It was a plan that President Lincoln endorsed, signaling his agreement with the trans-continental ambitions that had always characterized "manifest destiny,"[11] never mind the fact that the local populations, not to mention Mexico, might object, and never mind the fact that the American black population might not wish to be deported to what would probably have been more hostile economic and social conditions than they were already enduring.

This was nothing, however, compared to Blair's "brilliant idea," which would accomplish three objectives, all at once, by saving the Union, rescuing his beloved South from "defeat and occupation," and rescuing it from the Reconstructionist plans of the Radical Republican "Jacobins," while emancipating the slave "all at the same time." Indeed, if there was anyone on either side of the lines that could pull all of this off, "it was Francis Preston Blair, counselor to Abraham Lincoln and father figure to Jefferson Davis."[12]

By July of 1864, Lincoln's re-election hopes were at their lowest nadir. Providing a political shock to the these hopes, the Confederacy had proven that raids on the enemy's capital was a game that two could play, and returned the favor of the Dahlgren raid when Confederate General Jubal Early, heading Stonewall Jackson's old corps in the Shenandoah Valley,[13] and with Union armies preoccupied with offensive

[11] James B. Conroy, *Our One Common Country*, p. 20.

[12] Ibid., pp. 20-21, 24.

[13] General Jackson had fallen to friendly fire during the battle of Chancellorsville the previous year. Q.v. Conroy, op. cit, p. 25.

campaigns in the Wilderness and Georgia, poured out of Virginia and came within sighting distance of the Union capital dome in Washington, brushing aside the light defenses around the city. In these circumstances, Blair traveled to New York to confer with the one man with the political clout to back Blair's peace plan to Lincoln, newspaper publisher Horace Greeley.

The two men each argued for what they thought was the best path to peace, with Greeley maintaining that the best window of opportunity was *now*, *before* the 1864 election which Lincoln, in Greeley's estimation, would lose. Blair, conversely, thought that peace talks must be delayed until after Lincoln *won* the election, making it clear that the South's cause was hopeless, and that peace talks would have to be begun lest the South be completely subjugated under the Radical Republican Jacobin boots. With an election safely won, Blair reasoned (rightly as it would turn out) that Lincoln could afford to be magnanimous.[14] The problem was, of course, that neither man was thinking in terms of an assassination of the President, and a radical restructuring—pun intended—of the political landscape.

While neither man had retreated from his position, Blair had at least built a bridge to the influential New York publisher and political press power broker. By September of 1864, however, the political climate in the Union had changed dramatically against Greeley and the political moderates advocating for "peace now" and in favor of Lincoln, and Blair. The long and bloody Wilderness Campaign between Grant and Lee was drawing to its close. Grant had indeed thrown men and materiel at Lee in staggering numbers. He had indeed, "lost an army," but also left the Army of Northern Virginia a skeleton of its former self, depleted in numbers,

---

[14] James B. Conroy, *Our One Common Country*, p. 24.

materiel, and maneuverability, and pinned to the defenses of Richmond and Petersburg, the railhead supplying the Confederate capital. In Georgia, the long campaign between Union General William T. Sherman and Confederate General Johnston had drawn to a close when Davis, ever looking for a decisive victory, replaced the calculating Johnston with the bold, brave, and foolhardy John Bell Hood, who promptly lost Atlanta to Sherman in September 1864, after months of Johnston's having denied it to him.[15]

4. Lincoln's 1864 Post-Election Message to Congress

With the election of 1864 passed, and Lincoln returned overwhelmingly to a second term in office, the President turned to the prickly matter of ending the war quickly. On November 25, 1864 Lincoln convened a cabinet meeting in

---

[15] Hood went on to obligingly lose his army by sidestepping Sherman's army, and marching on Nashville in yet another foolhardy offensive, which ended in catastrophe and the decisive loss of his army in December of that year. Davis, who had removed Johnston many times before, once again realized his mistake after the fact, and reappointed him to the command of Confederate forces in Georgia and the Carolinas. The only result of Hood's sidestepping maneuver and offensive into Tennessee was to enable Sherman's march to the sea and capture of Savannah much sooner than it would have with significant Confederate forces barring the way. It never seemed to have occurred to Hood that if there had been a military advantage to this maneuver, Johnston would probably have pursued it. This fact should be born in mind when assessing Johnston's and Beauregard's forces' strength in 1865 when they surrendered to Sherman, for their significant numbers had been considerably *reduced* by Hood's "strategy." Had Hood not pursued it, and Johnston remained in command, Davis's Continuity of Government flight operation might have had a better chance of success.

which he read a draft of his state of the union message which he intended to submit to the Congress, and in it stressed that a quick end of the war was uppermost on his mind. But the question uppermost in the President's *private* mind was with whom on the Southern side should he deal? His Secretary of the Navy, Gideon Welles, observed that Lincoln's heart was not in it, and that the address seemed to lack direction and conviction. Lincoln made it clear that he would not deal with Davis. And James B. Conroy summarized Welles' reaction "If the war were to end short of abject conquest, if Southern voices were to be heard on the shape of the postwar future, someone must speak for the South. If not Jeff Davis, who?"[16]

By December of 1864, Lincoln had resolved his difficulties, and submitted the text of his State of the Union message to Congress. In it, Lincoln reiterated that there would be no retreat from his position in his Emancipation Proclamation, nor, more importantly, from his position on the indissolubility of the Union. But there *was* one significant change vis-à-vis the problem of peace negotiations: "On careful consideration of all the evidence accessible, it seems to me," Lincoln wrote,

> "that no attempt at negotiation *with the insurgent leader* could result in any good. He would accept nothing short of severance of the Union, precisely what we will not and cannot give. His declarations to this effect are explicit and oft-repeated. He does not attempt to deceive us. He affords us no excuse to deceive ourselves. He cannot voluntarily re-accept the Union; we cannot voluntarily yield it. Between him and us the issue is distinct, simple, and inflexible. It is an issue which can only be tried by war, and decided by victory. If we yield, we are beaten; if the

[16] James B. Conroy, *Our One Common Country*, p. 37.

> Southern people fail, he is beaten. Either way, it would be victory and defeat following war."…
>
> And then came the salient point: "What is true, however, of him who heads the insurgent cause is not necessarily true of those who follow. Although he cannot re-accept the Union, *they can.*" *It was a call to the Southern people to ignore their elected leader….*
>
> The president set only one other condition for peace. "I retract nothing heretofore said as to slavery." He would never revoke the Emancipation Proclamation, nor return to slavery any person freed by its terms, or by any act of Congress. "If the people should, by whatever mode or means, make it an Executive duty to reenslave such persons, another, and not I, must be their instrument to perform it."[17]

The speech was a hit, particularly with the Radical Republicans. Thaddeus Stevens welcomed the speech as indicating the war would go on without seeking any negotiated, compromise peace with the South or slavery.

But, observes James Conroy, Lincoln had actually said no such things. "There were *reasons*," Conroy writes,

> why his message had been so difficult to compose. It did not invite negotiations, but nor did it preclude them, so long as they included reunion and no *backward* steps on abolition. It said not a word about fighting the South to the death, or warring until slavery was gone. In practical effect, the Emancipation Proclamation had only freed the slaves in the conquered parts of the Confederacy, and the Constitutional amendment banning slavery had not yet passed the Congress, let alone been ratified by the states. If peace came now, there was room for negotiation on the timing, particulars, and rewards of moving *forward* with

---

[17] James B. Conroy, *Our One Common Country*, pp. 38-39, emphasis added.

> abolition, a priority that Lincoln embraced but had always ranked second to the restoration of the Union.
>
> In the end, Lincoln had invited the Southern peacemakers to proceed where "the insurgent leader" would not go.[18]

No one seemed to have noticed, however, that in couching his appeal in the specific terms that he did, Lincoln *was* tacitly acknowledging the legality of Davis' government by acknowledging the power and authority of the underlying states that had formed it. It was the ultimate *reductio ad absurdum* of the Lincolnian metaphysics of the Union: he was inviting the Southern states to break with the Union that they had formed to rejoin the Union they could never leave. And no one seemed to have noticed that, by making the principal nature of the union itself the central feature of his position, Abraham Lincoln had said almost exactly the same thing as Jefferson Davis had said to the Methodist peace envoy, Colonel Jacques!

5. Former Supreme Court Justice John Campbell

It was one week prior to the delivery of the text of Lincoln's 1864 State of the Union address to the Congress that former Supreme Court Justice John Campbell and Assistant Secretary of War for the Confederacy, wrote Justice Samuel Nelson, a New Yorker and a friend of the Union Secretary of State (and former Davis friend) William Seward.[19] Campbell had been appointed at the young age of forty-two to the Supreme Court by President Franklin Pierce at the urging of his Secretary of War, Jefferson Davis.[20]

---

[18] Ibid., p. 40.
[19] James B. Conroy, *Our One Common Country*, p. 41.
[20] Ibid., p. 42.

Additionally, while opposed to his home state of Alabama's secession, Campbell nonetheless agreed to be Davis's envoy to the federal government when the Confederate government was still drafting its constitution, negotiating the surrender of the federal forts in Southern ports. It had been Secretary of State Seward who informed Campbell that Mr. Lincoln would not receive them, as that would imply "recognition," but conveyed to him that the forts would be surrendered.[21] In any case, Campbell wrote his old friend on the court that he was reaching out to see if something could be arranged for a frank exchange *"between the two sections."*[22] The letter—in what will prove to be an important point later—was shown to President Davis, who allowed it to be sent and the contact attempted. The letter was successfully passed to Washington City by the Confederate "secret signal service," but no answer to it ever came…

… except Francis P. Blair himself.[23]

B. The Blair Peace Plan

1. Lincoln Issues Blair a Pass through the Lines

Blair had originally contacted Lincoln on December 22, 1864, reminding him of his family's friendship with Jefferson Davis, and that he, Blair, might be able to make a contribution to bring about a peace. Lincoln sent Blair away,

---

[21] James B. Conroy, *Our One Common Country*, p. 42 This of course, as is now known, was most probably a delaying tactic while the federal forts were resupplied, indicating that there was no intention to surrender them at all.

[22] James B. Conroy, *Our One Common Country*, p. 44, emphasis added.

[23] Ibid., p.45.

telling him to return *after* Savannah fell, which it did the next day, though the news took two days to reach Lincoln.[24]

When Blair returned to Lincoln on December 28, 1864, this time Lincoln heard his proposal, and decided at once to grant him a pass through the Union lines. "You will have," Lincoln informed him, "no authority to speak for me in any way whatsoever." The pass, written on a small card like an index card by Lincoln himself, and signed by him, simply stated, "Allow the bearer, F.P. Blair, Sr., to pass our lines, go South, and return. December 28, 1864. A. Lincoln."

While Lincoln may have informed his Secretary of State, William Seward, he did not inform the rest of his cabinet.[25] This was both very informal, and very high level, diplomacy, for Lincoln no doubt knew, or at least had a very good idea, from whom Blair was seeking a meeting once he reached Richmond. After all Blair had stressed his friendship with the Confederate President and his wife in his first meeting with Lincoln.

2. Blair's Two Letters to Jefferson Davis

Travel between the Union and the Confederacy during the War Between the States was not uncommon, but it was nonetheless a procedure with its own protocols. In general, a pass had to be issued from a civilian authority to be presented to the military authorities on either side of the lines. These in their turn would issue their own written request to the military authorities to pass the persons through their lines. The higher the authority making the requests, the more likely and swiftly the pass would be allowed.

After receiving his pass from President Lincoln himself, Blair travelled to General Grant's headquarters,

---

[24] Ibid., p. 47.

[25] James B. Conroy, *Our One Common Country*, p. 52.

where he presented his pass to the general, along with two personal letters, both addressed to President Davis himself, and requested permission to come to Richmond. Both letters gave reasons for this unusual request. One reason was true, and the other, false. The false reason, or rather, the cover story provided by the first letter was that Blair was seeking to recover documents that had been taken from his home when it was occupied and burned by Confederate forces during Jubal Early's raid on Washington. The second letter indicated that he would only talk with Davis personally, to "explain his views on the state of 'our country'," and, in a very cryptic comment, the "welfare of other nations that have suffered from it." Blair promised to unburden his heart and mind to Davis on these subjects, provided Davis do the same, and both in full acknowledgement that Blair possessed no official status, nor would convey any of Davis's thoughts that he, Davis, speaking privately between two friends, did not wish to be conveyed. Davis authorized a pass to be issued and conveyed to Blair through the lines that allowed him to come to Richmond for "the purposes indicated in his letter of application."[26]

3. Misdelivery of Davis' Pass? Or Deliberate Interception and "Pass Interference"[27]

Davis's response was, unfortunately, delivered to the wrong portion of Union lines, and consequently, Blair thought he had been rebuffed by the Confederate President, and returned home. By the time he had done so, Washington was abuzz with rumors about the trip to such an extent that Horace Greeley himself came to Washington to confer with his friend and confirm the details. Greeley

---

[26] James B. Conroy, *Our One Common Country*, p. 55.
[27] Sorry, but I could not resist.

> ...shared a suspicion that Stanton, the fiercest of all hawks, had sabotaged his mission, out of enmity for the Blairs, for peace negotiations, or both. In 1862, when Secretary of War Stanton was being vetted for the Cabinet, Montgomery (Blair, Francis' son) had described him to Lincoln as an able lawyer, faint praise for a prospective Secretary of War, especially with the addendum that Stanton was corrupt. Whether Stanton got wind of this particular slander or not, others had come to his attention.
>
> On Wednesday, January 4, Greeley's *Tribune* ran a special dispatch, from Washington, the accuracy of which "we have no doubt." Blair's mission had died...it said, because the Secretary of War had told General Grant he did not approve of it, which the *Tribune* much regretted. "We do not know, and at no time have felt confident, that the rebels are yet prepared to agree to any terms of pacification that our Government either would or should deem acceptable; but we can imagine no possible harm that would result from ascertaining precisely what they are ready to do."[28]

By this time, however, Blair's pass from the Confederate government had reached General Grant's headquarters, and he promptly forwarded it to Blair.[29] This time when Blair attempted to pass through Union and Confederate lines to Richmond, everyone was ready.

4. Blair and Davis Meet

In the second week of January, 1865, Francis Blair was finally able to meet his old friends, Jefferson and Varina Davis, at the executive mansion in Richmond, a large

---

[28] John B. Conroy, *Our One Common Country*, p. 56.

[29] Ibid.

rambling classical structure that had once belonged to a prosperous Richmond merchant. After the pleasantries, the men were left alone to converse. Blair began by reminding Davis—repeatedly—that he came with no official position nor commission, with no messages, no credentials nor instructions nor anything properly qualifying an ambassador and an embassy. "His private status," he emphasized, "entitled him to no reply" and that because Davis' responsibilities were both so high and deep, it was his decision entirely whether to reply to anything, or not. Davis's Secretary of State, Judah Benjamin, when queried by Davis of what he thought about the approach, stated that one denial of any status with Lincoln would have meant that it was the truth. Blair's repeated denials, however, meant that Blair was in Richmond with the direct, though informal, consent of Lincoln.[30]

Blair then came to the point of the meeting. Removing a thin sheaf of papers, he explained that what he wanted to propose was simply a "rough memorandum," which he wished to read aloud. Davis injected, stating he was assured, by their long friendship and familial ties, that he knew Blair was honest, and that Blair's role, being private, gave the presentation a certain character. He would allow Blair to read it in its entirety, and without interruption.[31]

Once the memorandum was read – its breathtaking contents no doubt not lost on Davis—Blair then indicated that the plan he had just outlined to Davis he had yet to outline to Lincoln, *but*, he insisted, he believed that Lincoln would be amenable to send, or receive, a peace negotiation delegation, though again, he reminded Davis, he could not, as a private individual only, give any assurances. Besides, he pointed out, Lincoln had his own internal radical opposition, and it would

---

[30] James B. Conroy, *Our One Common Country*, pp. 80-81.
[31] Ibid.

only probably increase in the next Congress. The time to strike for peace was now.[32]

The conversation then again returned for a few more points regarding the main contents of Blair's proposal—which we have not yet revealed—and then President Davis turned to the subject of the Union leaders, specifically his old friend William Seward, the Union Secretary of State, and President Lincoln himself, whom Davis had never met nor known personally. While Blair gave a less than ringing endorsement of his old friend Seward, he assured the Confederate President that Lincoln would sacrifice virtually anything for the good of the country, and that his word was absolutely inviolable. This pleased Davis, who informed his old friend that, on the basis of his proposal, he was "willing to appoint commissioners to pursue it, without regard to forms."[33] Additionally, Davis told Blair to relay to Mr. Lincoln that he was ready to discuss the plan. Writes Conroy,

> We may suppose that Blair could hardly keep still. He spoke of the fame that Davis would win for "relieving the country from all its disasters, restoring its harmony, and extending its dominion to the isthmus." He did not bring up the fame that the author of the plan would win.
>
> "What my name might be in history," Davis said, "I care not, if I can restore the prosperity and happiness of my country. That is the end and aim of my being. For myself, death will end my cares, and that is very easy to be accomplished."[34]

[32] Ibid., p. 83.

[33] James B. Conroy, *Our One Common Country*, pp. 85-86, the quotations are from p. 86.

[34] Ibid.

The day after their meeting, and while Blair was yet in Richmond, Davis sent to him to come for a written memorandum of their meeting, written on the day of their meeting and after Blair's departure.

This letter is very revealing, not so much for what it says, but for how it has been interpreted by scholars ever since, and in such a manner as to ignore other possibilities of what Davis was perhaps really trying to accomplish. It read:

> Richmond, Va., January 12, 1865
>
> Sir: I have deemed it proper and probably desirable to give you in this form the substance of remarks made by me, to be repeated by you to President Lincoln, etc. I have no disposition to find obstacles in forms, and am willing, now as heretofore, to enter into negotiations for the restoration of peace; and am ready to send a commission, whenever I have reason to suppose it will be received, or to receive a commission, if the United States Government should choose to send one. That notwithstanding the rejection of our former offers, I would, if you could promise that a commissioner, minister, or other agent would be received, appoint one immediately, and renew the effort to enter into conference, with a view to secure peace to the two countries.[35]

Conroy observes quite truthfully that "As Davis well knew, the last two words were fatal."[36]

5. The Interpretation of the Last Two Words of Davis' Letter to Blair to Relay to Lincoln

[35] James B. Conroy, *Our One Common Country*, p. 89.
[36] Ibid.

Indeed, as we shall discover later, Davis would buttress this reading of the phrase "two countries" by using it again, and in a clear context that he well knew the effect it would have on Lincoln. But *while this **is** the most obvious and plausible explanation,* it again does not do justice to what he may have been trying to accomplish. Far from being an example of the fanaticism or intransigence of which the Confederate President has been accused, his own remarks in his post-war memoir *The Rise and Fall of the Confederate Government* indicate that, at this stage of the war, he was trying to avoid a surrender at the "pleasure" of the Union,[37] and as his remarks there make clear, *and as the as yet unknown details of Blair's peace proposal also make clear*, there was some reason that Davis had to believe this approach was the required one. He could hardly surrender the principle of sovereignty, because there would be no point to negotiations if they were to be legitimate, and not a simple Union dictat. If there *was* intransigence and fanaticism, it was shared equally by both leaders, who might have met to discuss other issues, and found some way to negotiate through the principle hanging everything up and perhaps even to find some resolution to it: was the Union "indissoluble"? Or was secession, though a last resort, an essential component of state sovereignty? Or was war the inevitable result because no middle has ever existed nor could ever be found between the two throughout human history? And if the last point was true, then all talk of legal compacts was ridiculous, for even adhesion contracts – like indissoluble unions – are voluntarily entered into. There was little else, in the final analysis, that Davis could do. In this respect, it should be recalled that the Radical Republicans, for whom the Union was "indissoluble" and therefore a kind of "suicide pact," reinforced the South's

---

[37] Q.v. my *Rialto in Richmond*, pp. 36-39.

reading of the very same principle of indissolubility, in a kind of round about way, by insisting that in secession the southern states had committed suicide!

6. Blair's Return to Washington and 2nd Meeting with Lincoln

Blair returned to Washington with the Confederate President's written memorandum in hand, and promptly met with President Lincoln on January 16th, 1865. This meeting would be the first time that the Union leader would hear Blair's proposal. Blair again removed a small sheaf of papers, the very same which he had read to Davis, and read them to Lincoln. When he was finished, Lincoln took the memorandum, and wrote a disclaimer on them: "This paper first seen by me on this 16th day of January 1865…. I having no intimation as to what Mr. Blair would say or do while beyond our military lines."[38] When this was done he inquired of Blair if he thought Davis would send a copy of the subject of the memorandum, and Blair responded that there was nothing for Davis to send, as he had not been given a copy.

What happened next is unknown, as there is no record of what Lincoln thought of Blair's plan. On the one hand, it is known that Lincoln had remarked to an interested party that "there has been war enough."[39] On the other hand, however, whatever Mr. Lincoln *did* say to Blair, it must have given him cause to think that the President would at least ponder the plan, because Blair's actions after this meeting imply that his proposal was not outright rejected.[40]

At this juncture, it is important to note that another factor had entered the delicate political calculus operating, for by this point there was no more denying that the South was

---

[38] James B. Conroy, *Our One Common Country*, p. 93.
[39] James B. Conroy, *Our One Common Country*, p. 93.
[40] Ibid.

losing the war, and Davis faced open revolt in the Confederate Congress, with many senators and representatives urging an end to the war. Indeed, the Confederate Secretary of War, Seddon, had already resigned, and the Confederate Congress was demanding the resignation of Davis' entire cabinet, or face a vote of no confidence. While such a vote would have no effect under the Confederate constitution, it would nonetheless have sent a clear message. The very fact it was openly debated signaled that the end was near. This fact was known to Lincoln and the rest of the Union leadership when he summoned Blair the next day, handing him a hand-written memorandum, addressed to Blair, but really intended for Blair to deliver to Davis, in a reversal of the letter Davis had given to Blair to show to Lincoln. Lincoln's response to Blair/Davis took advantage of this situation. It read:

> Sir: Your having shown me Mr. Davis's letter to you of the 12th instant, you may say to him that I have constantly been, am now, and shall continue to be ready to receive any agent whom he, or any other influential person now resisting the national authority, may informally send to me with the view of securing peace to the people of our one common country. Yours, etc., A. Lincoln.[41]

The response was carefully calculated, for it opened the door to "any *other* influential person" in the South to send informal agents and representatives to a conference if Davis would not. While Lincoln fell far short of saying so, the intention of the note would have been clear to Blair: if Davis would not send representatives, perhaps the leaders *around* him and in the Confederate Congress would do so.

7. Blair's Return to Richmond

[41] James B. Conroy, *Our One Common County*, p. 94.

Blair returned to Richmond on January 22nd, 1865, and that evening dined with the Davises at the Confederate executive mansion. After the dinner, when the men were alone, Blair delivered the letter from Lincoln to Davis. The Confederate President read it twice. After drawing Davis' attention to the phrase "our one common country," which Davis would hardly have missed, Blair then noted that the central idea of his proposal had not been outright rejected by Lincoln. He added, however, that Lincoln's own political position within his party was not secure, and that the Radical Republicans were impelling him to adopt sterner and more strenuous post-bellum policies vis-à-vis the South than his own inclinations favored.[42]

Blair then proposed something that exceeded his "informal authorization" from Lincoln, but which was a brilliant move around the principle that had held everything up: the Union and its nature. Blair proposed that if anything at all could be done to bring a peace, its most likely route would be via military conventions between the opposing generals, Grant and Lee, and Sherman and Johnston. Davis indicated his wholehearted support for any negotiation done by General Lee, and Blair departed Richmond.

He returned to present the results of his second meeting with Davis to President Lincoln on January 28th. Blair underscored that Davis had read his letter twice, and that he had "acknowledged Lincoln's rejection of 'two countries.'"[43] The way was now clear for a peace conference.

C. The Hampton Roads Peace Conference
1. The Confederate Commissioners

---

[42] Ibid., pp. 98-99.

[43] James B. Conroy, *Our One Common Country*, p. 103.

The day before Blair returned to Washington to confer with President Lincoln, President Davis summoned his Vice President, the slight Alexander Hamilton Stephens,[44] to the executive mansion for the purposes of heading a Confederate delegation to peace talks with Mr. Lincoln. Stephens, who had been back in the Confederate capital for a month and a half, was a logical choice, for he and Lincoln knew each other personally, both having not only served in Congress, but both having sponsored a political "club"—today we would call it a "political action committee" – for the purpose of promoting the presidential candidacy of General Zachary Taylor in the Whig party.[45] Additionally, Stephens was a logical choice for yet two more reasons: he had never been in favor of the Southern secession to begin with, becoming a member of the Confederate government out of loyalty rather than conviction, and in the name of states' rights, was even opposed to some of Davis' wartime measures which he regarded as unconstitutional infringements of states' rights on the part of the Confederate government![46] Stephens had, in fact, been contacted by General William Tecumseh Sherman after the fall of Atlanta for the purposes of negotiating a peace. Stephens expressed his willingness, but added that he had no official capacity nor authority to do so, and suspected the same was true of General Sherman.[47] When the request for his presence came from Davis, the quick-witted Stephens

---

[44] Conroy notes that Stephens only stood about five feet seven inches tall, and never weighed much more than one hundred pounds. (Q.v. p. 62.)

[45] Ibid., p. 61. Conroy notes on p. 119 that Stephens had a high regard for Lincoln, and that Lincoln had actually considered Stephens for a cabinet appointment prior to Stephens' home state of Georgia's secession.

[46] James B. Conroy, *Our One Common Country*, p. 66.

[47] Ibid., p. 69.

must have known something was afoot. For one thing, he and Davis had not spoken directly to each other since 1863, and Stephens' opposition to Davis was well-known. For another thing, the entire city was abuzz with speculation about why Francis Blair had been seen in the city, and meeting with Davis.

Stephens, while probably having at least some good general idea of the purpose for the summons, was no doubt shocked and flabbergasted when Davis relayed the actual contents of Blair's proposal, showed Stephens the letters that had passed between him and President Lincoln, and added that he had not discussed the matter with his cabinet at all. Davis also added that Mr. Lincoln was under pressure from the extremists in his own party to pursue a harsh and punitive policy with regard to the post-bellum South, including ultimate measures against its leadership, "Davis and Stephens being leaders one and two."[48] The plan, and the political context thus surveyed, Davis solicited Stephens' thoughts on the whole matter.

> Stephens asked him if he believed that Mr. Blair really spoke for the Lincoln administration. Mr. Blair had denied it, Davis said, but with confidence that Mr. Lincoln would back him. Davis said he was sure that Mr. Lincoln understood what Mr. Blair proposed, despite Mr. Blair's disclaimers.
>
> Stephens, endorsed it on the spot. If nothing else, it would open a channel to Mr. Lincoln.[49]

Stephens went on to stress that it had to be carried out in utmost secrecy, lest the Jacobins in Lincoln's own party learn of the effort, and sabotage it. He then added that the most

---

[48] Ibid., p. 107.

[49] James B. Conroy, *Our One Common Country*, p. 107.

logical delegates to such an informal conference had to be Lincoln and Davis themselves, and they could meet at Grant's headquarters near City Point, Virginia, and no one would be thc wiser other than Grant's and Lee's staffs. President Davis, however, vetoed the idea. If the negotiations failed, he would be blamed. He would send three commissioners, Stephens himself, former U.S. Supreme Court Justice Campbell, and Virginia Senator Hunter. If the negotiations failed, then the responsibility could be assigned to the commissioners.[50]

The choice of commissioners made, Davis then gave them rather broad instructions and latitude. They could accept any arrangement "that did *not* include reunion," but beyond this, he instructed them that they were not "to deceive Mr. Lincoln," but that he, Davis, "was willing to secure an armistice even if they were satisfied that Mr. Lincoln might accept one under the mistaken impression that reunion must follow." Other than this, they were to receive, rather than to tender, propositions.[51]

[50] Ibid., pp. 107-109.

[51] James B. Conroy, *Our One Common Country*, p. 113.

Confederate Vice President Alexander Hamilton Stephens; he and Lincoln had served together in the US House of Representatives, and had mutually founded a "political action committee" to back the candidacy of Zachary Taylor for President. Stephens headed the Confederate delegation to the Hampton Roads peace conference with Lincoln.

Former U.S. Supreme Court Justice John Campbell, One of the three Confederate delegates to the Hampton Roads peace conference with Confederate Vice President Alexander Hamilton Stephens

After some more internal wrangling between Davis and his Secretary of State Judah Benjamin over the exact wording of the commissioners' credentials,[52] the commissioners, under the inspired idea of the crafty Confederate Vice President, drafted a communication to General Grant which carefully avoided all the problematical language of the two Presidents and requesting safe conduct through Union lines:

> Sir: We desire to pass your lines under safe conduct and to proceed to Washington to hold a conference with President Lincoln upon the subject of the existing war,[53] and with a view of ascertaining upon what terms it may be terminated, in pursuance of the course indicated by him in his letter to Mr. F.P. Blair of January 18, 1865, of which we presume you have a copy; and if not, we wish to see you in person, and to confer with you upon the subject.

The three men signed their names "very respectfully," thinking that Grant knew of, and endorsed Blair's mission, and that "Grant and Lee could end the war if Lincoln and Davis could not."[54]

Grant, as anxious for an end to the war as everyone else, replied immediately, but in doing so, he conveyed

---

[52] Q.v. James B. Conroy, *Our One Common Country*, pp. 114-115. The problem, of course, was over Lincoln's phrase, "our one common country," and Davis's phrase "our two countries," and other words and phrases in Benjamin's initial draft of the credentials, one of which was the phrase that the commissioners came "in compliance with" the Union President's terms, a phrase which Davis changed to "in conformity with," and so on.

[53] The phrase, "the subject of the existing war" was a return to the wording of the original commissioners' credentials drafted by Confederate Secretary of State Judah Benjamin.

[54] Conroy, op. cit., p. 126.

information to the Confederate delegates that must have given them pause that the whole desperate scheme could unravel at any moment due to the interference of those who might have a lot to lose if it were successful. Grant wrote:

> Gentlemen!
> Your communication of yesterday requesting an interview with myself, and a safe conduct to Washington and return, has been received. I will instruct the commanding officers of the forces near Petersburg to receive you, notifying you at what part of the line and the time when and where conveyance will be ready for you. *Your letter to me has been telegraphed to Washington for instructions.* I have no doubt that before you arrive at my Head Quarters (sic.), an answer will be received, directing me to comply with your request. *Should a different reply be received, I promise you a safe and immediate return within your own lines.*[55]

Grant's communication to the Confederate commissioners is worth pondering for a moment. By indicating to them that he had to telegraph the communication to Washington, he was tacitly informing them that Union Secretary of War Edwin Stanton, and through him, the radical Republican "Jacobins," would inevitably be alerted to the purpose of their visit. That this reading of the communication is accurate seems to be implied by the last sentence in it, for Grant leaves open the possibility that permission to journey on to Washington might be denied. In saying this, Grant is also subtly informing the commissioners that he himself would not initiate and was not responsible for any such reply.

Grant had good reasons both for his concerns, and for his subtle diction and messaging to the commissioners, for

---

[55] James B. Conroy, *Our One Common Country*, pp. 130-131, emphasis added.

Stanton first dotted the I's and crossed the T's of propriety, conveying Grant's news to Lincoln, and requesting instructions. But he then fired off an angry snort to Grant: "This Department has no knowledge of any understanding by General Grant to allow any persons to come within his lines as commissioners of any sort. You will therefore allow no one to come into your lines under such character or profession until you receive the President's instructions."[56] Having huffed his best puff and puffed his best huff, Stanton then ordered his cipher and telegraph office chief, Major Thomas Eckert – the very man whom Lincoln would request for a body guard, and whose service in that capacity Stanton and Eckert would both refuse on the night of Lincoln's assassination—south to personally investigate the commissioners and their purpose. Meanwhile, he also huffed and puffed to Lincoln, urging that the conference was a trap and that by sending such commissioners rather than coming himself, Davis was leaving any decisions or agreements as might be obtained by the commissioners open to disavowal.[57] Henry Ward Beecher, the fiery abolitionist preacher and son of Harriet Beecher Stowe was in Washington, and urged Lincoln to accept no lenient peace. Beecher's presence is yet another indicator of the deep geopolifinancial interests at work behind the scenes.[58]

In any case, Major Eckert successfully made contact with the Confederate commissioners, and conveyed to them that they would only be permitted to proceed with their mission if they acceded to Lincoln's initial letter and the premise of negotiations to be based upon his phrase "one common country." To reinforce the point, a copy of Lincoln's original letter was appended to the back of Eckert's own

[56] James B. Conroy, *Our One Common Country*, p. 121.
[57] Ibid., p. 123.
[58] Ibid., p. 152.

communication, and additionally, a *written* response from the commissioners was required before Eckert would pass them through the lines.[59]

The dance, however, was not over.

Once again the lawyer in Alexander Hamilton Stephens came up with a way around the impasse of the two presidents' blocking language, arguing that, rather than haggling over one or two countries, thirty-six states and therefore, legally, thirty-six countries were involved. Rather than haggle, Stephens reasoned, surely it would be better to meet and discuss what *might* be done, rather than to let slip the opportunity to meet. General Grant, whose headquarters had hosted all this diplomatic theater, quickly agreed with Stephens' modify-cation.

But Stanton's servant Major Eckert was having none of it, and he quickly composed a letter to be telegraphed to Lincoln that the whole effort had failed, and that the Confederate commissioners had refused to comply with Lincoln's demands.

2. The Sometimes Conveniently Malfunctioning, and Sometimes Conveniently Functioning, Telegraph

As if this comic opera were not enough, after composing his telegraph to Lincoln, Major Eckert then composed a much more lengthy and detailed version of the events to be telegraphed to his immediate boss, Secretary of War Edwin Stanton. But, as "luck" would have it, just when Eckert was about to send the message, the normally well-functioning telegraph, which only occasionally went down, suddenly did so, preventing Eckert from telegraphing his message just long enough for General Grant to compose *his*

---

[59] James B. Conroy, *Our One Common Country*, pp. 156-158.

own version of the events to Stanton, which Grant knew Lincoln himself would read, because it was his custom to read all communications passing between his War Secretary and his chief general. The general made it clear that, on this issue, his sympathies were with the Confederate commissioners, and not with Stanton, Eckert, and the Radicals; Grant wrote:

> Now that the interview between Major Eckert, under his written instructions, and Mr. Stephens and his party has ended, I will state confidentially but not officially, to become a matter of record, that I am convinced, upon conversation with Messrs. Stephens and Hunter, that their intentions are good and their desire sincere to restore peace and union. I have not felt myself at liberty to express even views of my own or to account for my reticence. This has placed me in an awkward position, which I could have avoided by not seeing them in the first instance. I fear now their going back without any expression from any one in authority will have a bad influence. At the same time I recognize the difficulties in the way of receiving these informal commissioners at this time, and do not know what to recommend. I am sorry, however, that Mr. Lincoln cannot have an interview with the two named in this dispatch,[60] if not all three now within our lines. Their letter to me was all that the President's instructions contemplated, to secure their safe conduct, if they had used that same language to Major Eckert.[61]

While the telegraph lines had conveniently malfunctioned when Major Eckert tried to send his detailed report to Stanton, they were conveniently functioning once again, a few minutes later, when General Grant sent *his* report to

---

[60] Conroy adds an editorial comment noting that the former justice Campbell had fallen ill.

[61] James B. Conroy, *Our One Common Country*, p. 161.

Stanton, a report that Grant knew Lincoln would read. It is thus difficult to believe anything but that Grant, or someone on his staff and with Grant's knowledge and permission, had interfered with the transmission of Eckert's report, allowing Grant's report to go through first, and influence President Lincoln's views on the events.

That Grant was bending every effort to bring about a conference is revealed by the next scene in the act, for again the wily Confederate Vice President had contrived a written response, as demanded by Eckert, and one that, again, did not abandon the principles upon which Davis had instructed them while at the same time it did not use Davis's troublesome "two countries" phrase:

> February 2, 1865
> Maj. THOMAS T. ECKERT;
> Aide-de-Camp
> MAJOR: In reply to you verbal statement that your instructions did not allow you to alter the conditions upon which a passport could be given to us, we say that we are willing to proceed to Fort Monroe, and there to have an informal conference, with any person or persons that President Lincoln may appoint, on the basis of his letter to Francis P. Blair of the 18th of January ultimo, or upon any other terms or conditions that he may hereafter propose, not inconsistent with the essential principles of self-government and popular rights, upon which our institutions are founded.
>
> It is out earnest wish to ascertain, after a free interchange of ideas and information, upon what principles and terms, if any, a just and honorable peace can be established without the further effusion of blood, and to contribute our utmost efforts to accomplish such a result.
>
> We think it better to add, that in accepting your passport we are not to be understood as committing

> ourselves to anything, but to carry to this informal conference the views and feelings above expressed.
>
> Very respectfully yours, etc.
>
> Alexander H. Stephens, J.A. Campbell, R.M.T. Hunter[62]

Having heartily endorsed this response, Grant had this reply forwarded to Eckert, who by this time was already on his way to Fort Monroe. He returned to the Confederate commissioners with—as Stephens described it—"an anxious disquietude upon his face." Grant informed the commissioners that the reply was still unacceptable to Eckert.

There was, however, good news, for the general had had enough of this black comedic opera, and informed the delegates that he was going to forward them on to Fort Monroe upon his own responsibility.[63] Grant's gamble with the telegraph had paid off, for just as the steamer taking the commissioners to Fort Monroe was about to depart, Grant

> …came pounding down the stairway almost at a run. He was "beaming with joy" as Stephens caught sight of him, waving a ribbon of telegraph paper, shouting to his coconspirators. "Gentlemen! It's all right! I've got the authority!" In his hand was a wire from the president. Almost out of breath, Grant read it aloud on the paddle wheeler's deck. "Say to the gentlemen I will meet them personally at Fortress Monroe as soon as I can get there. A. Lincoln."[64]

---

62 James B. Conroy, *Our One Common Country*, p. 162.
63 Ibid.
64 Ibid., p. 164.

Additionally, Lincoln had *not* informed Stanton nor the rest of his cabinet, with the exception of Secretary of State Seward, whom he sent ahead of himself.

3. The Conference is Finally Convened at Hampton Roads, Virginia

On February 3, 1865, in the main salon of the paddlewheel steamer *The River Queen*, a meeting of leaders of the two belligerents finally took place after nearly four years of the bloodiest fighting in American history. There would be no stenographer to record the exact conversation. The Confederate commissioners were ushered into the salon first, and the Union Secretary of War Seward and President Lincoln then entered. Lincoln watched as the small and slender figure of Stephens unwrapped himself from a bundle of clothing. Lincoln quipped that "He had never seen so small an ear emerge from so much husk. Happily for diplomacy, Stephens led the laughter."[65] Jokes and reminiscences and pleasantries were exchanged between the five men, and especially Stephens and Lincoln recalling their time together in the House of Representatives

The Confederate Vice President brought the conviviality to a halt by getting down to business and inquiring if there was nothing that could "restore the good feelings that existed in those days between the different States and sections of the country?" Lincoln's reply was blunt, but not unexpected: to do so would require all resistance to the "national authority" to stop. But Stephens was not deterred, and raised the central matter of "Blair's brilliant business": was there not something else, something more pressing as a

---

[65] James B. Conroy, *Our One Common Country*, pp. 173, 175, 176.

potentially bigger problem that might confront both belligerents, that might divert their military efforts and attentions elsewhere?[66]

Lincoln at once understood the allusion, and replied that he had not heard Mr. Blair's initial proposal when he allowed him to proceed to Richmond the first time; had had only learned of it upon Blair's return from Richmond, when Blair had read to him the same memorandum as he had read to Davis. He had allowed Blair to proceed, with the understanding that he did not in any way speak for Lincoln nor for his administration in any official capacity whatsoever.

Faced with this stunning revelation, the Confederate commissioners realized that Blair had misled their President. The rest of the conference discussed a number of other issues: would the southern States resume their position in Congress, would property be restored, would slaveholders be compensated for the loss of their slaves and the land given to them? What would happen to the Confederate leaders? And in each instance, Lincoln's position was basically that the South must rely on his liberal use of his executive powers. It was, as Davis was to write in his memoirs, a surrender at pleasure of the Union.[67] But ultimately, Lincoln also informed them that much, constitutionally, was out of his hands and in the hands of his Congress, a position remarkably similar to that of Jefferson Davis; neither man could, nor would, act counter to the popular will that they believed had put them into their positions. Neither had the constitutional authority to commit suicide.[68]

---

[66] Ibid., p. 177.

[67] Q.V. James B. Conroy, *Our One Common Country,* pp. 183-194 for a detailed presentation of the rest of the conference.

[68] Ibid., pp. 208-209.

*D. But What **Exactly Was** the Blair Peace Plan?*

The reader will have noted that, thus far, absolutely no particulars about "Blair's Brilliant Idea" or peace plan have been disclosed. What "out-of-the-box" absurd idea led to this black comic opera of conveniently malfunctioning telegraphs, huffing and puffing secretaries of war, adroit linguistic finesses, and finally, *to a Union President approving of a private and personal delegation to Jefferson Davis without even hearing any initial details of the plan, preferring to learn of it only after Davis heard it and responded?* It is when the question is put this way that the plan may not seem as crazy as it sounds.

But again, *what **was** it?*

When Blair first passed through City Point—Grant's headquarters—on the way to Richmond to propose his idea to the Confederate President, he shared the idea with the general, just as he had some months earlier with New York publisher Horace Greeley. The War Between the States was creating a dangerous situation, a dangerous *geopolitical* situation, one also entailing a dangerous *financial* situation. The Emperor Napoleon III had installed a French puppet regime under the Emperor Maximillian in Mexico, and while not formally a part of Blair's proposal to Davis, neither he, nor Greeley, nor Lincoln nor Stanton nor the whole Union leadership, could have been unaware of the strong British interest in the Erlanger cotton loan. The British, as will be seen in Part Three, had even stationed troops in Canada to secure their bridgehead in North America. With 35,000 French troops garrisoned in gold-, silver-, and resource-rich Mexico, and British troops in Canada, the geopolitical situation was clear, and dangerous, and while the Tsar's fleets in San Francisco Bay and New York might forestall the European powers, it might not. *Best to eliminate the last vestiges of European power once and for all.* But to do that, the Confederacy and the Union would have to table their differences, combine forces, and resume the enforcement of the Monroe doctrine, and drive the foreign troops from the North American continent. That, in a nutshell, was Blair's Brilliant Business.[69] Grant himself raised the problem of Mexico with Stanton and Lincoln, and while both did not like the presence of the French emperor, "one war at a time was enough". But Blair had proposed a way around one war: cease fighting it, in order to fight another.[70]

If Blair's proposal had been limited to merely a general statement of geopolifinancial principles, his scheme could easily have been dismissed. But Blair had backed it up with a breathtakingly detailed strategy for how to execute it, and here is where its connections to subsequent events becomes downright eerily "coincidental" if it did not play an actual role in them, and in the secret and deep counsels behind them of which we know little to this day. In his initial meeting with the Confederate President, Blair pointed out that Davis and the Confederacy itself was in the best geographic position to drive Napoleon III and France out of Mexico, if substantial field armies could be brought to the region, where they could combine forces with revolutionary Benito Juarez and drive Maximilian, and with him, Napoleon III, out of Mexico.[71]

But Blair's plan was even more detailed than this, for just exactly how was one to extricate the Confederate and Union field armies that were entangled with each other in a

---

[69] James B. Conroy, *Our One Common Country*, p. 76.

[70] James B. Conroy, *Our One Common Country*, p. 79.

[71] In the light of what was mentioned in chapter two covering the Johnson impeachments, mention must again be made that Juarez, like many revolutionaries in history, was a Mason.

deadly dance, in order to pursue the idea of a common campaign against Mexico? Simple, Blair said:

> Lee would abandon Richmond and retreat southwest, "to more defensible positions." Grant would follow in hot pursuit, *but not so hot as to catch him*, until he had driven him into Mexico, where Lee would provoke the French. With one American army attacked by a foreign fore, the other would leap to its side. Together they would decimate Napoleon's legions, embrace once again on the old familiar battlefields, reenact the triumphal march into Mexico City. After fighting Mexico twice in twenty years, "our people" could not be made to leave. Once they had joined hands to win a second Mexican War, no elaborate political devices would be needed to forge a reunion. It would follow as night the day.[72]

What will immediately be apparent from this summary and to the reader of the previous volume, *The Rialto in Richmond*, is that *this is remarkably similar to what actually happened.* When Jefferson Davis mounted his Continuity of Government flight from Richmond, the original intention was to link up with the remainder of Lee's Army of Northern Virginia, and Davis' party and the army would then link up with the armies of Joseph Johnston and Pierre G.T. Beauregard, and make—or fight—their way to the Trans-Mississippi Department, and continue the war from a "rump Confederacy" until better terms for a peace could be had.

It was a clever plan, for on the one hand, via the common border with neutral Mexico, the "mini-Confederacy" had a line of international supply and trade through its ports, and on the other hand, it could use the leverage of Blair's plan

---

[72] James B. Conroy, *Our One Common Country*, p. 83, emphasis added.

of an invasion with the North in return for more agreeable terms of reunion.

1. The Confederate Appeal to Europe

While all of this must seem the flight of purest fantasy, there are three indicators that, far from representing a private geopolifinancial fantasy of Blair, it may have been the indicator of deep eddies and currents swirling beneath the surface, and ready to boil over into a full-blown world war. In late December of 1864, the Confederate Department of State's Secretary, Judah Benjamin, sent a communication to John Slidell, the Confederate financial agent in Europe who had made the initial contact with Emil d'Erlanger, a contact that developed into the 1863 Erlanger Cotton Loan, with its heavy subscribers' list of British power brokers.[73] In this communication, Slidell is directed to remind both France and England that the Confederacy "was fighting France's battles against the United States" and "England's too." Their failure to recognize the Confederacy would only necessitate the South seek terms for an end to the fighting. When the communication was discovered by Union authorities after the war, it was quickly interpreted to be a cry of despair.[74]

---

[73] In this regard, the reader will have noted a distinct *lack* of a similar list for French and Prussian subscribers. Given the contacts between Union leaders and Bismarck's remarks, there probably were not many such Prussian backers of the Confederacy, since the Confederacy was aligned with Prussia's biggest continental competitors, France and Britain. There is, however, also a distinct lack of information concerning the *French* subscribers to the loan. I have searched for information on this score, but without much success.

[74] James B. Conroy, *Our One Common Country*, p. 51.

But such an interpretation excludes another possibility, one suggested by the apocryphal statements of Chancellor Bismarck that the war was instigated by the high financial powers of Europc for the purposes of weakening an up-and-coming competitor, for the communication may indicate that the Confederacy well understood that it was the representative of deep geopolifinancial interests. If it was a communication or cry of despair, it was the despair of the abandonment, or the despair of the sudden realization that it had been used, and then thrown away.[75]

2. Grant's Strange Connections, and his Mexico Initiative

The second indicator that Blair's plan is less the personal brainchild of an influential eccentric, and more the indicator of deeper players and deeper politics is General Grant himself. Grant was related to the Confederate general James Longstreet via his wife, Julia Dent Grant. Longstreet was one of Robert E. Lee's key corps commanders. Like many families during the war, Grant thus had eyes and ears and connections on the other side of the conflict. Whether or not this played any role in the following event is unknown, but *something* was in the air, and it was not just Blair's first trip to Richmond, for on the very day of Blair's arrival in Richmond, Grant sent a subordinate general, Lew Wallace "on an odd little mission of his own." The purpose? Wallace informed Grant that he had learned from an old school friend of his in Mexico that the Confederate forces in Texas would "gladly unite with us" in invading Mexico across the Rio Grande. "Independently of Blair, and ignorant of his plan, Wallace told Grant that a joint invasion of Mexico would 'stagger the rebellion.'" Grant acceded to Wallace's request

[75] For the apocryphal quotation of Chancellor Bismarck and its ramifications, see my *Rialto in Richmond*, pp. 233-240.

be sent to Texas covertly for the purpose of a secret approach to the Confederate commander to sound out the idea. "Wallace would soon report that the Rebel general endorsed the idea "heartily."[76]

Might this general have been Confederate Lieutenant General Kirby Smith, the military governor of the Trans-Mississippi, himself? Possibly, but even if not, given Smith's tight control and watchfulness over his chain of command, it is unlikely that he did not know of Grant's secretive inquiries. In any case, Grant's secret assignment to Wallace now provides the necessary context for why he and General Sherman—with whom he no doubt shared the results of the inquiry—were so worried and concerned about the success of Davis' Continuity of Government flight, and the prospects that a kind of "mini-Confederacy" might survive to continue the fight, or, conversely, use its leverage to gain more favorable terms.

In any case, there is also one final vignette to report regarding General Grant and "the Mexico option," as we might call it. On April 11th, 1865, two days after General Lee's surrender at Appomattox, Grant and his staff returned to City Point, where he "signed a few dispatches, then rose and turned wryly to an aide," and then said, "On to Mexico."[77]

While much, much more could be said about this whole very black comic opera of errors and miscalculations, it is best to end it with what is perhaps the most dramatic irony of them all. When word finally spread that Mr. Lincoln had secretly left the capital with his Secretary of State Seward for a clandestine meeting with a Confederate delegation, the Radical Republican Jacobins in the U.S. House of Representatives had a meltdown of hysteria and there was

---

[76] James B. Conroy, *Our One Common Country*, p. 88.
[77] James B. Conroy, *Our One Common Country*, p. 278.

open talk of impeaching Lincoln. On the House floor, Thaddeus Stevens was in a purpled rage.[78] Lincoln would not survive to see either his policies initiated, nor himself impeached. It would be Andrew Johnson who would suffer the outraged sense of betrayal from the Radicals. As for Thaddeus Stevens, there was one more irony with which to ring down the curtain, for Stevens offered his legal services to defend Davis should a treason trial ever occur! Stevens told Davis that he would argue that the Confederacy was merely a conquered territory, and conquered princes are never hung for treason. "That," Davis replied, "would have been an excellent argument for me, but not for my people."[79]

---

[78] Ibid., p. 174.

[79] James B. Conroy, *Our One Common Country*, p. 293.

The Confederate Financial Agent in Europe, John Slidell, whose initial contact with Emile d'Erlanger brought about the 1863 Cotton Loan, and to whom Confederate Secretary of State Judah Benjamin directed the late 1864 Communication to France, reminding that country that the Confederacy was fighting Europe's battles

Confederate Lieutenant General Edward Kirby Smith, Military Governor of the Confederacy's "Trans-Mississippi Department," the center of the Blair and Grant "Mexico Option"

The Luckless Hapsburg "Emperor" of Mexico, Maximillian, puppet of French Emperor Napoleon III

Louis Napoleon Bonaparte,
Emperor Napoleon III of France

PART THREE: THE THIRD AND DEEPEST LAYER: THE SERPENTS OF THE CITY, THE WEASELS OF WALL STREET, AND BISMARCK'S BANKSTERS

"Lord Palmerston followed Disraeli in the debate, and at considerable length, but he did not deny that statesman's allegation that Gladstone spoke with the authority of the Government at Newcastle, nor refer at all to American affairs: a reticence more significant than any words he could with propriety have uttered."

—John Bigelow, LL.D., Union Minister to France, *Lest We Forget: Gladstone, Morley, and the Confederate Loan of 1863*, p. 55

"Many in British North America did not see why America's Southern states should not be allowed to ***voluntarily*** *leave a union they had* ***voluntarily*** *entered. It was the individual states who together had created the United States and not the other way around. Yet the absurd concept that Washington created the Union or the Union created itself, was precisely Lincoln's legal argument for raising an army to invade the South. It was a facile legal case but it justified the use of force to coerce the South into remaining in the Union."*

—Barry Sheehey, *Montreal, City of Secrets: Confederate Operations in Montreal during the American Civil War*, p. 36

A view of Montreal in the mid-nineteenth century

7
Montreal, Canada:
Conferences, Cabals, Conspiracies, Confederates, Carpetbaggers, Money, and Mexico

"Trowbridge told U.S. Consul John Potter in April 1865 that he was in Montreal to meet Lafayette Baker, head of the War Department's National Detective Police. What business Trowbridge had with the War Department's chief spy is unclear, but it may have had to do with cotton."
—Barry Sheehy[1]

NEUTRAL COUNTRIES ARE HOTBEDS of intrigue, politics, and financial activity of every stripe from legal, highly speculative ventures, to illegal black market smuggling and trading with the enemy, and to financing deeply covert agendas and projects. They are, in short, hotbeds of what this book has called "geopolifinance," and one must repair to them to detect its oftentimes subtle and sometimes very overt footprints. During World War One, for example, the neutral Netherlands was the one country in western Europe with which Germany shared a border, and whose ships could consequently conduct overseas trade for the Kaiser in spite of the British blockade. It quickly became a center of espionage, smuggling, and for the financial

[1] Barry Sheehy, *Montreal, City of Secrets: Confederate Operations in Montreal During the American Civil War* (Montreal, Quebec, Canada: Baraka Books, 2017, ISBN 978-1-77186-123-6), p. 51. Sheehy's book is ***absolutely*** indispensable and magisterial for any approach to an understanding of the Confederate and Union machinations surrounding the end of the war and its aftermath.

networks sustaining them, some of which endured into World War Two. One need only think of Prescott Bush and German steel magnate Fritz Thyssen's *Vereinigte Stahlwerke* and the Dutch bank that functioned as the liaison between the two. In World War Two a bank in a neutral once again served as the point of contact between the Axis powers and occupied Europe, and the United States, with the Bank of International Settlements' American President William McKittrick serving on a board with prominent Nazi leaders, and traveling freely in Axis Europe on the business of the bank.[2] The same patterns, and then some, are on display during the American War Between the States, and particularly with respect to one "neutral," Great Britain, and its North American dependency, Canada.

A. Background: The Confederacy and Britain

The first Confederate diplomatic commissioners to Europe were not, in fact, representatives of the Confederacy at all, but rather, a commissioner from the State of Georgia appointed in January 1861 by its governor, Joseph F. Brown, to represent the state's interests to Napoleon III, and to the government of Queen Victoria under Prime Minister Henry John Temple, the Lord Palmerston. It would not be until March, 1861, when the seceded states had met and formed a provisional government with Jefferson Davis as its provisional president, that Davis would send three commissioners to represent the new Confederate government to Europe.[3] The three commissioners were not particularly

---

[2] Q.V. my books *Covert Wars and Breakaway Civilizations*, and *Covert Wars and the Clash of Civilizations*.

[3] John D. Bennett, *The London Confederates: The Officials, Clergy, Businessmen and Journalists Who Backed the American South*

good choices but one of them did succeed in gaining an approach to the powerful British bank, Barings Brothers, a bank at that time so powerful that it was nicknamed the sixth Great Power. This approach, for the purpose of obtaining a loan from the bank, was rebuffed by one of its board members who held a low opinion of the provisional president of the provisional Confederacy.[4] Barings Bank was a logical choice for such an approach, because Barings had underwritten the bonds that enabled the United States to purchase Louisiana from Napoleon I.

If the initial Confederate approaches to Great Britain were not successful, the Union's fortunes were no better, as its ambassador, Charles Francis Adams, the son of President John Quincy Adams, arrived in Britain to replace the previous American ambassador, two months later than the Confederate commissioners, and just in time for the British Proclamation of Neutrality.[5] This recognized the Confederacy as a belligerent in the upcoming war, a status that, under British law, allowed trade, including the sale of arms, to be conducted with the Confederacy. By early August, the situation for the Union in Great Britain had soured after news reached Britain of its rout at the hands of the Confederate army of P.G.T. Beauregard and Joseph Johnston at the Battle of First Manassas outside of Washington. The *London Times* wrote:

> One thing is clear, and that is that the contest now going on is upon the people of the Confederate States for the right to govern themselves, and to resist subjugation by the North… In defense (sic) of their liberties and sovereign

---

During the Civil War (Jefferson, North Carolina: McFarland and Company, Inc., Publishers, 2008 [ISBN 978-0-0764-6901-7]), p. 25.

[4] John D. Bennett, *The London Confederates*, p. 27.

[5] Ibid., p. 28.

> independence, the Confederate States and people are united and resolute. They are invaded by a power numbering 20,000,000; yet for eight months has the Confederate Government successfully resisted—aye repelled—that invasion, along a frontier of 1,000 miles.[6]

In spite of the thaw of attitudes toward the South in anti-slavery Europe, the Confederate commissioners were unable to convert their victories in the field against Union arms into diplomatic success and recognition, and Davis, now elected President of the fully-formed Confederate government, recalled the Commissioners and appointed new ones, James M. Mason to Britain, and John Slidell to France.[7] Slidell, of course, was the commissioner who had a direct hand in bringing about the Erlanger cotton loan of 1863.

1. The Trent Affair

It was the appointment of Mason and Slidell as the new Confederate commissioners to Great Britain and France that was the occasion of the incident that nearly brought Great Britain into the war on the Confederate side in 1861. Mason and Slidell boarded the *Theodora,* managing to evade the Union blockade of Wilmington, sailed to Havana, Cuba, where they changed ships to the British mail carrier steamer, the *Trent* bound for St. Thomas in the British West Indies.

Unfortunately—or, in hindsight, perhaps fortunately—for the Confederate commissioners, the *Trent* was intercepted and boarded by the Union warship *San Jacinto,* and its Confederate representatives taken prisoner and interred in

---

[6] John D. Bennett, *The London Confederates*, p. 30, citing *The London Times*, November 12, 1861.

[7] Ibid.

Boston. This provoked an entirely predictable outrage in Britain, against which the United States had declared war scarcely forty years before, and for precisely the same thing: the stoppage and boarding of a neutral ship, under its own flag, in international waters, and the impressment of some or all of its passengers and crew as prisoners. There were open calls for war in most of the British press, and Lord Palmerston and his cabinet quickly dispatched troops to protect British Canada, and an ultimatum to the Union: release the property and the prisoners, or it was war. Some British regimental bands, departing the docks, were heard playing "Dixie."[8] Lincoln's administration soon bowed to the pressure, disavowing the actions of the captain of the *San Jacinto*, the Confederate commissioners Slidell and Mason were released, and were allowed to sail on to Europe without further incident. The British satirical magazine *Punch* "marked the occasion with a rhyme:

> A Masonic Ditty
> Sing high diddle diddle
> The colleague of Slidell,
> Released from the stone-jug, or basin,
> And by England received,
> May now be believed,
> A free, and accepted, Mason.[9]

Once in London, the newly "freed and accepted" James Mason lost little time in seeing the British Foreign Secretary Lord Russell, and making the rounds of British society and

---

[8] John D. Bennett, *The London Confederates*, p. 32.

[9] Ibid., p. 32, citing *Punch*, January 18, 1862. Bennett notes that the term "stone-jug" was British slang of that time for a prison.

social circles, but the sought diplomatic recognition never came.[10]

2. Union Counter-Intelligence Operations in Great Britain

Great Britain was the host not only of Confederate agents seeking diplomatic recognition and financial favors, but was also the host to the Union's own intelligence and counter-intelligence efforts. The Confederacy itself played the game rather well, given its meager resources compared to the Union, running a variety of fake "defectors" from the Confederacy who would "defect" to the Union in Great Britain, offering "information" to the Union ambassador, Charles Francis Adams. This "information" the Confederates knew would be forwarded by Adams to the Union Secretary of State Seward in Washington.

The Union, however, was not idle, and picked its own infiltration and espionage targets very carefully, bribing its way into possession of operatives inside of Lloyd's Maritime Insurance,[11] the perfect place for spies monitoring Confederate arms purchases and insurance to operate! And the most successive Confederate financial agent in Britain, Confederate naval officer James Bulloch would complain to the Confederate Navy Department in Richmond that the Union had "succeeded in converting a portion of the police of

---

[10] Bennett notes that in February 1865, Duncan Kenner, a member of the Confederate House of representatives, traveled incognito to London via a stopover in New York, conveying a secret proposal from Jefferson Davis to emancipate all slaves in return for diplomatic recognition. Q.v. p. 37f.

[11] John D. Bennett, *The London Confederates*, pp. 78-79.

this country into secret agents of the United States."[12] In picking these types of targets, one may detect not only the sure hand of Union Secretary of State William Seward at work, but those of his fellow cabinet members, Navy Secretary Gideon Welles, and, of course, Secretary of War Edwin Stanton.

3. The Hidden Geopolifinance of the Erlanger Cotton Loan

In the previous volume, *The Rialto in Richmond,* I observed that the terms of the loan, while onerous to the Confederacy, at least gave it some access to substantial international liquidity and investment by collateralizing the bonds with cotton or other commodity, namely gold.[13] There I also observed that the Rothschild interests had flip-flopped on the idea of the bonds, particularly its notorious *Economist* magazine.[14] But while I hinted at the wider geopolifinancial implications in that book by noting the high political positions of some of the subscribers to that loan, here we must press these connections further, for they indicate the wider context in which the Montreal Canadian Confederate and Union operations must be viewed. In its reportage on the loan, *The Economist* also observed that:

> the Corporation of the City of London had lent money to the Greek insurgents at the time of their War of Independence (1821-1827), and concluded: "If the greatest Corporation in

[12] Ibid., p. 84, citing Harriet C. Owsley, "Henry Shelton Sanford and Federal Surveillance Abroad, 1861-1865," *Mississippi Valley Historical Review, 48*(1961-1962): p. 425.

[13] Q.v. my *Rialto in Richmond*, pp. 241-250ff. Q.v. also John D. Bennett, *The London Confederates*, p. 87-88.

[14] Joseph P. Farrell, *The Rialto in Richmond*, pp., 251-252. Q.v. also Bennett, op. cit. p. 88.

> England may subscribe in aid of rebellion, unquestionably mere individuals may be so bold as to lend to rebels."[15]

But as was seen in *The Rialto in Richmond*, some of these "mere individuals" included the personal secretary to the Prime Minister, the Lord Palmerston, himself, the keeper of the Great Seal, and the Chancellor of the Exchequer (and future Prime Minister William Evert Gladstone himself). It is as if, through the formation of such a loan by private subscribers, a geopolifinancial agenda and objective could be pursued until it was safe to make that agenda an open, public, and *official* one, and if that agenda should fail, plausible deniability of any *official* policy could be maintained.

British Prime Minister Henry John Temple, 3rd Viscount Palmerston

[15] John D. Bennett, op. cit, p. 88, citing *The Economist* March 21, 1863.

William Evert Gladstone, Chancellor of the Exchequer in Lord Palmerston's Government, and later himself Prime Minister

Gladstone nemesis and Prime Minister Benjamin Disraeli

That this may be a plausible interpretation of why so many influential and powerful figures within British finance and politics chose initially to be involved only at a personal level and not in any official capacity is revealed by the deeper controversies that followed the cotton loan after the end of the War Between the States, when the Union press published the list of some of the bonds' prominent British subscribers, chief among whom was the then British Chancellor of the Exchequer and subsequent Prime Minister, William Evert Gladstone, who strenuously objected to the presence of his name among the subscribers in the British press, and demanded his name be omitted from the list.[16]

As the debate raged in the British press over whether the names on the list of subscribers to the Erlanger loan was legitimate or a well-planned Confederate forgery planted in the Union press,[17] a *second* expanded list was published in *The New York Times*, a list many think ultimately was leaked to the newspaper by Secretary of State William Seward, who in turn maintained that it had been obtained from the Confederate agents in Paris.

> This was a very long list of approximately three hundred names, of whom some two-thirds turned out to have London addresses, and included titled persons, Members of Parliament, naval and military men, clergymen and a number of firms; about forty were known Confederate sympathizers.[18]

But while Secretary of State Seward was defending this list as having been obtained from former Confederate agents in

---

[16] John D. Bennett, *The London Confederates*, p. 91f.
[17] Ibid., p. 92.
[18] Ibid., p. 93.

Paris, the list was being denounced in the British press as being a forgery, since some of the handwriting in the marginalia of the list was that of John Bigelow, Union ambassador to Second Empire France, who had deceived Seward as to its nature as a fraud that he had concocted to incriminate the British government.[19]

4. The Union Ambassador to France, John Bigelow, Exposes the Hidden Geopolifinance After the War

Bigelow was not about to take these accusations lying down, however, for after the war he would publish his own version of events. He began his review and analysis of the general history of the list, and especially of the remarks of Gladstone shortly after subscribing to the Erlanger bonds, with the following geopolifinancial observation about the deep politics of the deep event that *was* the Erlanger loan:

> Is it to be supposed that many, if any, of these gentlemen put up their money, and in such large amounts, on a gamble of this peculiarly risky nature, unless they had satisfactory reasons for believing that the army and navy of England were behind them? And what better security could they ask than the names on this list?[20]

For Bigelow the list itself—the names of the people on it with their subscription amounts—was an all but certain indicator

---

[19] John D. Bennett, *The London Confederates*, p. 93.

[20] John Bigelow, LL.D., *Lest We Forget: Gladstone, Morley and the Confederate Loan of 1863* (New York: Gramercy Park, 1905, University of California Reprint), p. 42f.

that there were deep geopolifinancial implications and agendas at play in the Erlanger loan.[21]

As was seen, when the expanded list of subscribers was published in the British press, Gladstone denounced his inclusion as a "mistake" and demanded his name be withdrawn. This prompted another broadside from Bigelow:

> ...(The) Confederate bankers were among the most widely known bankers in Europe: Fraser, Trenholm & Co., of London; James Spence of Liverpool; Erlanger & Co., of Paris; and Schroeder & Co., of Holland. Any of these houses could have told any inquirer whether his name was on their list, and, if there, how it came there. Has any newspaper in London or elsewhere informed its readers that Mr. Gladstone, or any of the repudiating editors... or indeed any single one of the three hundred on the list, ever asked either of the bankers, before or since the publication of the list, by whom or by whose authority their names were placed there?[22]

---

[21] I should add that in my research for *The Rialto in Richmond*, and for this book, I was struck by the fact that neither sources of that time, nor current research, have made any deep inquiry into who the holders and subscribers to the bonds may have been on the *continent* of Europe, and particularly in France. This is all the more surprising since, on the French side, the loan was largely intended for the purchase of ironclads to be built in French shipyards. Napoleon III's government had given quiet assurances to Slidell—who was related by marriage to d'Erlanger—that the ships would be built and conveyed to the Confederacy. However, Napoleon III, when pressed by Confederate agents to declare publicly that the ships were headed for the Confederacy, reversed course, and refused to back the project any further. In any case, this implies that the French subscribers would be a list of similarly wealthy and powerful individuals.

[22] John Bigelow, LL.D., *Lest We Forget*, p. 44.

Needless to say, the answer to all of Bigelow's questions was a firm No. "It is unnecessary to look for an explanation of this persistent silence," he writes, because "From every quarter it leaps to the eyes."[23]

Bigelow pressed his point home by pointing out that there were other very public, as well as very private and secret, indicators that the threat of British recognition of the Confederacy and intervention in the war was very real, for in 1862, at Newcastle, Gladstone delivered a speech, in which he attempted "to prepare the world for England's recognition of the Confederates by the following statement:

> We know quite well that the people of the Northern States have not yet drunk of the cup—*they are still trying to hold it far from their lips—which* ALL THE REST OF THE WORLD SEE *they must nevertheless drink of.* We may have our own opinions about slavery; we may be for or against the South; but THERE IS NO DOUBT that Jefferson Davis and other leaders of the South have made an army, they are making, it appears, *a navy, and they have made what is more then either, they have made a nation.*[24]

If this was not enough to convince the skeptic, Bigelow then cites a letter from Gladstone to his wife, which one might assume came into Bigelow's hands via the efficient Union espionage and counter-espionage operation in Britain. In it, Gladstone explicitly states that, "Lord Palmerston has come exactly to my mind about some early representation of a friendly kind to America, if we can get France and Russia to join."[25] Bigelow goes on to add that:

---

[23] Ibid., p. 45.

[24] Ibid., p. 46, citing William E. Gladstone, speech at Newcastle, 1862, all emphases in Bigelow.

[25] John Bigelow, LL.D., *Lest We Forget*, p. 47.

> He (Gladstone), Palmerston and Russell, the three heads of the Government… were at this very time agreed that *even in the case of failure to secure the cooperation of France and Russia,* England alone if necessary ought to recognize the Southern Confederacy as an independent republic.[26]

Nor was this all. Having found the range, Bigelow unleashes full broadside after full broadside:

> In 1862, September 24th, Lord Palmerston wrote to Mr. Gladstone "that he himself and Lord Russell[27] thought the time was fast approaching when an offer of mediation ought to be made by England, France, and Russia, and that Russell was going privately to instruct the ambassador at Paris to sound out the French Government. "Of course," Lord Palmerston said, "no actual step would be taken without the sanction of the Cabinet. But if I am not mistaken you would be inclined to approve such a course." The proposal would be made to both North and South. If both should accept, an armistice would follow, and **negotiations on the basis of separation.** *If both should decline, then Lord Palmerston assumed that they would acknowledge the independence of the South.* The next day Mr. Gladstone replied. He was glad to learn what the Prime Minister had told him, and for two reasons especially he desired that the proceedings should be prompt."
>
> So far towards a recognition of the insurgents had the three heads of the Queen's government advanced when Mr. Gladstone went to Newcastle and let fall the sentence about the American War, already cited, "of which… he was destined never to hear the last"; "but a sentence which *he undoubtedly thought, and not without good reason,* as we

[26] Ibid., emphasis added.

[27] Lord Russell: the British Foreign Secretary.

> have seen, *expressed the views of the Queen's government* and foreshadowed its policy.[28]

Notably, the phrase boldfaced in the previous quotation makes it clear that the British government *preferred the permanent separation* of the Union and the Confederacy and that any negotiations which it might mediate would proceed upon that principle. That this was a real geopolifinancial danger and not just a private fantasy being discussed by the three most powerful ministers of office in Great Britain is revealed by the fact that, in his instructions to Ambassador Charles Francis Adams, Union Secretary of State William Seward issued specific instructions against the possibility of a British declaration of war against the Union.[29]

As if this were not enough to convince any reader of the deep events and deep geopolifinancial interests that were active behind the scenes, Bigelow had one more broadside to fire. "I will quote," he writes, "a few pertinent words from a speech delivered by Disraeli, the leader of the Tory Party, in the House of Commons, on the 5th of February, 1863, at the first session of Parliament after the Newcastle speech:

> "Her Majesty's Government," he said, "commissioned one of their members to repair to the chief seats of industry in the country to announce, as I understood it, an entire change in the policy which they had throughout supported and sanctioned: *the declaration* (about Jefferson Davis's army, navy, and country) *was made formally and avowedly with the consent and sanction of the Government.* Now, Sir, what did that declaration mean? If it meant anything, it

---

[28] John Bigelow, LL.D., *Lest We Forget*, pp. 48-49, boldface emphasis added by me, italicized emphasis in Bigelow.

[29] Ibid., p. 54. The entire text of Seward's instructions to Ambassador Adams is given on pp. 50-54.

meant that the Southern States would be recognized; because, if it be true that they have created armies, navies, and a people, we are bound by every principle of policy and of public law to recognize their political existence."

Bigelow goes on to observe,

> **Lord Palmerston followed Disraeli in the debate, and at considerable length, but he did not deny that statesman's allegation that Gladstone spoke with the authority of the Government at Newcastle, nor refer at all to American affairs: a reticence more significant than any words he could with propriety have uttered.**[30]

It is against this backdrop and context of the deep geopolifinance of the European Atlantic powers that the substantial Confederate secret service network in Canada must be examined, for there we find truly bizarre and highly suggestive connections... to the very Union from which it was trying to separate.

B. Montreal: Where Confederates and Yankees go to Talk and Plot Together

When we turn to a consideration of the Confederacy's intelligence and paramilitary operations in Montreal, Canada, here, as elsewhere in this book, we are confronted by the fact that the number of published sources are few and far between, in this case, there is only *one* book dealing exclusively with the subject, the invaluable work of Barry Sheehy, *Montreal, City of Secrets: Confederate Operations in Montreal During*

[30] John Bigelow, LL.D., *Lest We forget*, p. 55, italicized emphasis in Bigelow, boldface emphasis added by me.

the American Civil War.[31] Additionally, this book gives the deep geopolifinancial reasons behind the formation of the Canadian confederation as a response to the then perceived instability of the United States and its imperial ambitions and designs on British North America.

While the Confederacy's financial and intelligence operations in Great Britain and France were large and extensive, it was in fact Montreal which was the seat of the largest, and most well-financed operations of the Confederate Secret Service during the War Between the States. By 1864, these operations were funded by the Confederate Congress to the tune of approximately one million dollars in hard currency, in that day and time, British pounds sterling, or gold. The cell reported directly to Confederate Secretary of State, Judah P. Benjamin, and its importance may be judged by the fact that when his Continuity of Government flight had failed, and after his release from Union internment at Fort Monroe, former Confederate President Jefferson Davis and his entire family first travelled to Montreal, where they found help and shelter from fellow Confederates still living in Montreal.[32]

One of the purposes of this cell, as has been seen in previous chapters and in *The Rialto in Richmond*, was to fund and coordinate the election campaigns in the Union border states and swing states in favor of the Confederacy in the crucial 1864 elections. The other purpose was to function as a basis of espionage and covert operations of a paramilitary

---

[31] Barry Sheehy, with Photographer Cindy Wallace, *Montreal, City of Secrets: Confederate Operations in Montreal During the American Civil War* (Montreal, Quebec, Canada: Baraka Books, 2017 [ISBN 978-1-77186-123-6]). Sheehy's book is also full of period pictures of Montreal of many of the sites discussed in his book.

[32] Sheehy, *Montreal, City of Secrets*, p. 13.

nature, like the St. Alban's raid of that year when Confederate soldiers crossed the Canadian-Union border, and robbed a bank in St. Alban's, Vermont. It was the northernmost engagement of the American Civil War, and for the Confederacy, it was a long-overdue payback for the devastation caused by Union armies as they burned and pillaged their way through the South, and for the murderous raids of radical abolitionist John Brown prior to the war.[33]

Most importantly, however, Montreal served as a neutral hub that could be more or less easily accessed by the personnel of both belligerents of the war, where they could confer, and very often, conspire together.

> Not only were the Confederates present in strength in Montreal, but many of Lincoln's enemies from the North were as well, including Copperhead Democrats and Radical Republicans. We discovered much of Wall Street and America's nascent military industrial complex in Montreal, apparently doing business with the Confederacy. The level of corruption in the Northern war effort suggested by these American power brokers in Montreal is at once breathtaking and disquieting. Also present in the Montreal and Niagara areas were key members of the War Department, the Judge Advocate general's Office, the Federal National Detective Police, and the Treasury Department. Much of Secretary Salmon Chase's presidential committee appears to be on hand. What business called these American officials to Montreal, and to a hotel known to be closely associated with the Confederate Secret Service? *Civil War super banker Jay Cooke and Edwin Stanton's chief telegraph operator and confidant Thomas T. Eckert* were in Canada along with Radical Republicans like James Ashley, James Harlan, James

[33] Ibid., pp. 21, 177-178, 180.

> Wilson, John Bingham, *John Sherman*, and Alexander R. Shepherd, to name but a few. Lincoln haters like New York Mayor Fernando Wood and his brother, Congressman and newspaper editor Benjamin Wood, were regulars at St. Lawrence Hall.... *The full list of those present in Montreal will stagger anyone familiar with the era and certainly challenge the mainstream American narrative regarding the Civil War and Lincoln.*[34]

Jay Cooke, Lincoln's essential financier, the broker who sold much of the Union's sovereign securities, present in the center of a Confederate Secret Service cell? John Sherman, Ohio U.S. Radical Republican Senator and the brother of William Tecumseh Sherman, whose armies were laying waste to Georgia? *Thomas Eckert*, not only Stanton's telegraph operator, but the very man who had refused his protective services to his commander-in-chief, Lincoln, on the very day the latter requested them? And this is, as Sheehy himself observes, just scratching the surface of a very long list of people who frequented Montreal, or who were present in the city *at the same time* as some of the others. This list alone, as Sheehy avers, is enough to cast suspicion on the standard narratives about the War Between the States, and about Lincoln himself.

The presence of such people begs questions, and in some cases, an answer can be speculated. For example, in the above quotation, it was noted that Thomas T. Eckert, Union Secretary of War Edwin Stanton's close confidant, was present in Montreal during the crucial election year of 1864. One purpose, however, is suggested by the fact that Stanton had sent another close associate and friend, Judge Jeremiah

[34] Sheehy, *Montreal, City of Secrets*, pp. 13, 15, italicized emphasis added.

Black, to Montreal "to explore the possibility of a negotiated peace" with the Confederacy![35] Months later, of course, Stanton would be seeing to it that the assassination of Abraham Lincoln was all but guaranteed success by denying Lincoln the use of Major Eckert for his security, and by warning General and Mrs. Grant not to attend the Good Friday play at Ford's Theater with the Lincolns on the night of the murder.

1. An Example: Lincoln's Multi-Million Dollar Covert Cotton-for-Contraband Deal

One of the biggest indicators of a covert Union-Confederate collaboration via their overlapping operations in Montreal is President Lincoln's covert Cotton-for-Contraband deal, a deal worth no less than "half a billion dollars or more in greenbacks," and a deal whose details were negotiated between the belligerents' representatives in Montreal in 1864.[36] This deal was approved by both Richmond and President Lincoln, in the latter's case, because it stopped the hemorrhage of gold from the Union to purchase finished cotton (and other finished products) from Great Britain, and by the former because the cotton-for-contraband trade allowed the Confederacy to obtain military supplies and equipment directly from its foe! Needless to say, as word of this multi-million dollar deal leaked, Montreal was flooded with arms dealers, smugglers, and financiers from the Union, the Confederacy, and Europe, all hoping to cash in on the deal.[37] Some of these were even Radical Republicans whose hatred of Lincoln overcame their hatred of slavery, and

---

[35] Sheehy, *Montreal, City of Secrets*, p. 62.

[36] Ibid., p. 15, see also pp. 107-108.

[37] Sheehy, *Montreal, City of Secrets*, p. 23.

enabled their own participation in the deal.[38] They had some ammunition, as Lincoln's personal endorsement and signature on some of the permits authorizing the trade[39] provided them leverage over the President and by implication his cabinet.[40]

As was pointed out earlier in this book, there was a perverse effect of the Union blockade on the Union itself, namely, that it cut itself off from the cotton needed to make cloths for its citizens and more importantly uniforms for its soldiers, while it had nothing worthwhile to export to Europe. Lincoln came up with a spectacularly specious argument that the covert trade with the South might support "loyal southerners," but as Sheehy points out, there was no way to know if the cotton was coming from such southerners. The White-House-sanctioned black market trade was also a source of rich patronage favors which could be doled out to friends.[41]

2. New York City Mayor Fernando Wood's Threat to Secede, and New York's Confederate Currency Notes Production

The perverse effect that the Union blockade of the South had on the *North* was quickly felt in the ports of the Union, such as New York City, which could no longer export southern cotton, not import goods from Europe paid for by the export of cotton. This led New York City's mayor Fernando Wood to advocate that the city secede, declare itself a city state and "continue business as usual with the Confederacy," and indeed, Wood's brother, Congressman and

---

[38] Ibid., p. 22f.

[39] Ibid., p. 94.

[40] See Sheehy's summary of these risks on p. 110.

[41] The cotton-for-contraband deal also involved the participation of Louis Kuhn (to become Kuhn, Loeb and Co.), and of agents of Thomas Durant of the Union Pacific Railroad. (Sheehy, op cit., p. 114.)

New York Daily News publisher Benjamin Wood was "actually on the payroll of the Confederate Secret Service in Montreal, receiving a payment of $25,000 in 1864 from the Confederate-controlled Montreal branch of the Ontario Bank."[42]

New York City was also the site of another intriguing operation probably conducted under the supervision of, and arranged by, the Canadian Confederates, for prior to the war, many of the South's banknotes were printed in New York City under the auspices of the Importing and Exporting Company of Georgia jointly owned by Gazaway Lamar and his son Charles Augustus. When the war broke out, the Lamars arranged for the continued covert printing of Confederate currency and bonds in New York City and their trans-shipment to Florida via Halifax, Canada. This was the heart of other operations of a large Confederate Secret Service network in that city, again under the control of Confederate Secretary of State Judah Benjamin.[43]

It would be surprising if this operation was not piggy-backed with others, such as the counterfeiting of Union greenbacks, and the use of such notes to fund other covert activities.

3. The Montreal Banks and the Confederacy; Booth's Accounts on Wall Street, Money Laundering to Radical Republicans, and the Origin of the Davis Myth?

Mention has already been made of the de facto Confederate control over the Montreal branch of the Ontario Bank, and it was this control that permitted the Confederacy to launder money to various Radical Republican and

[42] Sheehy, *Montreal, City of Secrets*, p. 121.
[43] Ibid., p. 124.

Copperhead Democrat targets. This was done by issuing bank drafts to the employees of the bank, who in turn would endorse them to "the real intended recipients of the money." This was how the publisher Benjamin Wood received $25,000 of Confederate greenbacks. This is an important point, for Wood could hardly have been issued Confederate money, which would have been useless in the Union. Nor is it likely the money was in the form of specie, for that amount in gold coin would have raised Federal suspicions. Thus, Wood's money was likely in the form of greenbacks, which in turn might have been the result of a counterfeiting operation run out of New York City, and laundered through the Canadian bank! While this is pure speculation, it is worth entertaining, and to my knowledge, no one has raised nor investigated the possibility.[44] The tight connections between Union wheeler-dealers and those of the Confederacy in Montreal even go so far as to raise the possibility that Montreal, and these connections, were the reason behind the alleged but never proven role of Davis in the Lincoln assassination.

a. Montreal and the Missing Pages of the Booth Diary Again, and the Cashier's Cheque Found on His Body

In *The Rialto in Richmond* I spent a great deal of time covering the long-missing and recently-recovered eighteen

---

[44] Sheehy, *Montreal, City of Secrets*, p. 54. Sheehy also notes that Ohio Radical Republican Senator Benjamin Wade was heard declaring that "the sooner he (Lincoln) was assassinated the better." (p. 54). This statement, in view of the implications of the missing pages of the Booth diary, would constitute evidence of *mens rea* and could have been used at trial to prosecute Wade in connection with the assassination, had the missing pages been public in that time.

pages of John Wilkes Booth's diary, pages wherein a vast conspiracy to murder Lincoln is outlined, including the participation of well-known Radical Republicans in Lincoln's own northern Congress, people such as Indiana Representative George Washington Julian, Michigan Senator (and future Secretary of the Interior under Ulysses S. Grant) Zachariah Chandler, Ohio Senator Benjamin Wade and President *pro tempore* of the U.S. Senate during the impeachment trial of President Andrew Johnson, Senator John Conness of California, who would quickly call out the troops after learning of the assassination attempt on Secretary of State William Seward. Booth also wrote of receiving thousands of dollars in greenbacks and of the participation of New York financiers in the scheme. But there are three *direct* ties of Booth to the overlapping interests of the Confederacy and Union in Montreal, Canada:

(1)*Booth himself was present in Montreal, on or about mid-October of 1864, for he signed the St. Lawrence Hotel guest book on October 18 of that year; and,.*[45]

(2) *Shortly after this trip to Montreal, Booth established accounts at the Montreal Branch of the Ontario Bank,* ***and at the Washington branch of Cooke Brothers Bank***; and,

(3) *A bank draft signed by Ontario Bank president H. Starnes for the amount of £61 or approximately $450 to $550 was found on the body of "John*

[45] Sheehy, *Montreal, City of Secrets*, p. 22.

> *Wilkes Booth" after he was shot at Garrett's farm after the Lincoln assassination.*[46]

b. Booth's Strange Network of Associates in Montreal

These three indicators of Booth's wider network of overlapping Union and Confederate interests in Montreal and their possible connections were noted by Sheehy in his work. Sheehy describes this strange network of associations in the following way:

> This list includes Democrats, Republicans (some of them Radicals), bankers, business leaders, arms dealers, Treasury Department officials, and War Department agents, including Edwin Stanton's top spies; there was even a governor or two involved. Some of these individuals were in Montreal to trade cotton for contraband, but this put them into direct contact with senior members of the Confederate Secret Service. Others were in Montreal selling arms and food to the Confederacy or laying plans to defeat Lincoln at the polls. Some even wanted to displace him as the Republican nominee. All these powerful Northerners were at St. Lawrence Hall rubbing elbows with Confederates who used the hotel as an unofficial headquarters. This was the universe in which John Wilkes Booth circulated in Canada, and this circle is more interesting and eclectic than one would normally associate with a lone, brooding, assassin.[47]

---

[46] Sheehy, *Montreal, City of Secrets*, p. 53. I put Booth's name in quotations marks because of the difficulties encountered in identifying his body, as was detailed in *The Rialto in Richmond*, pp. 139-146.

[47] Sheehy, *Montreal, City of Secrets*, p. 133.

That, indeed, is the precise point, for Booth was not simply a "lone brooding assassin" but the trigger- and bag-man for a much broader and deeper conspiracy that included the deep geopolifinancial interests of the North, and via Canada, Britain.

c. And the Northern New York City Anti-Lincoln Assassination Plot

Sheehy himself notes this wider and deeper Northern geopolifinancial interest in the assassination and its connection to Booth as well, and in doing so, mentions names we have encountered previous in this book and in *The Rialto in Richmond*:

> There was a fourth scheme targeting Lincoln, the most mysterious of all, and it was centered in New York City. Those behind this latter conspiracy remain in the shadows even today. *Booth was in contact with them and expressed concern to George Atzerodt*[48] that they might get to Lincoln first. Booth spent considerable time in New York in the summer of 1864 and again in early 1865. He boasted to George Atzerodt of dining in the finest mansion in New York but never revealed the name of his host. This was precisely the time when a powerful movement was afoot to force Lincoln off the Republican ticket. This movement may have begun in New York but it soon developed national reach. It also crossed party lines, involving powerful Republicans and War Democrats. A number of influential newspaper editors were also involved. Meetings were held in private homes rather than hotels to avoid publicity. New York Mayor George Opdyke and

[48] Atzerodt, it will be recalled, was one of the members of Booth's conspiracy that was hanged for his part in it.

> businessman David P. Field hosted two such meetings; there may have been more. According to Thurlow Weed, who attended these clandestine sessions, the conspiracy was "vicious and powerful… involving more leading men than I would have thought possible." Security was tight. Even today, a century and a half later, we know the names of only about a dozen of the fifty or more people involved. *The ones we can identify include* Mayor George Opdyke, businessman D.D. Field, Hon. Henry Winter Davis, *Senator Benjamin Wade, Senator Charles Sumner,* James Van Dyck, George Wilkes, newspaper editor Parke Godwin, newspaper editor Theodore Tilton, Lewis Parsons, Governor J. Andrew, governor William Dennison, newspaper editor Manton Marble, and former Attorney General Jeremiah Black. *Salmon Chase,*[49] forever ambitious for the presidency, sent an observer.[50]

While most of these names have remained out of our narrative and, due to the focuses of this book must remain so, some of them by now will be well familiar to the reader.

This wider northern anti-Lincoln conspiracy and Booth's presence in it is further buttressed by the fact that at approximately a month prior to his presence in Montreal, several major figures in Union finance and industry were also present in the city, including William Fargo, the founder of Welles Fargo and American Express, James Brown (of Brown Brothers, and later known as Brown Brothers, Harriman), John D. Rockefeller, Charles Barney, Louis Kuhn

---

[49] Chase was initially Lincoln's Secretary of the Treasury, and Chase successfully placed his own portrait on the obverse of the Lincoln one dollar greenback certificate as a kind of free political advertising. He was later named by Lincoln and confirmed as the Chief Justice of the Supreme Court.

[50] Sheehy, *Montreal, City of Secrets*, p. 135, emphasis added.

(already mentioned), three bankers representing Jay Cooke and Company—A.S. Hatch, George Bliss and Henry Hatch—and Democrat Samuel Ward, who also was "the U.S. Representative for Barings Brothers Bank in London,"[51] the so-called "sixth Great Power." Perhaps most tellingly, Jay Cooke himself, along with his wife, was a guest at the St. Lawrence Hotel *at the same time* that Booth was also there.[52]

"The sheer weight of evidence," writes Sheehy, and, we might add, the sheer mass of powerful and influential persons present, "points to something powerful and unusual occurring in Montreal from the summer and fall of 1864 through the spring of 1865."[53]

4. The New York City & Confederate Efforts to Short the Greenback

With these powerful geopolifinancial personages and forces circling around Montreal, it should come as no surprise that, almost as soon as the Lincoln greenbacks made their first appearance in 1862, that the Confederacy, in league with the Lamars' company that minted the Confederate paper currency and bonds, began an effort in 1864 to short the greenback by buying large amounts (for that day) of gold, and shipping it to Britain. This was done with the participation of the Canadian banks, and predictably the Montreal branch of Ontario Bank, and with the participation of the financial houses of New York City, including J.P. Morgan. This important point gives yet more contextual evidence that the apocryphal statements attributed to Chancellor Bismarck about the Civil War and the assassination having been decreed by the "high financial

---

[51] Sheehy, *Montreal, City of Secrets*, p. 96.

[52] Ibid.

[53] Ibid., p. 103.

powers of Europe"[54] have some basis in actual truth and the financial policies of the day that were clearly opposed to Lincoln and his methods of financing the war.

5. German Purchase of Union Sovereign Debt And Grant's Visit to von Bismarck

That this interpretation of the Chancellor's apocryphal statements is probably true is further supported by yet another little known fact. While the Erlanger cotton loan to the Confederacy was being "over-subscribed in Europe," the Union was having severe if not extreme problems raising foreign credit due to the appearance of the greenback. Aware of the Montreal-based Confederate and New York City financiers' efforts to short the greenback, former U.S. Secretary of the Treasury R.J. Walker, was called upon to defend the greenback and the credit-worthiness of the Union, which he did in a series of pamphlets in early 1865. By this point, of course, the Union was clearly going to win the war, but nonetheless it could not raise credit in France or England. The one place that *did* by Union bonds were the various states of what would become Germany, including the dominant German state, Prussia. Here again we find yet another possible reason for President Grant's post-presidential visit to what had *become* Germany and his meeting with its imperial *Reichskanzler* Otto von Bismarck. They may have met not only to discuss the nineteenth century airship mystery and the Prussian involvement, but the German investments in the country at the end of the war and their status.

---

[54] Q.v. my *Rialto in Richmond*, pp. 233-240.

6. The Montreal Connection and the Lincoln Assassination

The connection and timing of John Wilkes Booth in Montreal with that of prominent union financiers, industrialists, and railroad men has already been noted, but now we must take note of some *truly* bizarre presences. It is known, for example, that in April of 1865, in the aftermath of Lincoln's assassination, that Secretary of War Edwin Stanton's intelligence chief of the National Detective Police, Lafayette Baker, along with representatives of Judge Advocate General Joseph Holt's office were in the city, ostensibly for the purpose of investigating the alleged Confederate connection to the murder.[55] But one individual, a Connecticut slave-trader named Nelson Trowbridge, stated that he was in Montreal to conduct cotton business with Baker.[56] While we will never know, the possibility remains that Baker may have been trying to do double duty in Montreal, accomplishing business while investigating the assassination links to the Confederacy. In any case, with the extensive size of Confederate operations in Canada, it is possible that one is looking at one half of what was planned should Britain ever recognize it and enter the war on its side.[57]

---

[55] Sheehy, *Montreal, City of Secrets*, p. 23.

[56] Ibid., p. 51.

[57] This seems an adequate juncture to point out that Sheehy also discusses the War Between the States as the geopolitical pressure that led to the formation of the Canadian confederation itself. He points out that the *Trent* affair actually led to the Palmerston government issuing an ultimatum to release both the ship and its interred Confederate prisoners, or else Britain would go to war. Plamerston's war plan called for an all-out naval offensive by British ironclads against the wooden ships of the Union, breaking the Confederate blockade, and for the blockade and

7. What was the Possible Purpose of the Confederacy's Investigations of the Dahlgren Raid in Canada?

We are not yet quite done with the strangeness of the Montreal Canadian connection. There are two final and exceedingly strange events that indicate that perhaps even the Confederacy was beginning to wonder just exactly what was going on. The first of these is the dispatch of Confederate Secret Service agent Daniel B. Lucas to Montreal. Prior to his dispatch to Montreal, it was Lucas who had been one of the main interrogators of the Federal prisoners of war *taken during the infamous Dahlgren raid on Richmond.* Sheehy does not speculate on what, if anything, this might indicate about the reasons for his posting to Montreal, but we are free to do so. As was seen in chapter five, there were—and are—questions about the origins of Dahlgren's orders and if, indeed, he actually composed them. They were certainly *found* on his body, but they could have easily been planted by someone intending to cast the Union in the worst possible light, and perhaps even to raise questions about the Confederacy itself. Perhaps Lucas' presence in Montreal is an indicator that the Confederacy had begun to suspect a dastard deep player in the mix, and was intent on following up any potential British connection to the Dahlgren raid. Perhaps the Confederacy had already encountered someone operating on both sides of the lines. If so, then where better to probe into that possibility than Montreal? It is perhaps significant in this regard that immediately prior to Lincoln's assassination, the

---

bombardment of northern ports in conjunction with joint Confederate-British land operations. (p. 40) British troops in Canada were quickly reinforced.

Confederate accounts in Ontario Bank were emptied and "headed for Europe."[58]

8. The Final, Most Significant and Suggestive Presence in Montreal

There is one final, most significant and most suggestive presence that was hovering over Montreal in spirit, and in that crucial summer and autumn of 1864 was actually there in body as well, a man who might have mixed and mingled with the movers and shakers of the day, the Fargos, the Kuhns, the Rockefellers, Cookes, and Durants. While the high and the mighty were meeting and talking and plotting and scheming with each other in the drawing room of the St. Lawrence Hotel, a journalist by the name of Sanford Conover was filing his reports on the goings on in the Canadian press, reports which included plots to kidnap Lincoln. But "his real name was Charles A. Dunham, but he operated under multiple aliases and was almost certainly a double agent."[59] Never one to be known for being flush with money, the source that paid for Conover-Dunham at the pricy St. Lawrence Hotel remains unknown. Regardless of who may have paid for it, however, Charles A. Dunham, the Impresario of Imposture, has finally appeared, amid a cast of characters all of whom connect him to all of the events surveyed in the preceding chapters of this book.

---

[58] Sheehy, *Montreal, City of Secrets*, p. 67. Sheehy notes that it was Jacob Thompson, one of the three original Confederate commissioners to Canada, who transferred the funds, along with himself, to Europe.

[59] Ibid., p. 148.

8
The Impresario of Imposture:
The Double- (or Triple?-) Dealing Career of Charles A. Dunham

"In short, he was a genius in the black arts of false information and dirty tricks....
"This summary is incomplete because much of Dunham's story is still unknown or in dispute."
—Carman Cumming[1]

THEIR NAMES, THEIR PICTURES, and their character (or lack thereof) have populated the narrative of this book and its predecessor: Generals Ulysses S. Grant, William Tecumseh Sherman, Joseph Johnston, Robert E. Lee, and Edward Kirby Smith, power brokers Francis Preston Blair and Horace Greeley, Secretaries of State Judah Benjamin and William Seward, Presidents Abraham Lincoln, Jefferson Davis, and Andrew Johnson, Senators Benjamin F. Wade and Zachariah Chandler and Charles Sumner, Congressman Thaddeus Stevens, Prime Ministers Henry John Temple (the Viscount Palmerston), William E. Gladstone, and Benjamin Disraeli, the Emperors Maximillian I, Napoleon III, and Tsar Alexander II, Chancellor Otto von Bismarck, intelligence chiefs Lafayette Baker and Thomas Eckert, spiders and serpents Edwin Stanton and John Wilkes Booth, bankers and financiers Emile d'Erlanger and Jay Cooke, noblemen, commoners, carpetbaggers and crooks and a host of others have all appeared in this confusing and

---

[1] Carman Cumming, *Devil's Game: The Civil War Intrigues of Charles A. Dunham* (Chicago and Urbana: The University of Illinois Press, 2004, ISBN978-0-252-07519-3), p. 9.

downright dark comic opera. It is therefore perhaps entirely and altogether fitting *and **telling*** that the ultimate scallywag, grifter, crook, monteback, archconspirator, fraud, swindler, hustler (and these are but euphemisms), the "Impresario of Imposture" himself, Charles A. Dunham, has no picture at all, not a photograph, daguerreotype, pen and ink or pencil sketch, watercolor, or oil painting. There is *nothing whatsoever* to give us a glimpse into the face of the man who may have been one of the most accomplished grifters of all time. There may, indeed, be a family portrait somewhere in an old box of forgotten memorabilia, but for the public record there is nothing but a trail of endless aliases, forged letters, faked newspaper articles, and a network of contacts that fanned out over a continent, ingratiating himself into the corridors of power in Richmond, Washington, and elsewhere. He is the ultimate enigma in a Civil War cipher wrapped in a code, boxed in a mystery and wrapped in a riddle.

The Impresario of Imposture,
Charles A. Dunham

For the one and only complete study of the life of this remarkable man, he is simply, and only, a consummate swindler. But I shall argue that everything which speaks for this interpretation of the man—the endless aliases, the forged letters and journalistic articles, the networks of contacts—argues even more emphatically for a different view: that he was a consummate spy and *agent provocateur*, a one-man chamber of mirrors worthy of a John le Carre spy novel, for these things may be seen as the props in the trade craft of *espionage*: aliases may be seen as professionally created *legends,* the forged articles and responses as the narrative preparations and social engineering of a consummate *agent provocateur*, and the networks of contacts as the manipulations of a master handler of cells, to invoke all the terms of tradecraft. Thus the methodology of previous chapters—that the research of others is capable of a very different interpretation than its authors gave it±is especially true here.

But if he was all of these things, if Charles A. Dunham was not simply a darkly brilliant swindler and grifter, but a master spy and *agent provocateur*, for whom did he ply the trade?

The Union?

The Confederacy?

Both?

Or neither, but someone else?

In seeking to answer these questions we shall rely on a summary of the only biography of the man available, that of Carman Cumming.[2] We can only hope to convey the impression left by a close reading of Cumming's research, the impression of a supremely gifted practitioner of the art of the grift. In attempting to summarize Cumming's thorough

[2] Carman Cumming, *Devil's Game: The Civil War Intrigues of Charles A. Dunham* (Chicago and Urbana: The University of Illinois Press, 2004, ISBN978-0-252-07519-3).

biography, I hope to demonstrate that when this career is viewed within the context of everything else that has preceded in this book, it is much more likely that Dunham's career represents that not of an accomplished con-man and swindler, but of an exceptionally brilliant spy and *agent provocateur.*

A. The Patterns of Perjury, Templates of Treachery, and Fundamentals of Fraud

1. The Basic Dunham Pattern: Multiple Aliases, Infiltrating All Sides, and Feigning Conflict

Dunham may safely be credited as being the first modern example not only of a fake journalist planting faked stories based on faked "sources" all of which culminated in himself, but he may be the first example of coordinated trolling, gaslighting, and all the other techniques that have been used in the modern social media era to promote false narratives. Dunham employed a veritable arsenal of aliases (or, as a spy would call them, "legends"), which he would often employ against himself as phony critics of his planted newspaper articles!

> Wallace...Margrave...Rhett...Haynes...Wolfenden... Conover ...Redburn... Dunham...
>
> In reports, letters, and newspaper articles, the cast became ever more elaborate and interconnected. At times, in letters or dispatches, one of these men would expose the doings of one of the others. At times they would accuse each other of notorious crimes and misdemeanors, such as the planning of Lincoln's assassination. At one point, Conover named Dunham as the head of this conspiracy and at another he told how Margrave had created the original plan. At still another, Wallace offered a reward for the

> capture of Conover, who had "personated" him in Washington. (He was shortly afterwards arrested by a Canadian policeman eager to collect the reward he himself had put up.
>
> Only very gradually and long after the war, would it become clear that all these men and several others (such as Harvey Birch of the *New York Herald* and Franklin Foster of the *New York World*) were all one and the same, the creation of an astonishingly clever and prolific fraud. A fraud who wrote constantly, creating multiple personalities and weaving them into a framework of deception that crossed the boundaries of North and South, exploiting wartime paranoia.[3]

We are thus already in the presence of the dilemma that is Dunham: was he merely a very clever fraudster and swindler, acting out his own narcissistic fantasies and deriving pleasure from his ability to manipulate people and events, or did all of this serve darker purposes and hidden masters? It is to be noted that the technique of multiple aliases and trolling and gaslighting his own aliases is a classic technique of the *agent provocateur*, as is the cover employment of journalism, a typical cover for espionage and spies.

He began this astonishing career by a standard grift, the "missing heir" scheme, to which he added his own special embellishments, including a pattern that would become a favorite: ingratiating himself into one faction, and then having one of his aliases accuse him of criminality, and then having yet a third, fourth, or fifth alias form a "committee" to investigate the rival competing claims of various "heirs" and previous aliases! One can guess the rest: "we cannot complete

---

[3] Carman Cumming, *Devil's Game*, p. 8.

our investigations, which are expensive to pursue, without your help and assistance; please send money."[4]

2. Some of Dunham's Peculiar Associations and Claims

Dunham also had a surprising talent for appearing in places or connections not only with impeccable timing, but that are in themselves highly suggestive, again, of an intelligence agent, rather than simply a one man fraud and grift show. He appeared in Washington in July of 1861, in the same time frame of the disastrous Union defeat the same month at the First Battle of Manassas.[5] While this coincidental appearance at this crucial time is not in and of itself incriminating nor indicative of any wider networks and associations behind him, it will become evident that it is often a pattern with Dunham. Thus the question occurs: Why would he appear in Washington in the same month as the first major clash of arms between the Union and newly-formed Confederacy took place? And the answer may be because he was reporting on the outcome and its implications to his superiors.

Worse, during these initial stays in Washington, Dunham was often in the company of a notorious and somewhat well-known Washington "character," an eccentric Canadian "herbal healer" collector of weird "medical specimens" by the name of Francis Tumblety, who liked to ride around the city on a white horse. According to one of many of Dunham's "newspaper articles," Tumblety was suspected of a role in the infamous Jack the Ripper murders in London because some of his "medical specimens" resembled those cut from the Ripper's murder victims. As if

[4] Ibid., pp. 21-22.

[5] Carman Cumming, *Devil's Game*, p. 29.

this were not enough, he was also suspected of having had some role in Lincoln's assassination.[6] And this is only 1861, and we are just getting started.

Dunham also was a member of various pre-bellum secret societies and what we would now call "political action committees" advocating for the creation of a vast "slave empire" composed from the southern states, Mexico, Meso-America, and the Caribbean islands, and was also allegedly a member of a secret society called the Knights of the Golden Circle, a group that conducted covert operations in Canada and the Union states of the Ohio Valley,[7] and which some suspect as having a relationship with the postwar Ku Klux Klan.

The Impresario of Imposture would not end this pattern of strange associations when the war ended, for he would claim to have known Andrew Johnson, whose career did indeed, as we saw in chapter two, run afoul of Dunham's "talents." Dunham would write yet another of his infamous newspaper articles for the Montreal press, claiming intimate knowledge of serious criminality on Johnson's part, including a role in the assassination of his predecessor, and offering Johnson's drunkenness on the day of his inaugural as "proof" of Johnson's low character and the type of deeds of which he was capable.[8]

B. Dunham in the Confederacy, 1862-1863

The period of from the spring of 1862 to the spring of 1863 is the most hidden part of Dunham's life during the war. According to one Northern newspaper source, he was

---

[6] Ibid., pp. 29-31.

[7] Carman Cumming, *Devil's Game*, p. 25.

[8] Ibid., p. 31.

recruiting for the Confederacy in the South, and Dunham would tell the Confederate authorities that he had come South after trying to recruit for the Confederacy in New York and Maryland.[9] Note that Dunham's story—if it *was* a story—was at least accurately (and thus perhaps professionally) conceived in case of the eventuality of capture or internment by the Confederate authorities, for as has already been seen, New York City *was* a scene of pro-secessionist sentiment since its own Mayor favored secession for the city, and Maryland, as a slave state that had remained in the Union, certainly had its fair share of Southern sympathizers. A trunk of Dunham's later seized in—you guessed it—Montreal contained a letter, dated December 2, 1862, that he was inspecting a new type of rifled cannon,[10] a letter that Dunham may have composed precisely for the purpose of being discovered, and alleging activities he never performed!

What *is* known is that Dunham acted as an army scout during the crucial weeks in the run-up to Union General Joseph Hooker's campaign against General Lee, the campaign that ended with yet another disastrous Union defeat at Chancellors-ville, a battle that many military historians regard as Lee's masterpiece. During this period, Dunham also managed to inspect the defenses of Richmond, and found them wanting.[11] Having completed whatever mission he may have been assigned in the South, Dunham attempted to return to the North, when he was apprehended by Confederate authorities and arrested as a spy. The reason?

He had produced for the Confederate authorities, as he was attempting to cross the lines back into the North, several incriminating papers, including a letter from Abraham

---

[9] Ibid., p. 33.
[10] Carman Cumming, *Devil's Game*, p. 33.
[11] Ibid., p. 40.

Lincoln himself approving a scheme to raise a regiment of troops and authorizing him—Dunham—to do so. His defense to the Confederate authorities was classic Dunham double-dealing and imposture:

> I did not bring these papers with me accidentally but purposely. I did not wait for them to be found on my person, but voluntarily produced them to prove my identity as the person I represented myself to be, and to show that I had been deemed competent and worthy of a command in the North, hoping it would be inferred therefrom that I could be of service to the South.
>
> If I had come here for an improper purpose, to act the part of a Spy, would anyone suppose that I would have brought and kept on my person papers that show me in the service of the federal Government; and papers, too, which a person acting such a part could possibly have not occasion to use? I am certain you will agree with me that such a proposition would be absurd.[12]

Faced with this ingenious and certainly duplicitous "explanation" for his presence in the South, the Confederate authorities and officers interviewing Dunham debated on whether or not to accept it, a debate that went all the way up to and including Confederate Secretary of War John Seddon himself. Eventually, Dunham's story was rejected for the simple reason that he could provide the South with nothing concrete to aid its cause. He was to be held simply "as an alien enemy, accused of no crime, until he could 'with prudence and propriety' be returned to the United States."[13] This the Confederacy did during Lee's invasion of

---

[12] Carman Cumming, *Devil's Game*, p. 43.

[13] Q.v. the discussion on pp. 44-46. The quotation itself is from p. 46.

Pennsylvania that would lead to the Battle of Gettysburg. It is not known whether or not the Confederate Secretary of War Seddon chose to allow Dunham to "overhear" a bundle of misinformation to take back with him to the North or not,[14] but it *is* known – in what can only be considered highly suggestive if not telling about Dunham – that the first person he saw upon his return to the North was Edwin Stanton's chief of the National Detective Police, Lafayette Baker.[15]

1. Plots and Proposals
a. For a Kidnapping Raid on Richmond

As noted, the first person that Dunham contacted upon his return to the North was Colonel LaFayette Baker, chief of the National Detective Police and, with Major Thomas Eckert of the War Department telegraph and cipher office, one of Union Secretary of War Edwin Stanton's key right hand men. Dunham wrote Baker stating that he brought information from one of Baker's agents imprisoned in Richmond, one John H. Sherman, and indicated that he would visit Washington to convey this information directly to Baker, it being unsafe to do so by the mails.[16]

But then Dunham wrote a second letter, this time directly to President Abraham Lincoln himself:

> Baltimore, Aug. 12, 1863
> His Excellency, Abraham Lincoln, President of the U.S.
>
> *I propose to aid your efforts to suppress the rebellion by rendering a special service. It is to deliver into the*

[14] Carman Cumming, *Devil's Game*, p. 47.

[15] Ibid., p. 9.

[16] Ibid., pp. 50-51, the text of Dunham's letter to Baker may be found on p. 51.

hands of the Government, alive, the person of Jefferson Davis, the rebel chief. All I require the Government to furnish, is 250 mounted men armed, &c.

I address this proposition to you because I believe you are less inclined, than most of the Government functionaries, to regard projects difficult of accomplishment, as impossibilities.

My scheme at first sight may appear to you visionary and unpromising, but I hope it will not be rejected as impracticable, until my plans, which I am willing to submit, have been seen and considered by you.

My intimate knowledge of Richmond, the fortifications around it, and the points at which picket-guards are stationed; the woods and marshes surrounding the Town, and the thoroughfares leading to it, together with my acquaintance with Mr. Davis' residence, enable me to promise, with perfect confidence, a nocturnal raid with the result I have suggested. *Desperate as the enterprise may appear to you, I am satisfied that upon hearing my plans, you will say it is worth trying.*

I intended to seek an interview, make my proposition, and submit my plans at the same time; but having suffered a long and severe confinement in Castle Thunder,[17] charged with being a spy, from which I was released only a few days ago, it will prove an advantage to my health if I remain quiet a few days longer. Besides, my letter will occupy less of your valuable time than an interview would.

Hoping I may receive a line tomorrow informing me of your pleasure in regard to my proposition, I am,

Respectfully, Your obt. servt.

C, A, Dunham// Baltimore, Md.[18]

---

[17] Castle Thunder, a Confederate prison in Richmond.

[18] Carman Cumming, *Devil's Game*, pp. 51-52, all emphases added by me.

> Cumming himself observes that the similarity of this letter to the actual Dahlgren raid a year later is hardly coincidental, but also states that the letter, while forwarded by Lincoln to his War Department (and thus, to Stanton), was apparently not taken seriously by Lincoln himself nor his officers, though Lincoln, by expressing disappointment that another raid, Stoneman's raid, had failed to penetrate the city and capture Davis, is an indication that Lincoln himself was sympathetic to the whole idea.[19]

b. Recycling the Plot into a Plot to Kidnap Lincoln

Having planted the idea of such a raid in Lincoln's War Department, and thus in my opinion having been the original instigation of the Dahlgren Raid, Dunham then followed this up, in classic Dunham fashion, with a newspaper article written under his alias of Sanford Conover in an article for Horace Greeley's *New York Tribune*, dated January 12, and which ran on January 25, 1864. In the article, Conover "cites" a letter from a Colonel Margrave (another Dunham alias!) to the Confederate War Department outlining a plan to kidnap, and if that failed, to assassinate Abraham Lincoln.[20] This is the first public discussion of the kidnapping-assassination plot of Lincoln, and it should be noted, it comes from one and the same man promoting a similar plot for Jefferson Davis in a private letter to Abraham Lincoln!

---

[19] Carman Cumming, *Devil's Game*, p. 52.
[20] Ibid., pp. 70-72,

c. The Relevance to the Discussion of the Authenticity of Colonel Dahlgren's Orders

We are now at last in a position to answer the speculative questions about the Dahlgren Raid raised in chapter five: whence did the "orders" found on Colonel Dahlren's body originate? One may speculate that *if* the orders to kidnap or kill Davis *had* been part of the original plan, design, and objective of the operation, then it is highly *unlikely* that any superior officer in the chain of command to Colonel Dahlgren would ever have committed such orders to writing, much less Colonel Dahlgren himself. More likely such orders were communicated only orally. *However*, it is entirely possible that written orders, in a reasonable imitation of Dahlgren's own handwriting, may have been entrusted to one or two members of Dahlgren's raiding party, for the express purpose of being planted on the Colonel in the case of his demise, and for the deliberate purpose of being discovered. Dunham, it must be remembered, was not only a consummate grafter, but an accomplished forger. If indeed this possibility was the case, and evidence planted to make the entire Dahlgren raid appear to be something it was not, then the *subsequent* action of "exposing" a Lincoln kidnapping-or-assassination plot maybe regarded as part of one operation, *an operation not of a clever grifter spreading chaos, but of an agent provocateur ensuring that the animosities of North and South against each other would continue long after the war and regardless of the outcome or kidnappings or deaths of their leaders.* Additionally, it should be noted that Dunham, if he *was* an *agent provocateur* as I believe he was, then he would have known it was hardly necessary to persuade Lincoln of the feasibility of his plan to kidnap Davis. *All he had to do was plant the seed in the War*

Department, and by means of carefully planned articles in the press, fan the fuel for its adoption.

To put it as plainly as possible, the links from the Dahlgren Raid to Charles Dunham, seem direct and all but ironclad.

2. Was There a Connection between Dunham and Stanton?

The connection between Dunham and Horace Greeley's *New York Tribune* has been noted, for Dunham orchestrated a campaign under his various aliases to broach the subject of a Lincoln kidnapping-assassination plot in that paper, in classic "narrative preparation" fashion. But during early 1864, as Dunham was advancing *that* idea, he was also, under yet another alias, Henry Birch, advancing the notion that General McClellan, Lincoln's likely presidential opponent on the Northern Democrat ticket, was a bumbling and incompetent general.[21] Dunham, under his various aliases, was subtly promoting a Lincoln candidacy at the same time he was talking about the kidnapping or assassination of the President under *other* aliases!

All of this apparent "pro-North" slant to Dunham's newspaper articles of this period, as does the kidnapping-assassination plot itself, implies that some sort of connection between the Union Secretary of War, Edwin Stanton, and Charles Dunham, existed, no doubt via Lafayette Baker as liaison.[22] One of the most damning bits of evidence in this regard is that Dunham, when being interrogated by the Confederate authorities upon his arrest for espionage under his "Wallace" alias, stated that he had met personally with

---

[21] Carman Cumming, *Devil's Game*, p. 57.

[22] Ibid., p. 59.

Secretary of War Stanton "on private business." When this affidavit was produced at the military tribunal trying the Lincoln assassination conspirators, Judge Advocate General Joseph Holt had the incriminating phrase struck from the record.[23] Given Holt's abject and almost servile submission and relationship with Stanton, this is particularly incriminating, for its suggests that at the minimum Dunham was a professional agent for the Union Secretary of War.

Cumming himself insists that there was some sort of deeply hidden relationship with Union intelligence, and most likely through LaFayette Baker:

> Any thought that Dunham might have operated as an independent, without the notice of intelligence officers, is thus hard to credit. He was, after all, claiming repeatedly to have had contacts with rebel officials. He was claiming intimate knowledge of Richmond's defenses, of "the points at which picket-guards are stationed; the woods and marshes surrounding the Town, and the thoroughfares leading to it." He was claiming to have seen an experimental gun in operation. He was claiming to have brought documents from the Richmond War Department on assassination planning. The intelligence officers would have been unhappy if they had not heard all of this first—and first-hand.
>
> But which official could have been his contact? While there is no sure answer two possibilities are Charles Dana, who ran some agents as part of his broad duties in the War

---

[23] Carman Cumming, *Devil's Game*, p. 19. Dunham would also assert to the Montreal Confederates while on a visit there in early 1865 that he had assisted Stanton in the latter's first use of the insanity defense of Daniel Sickles in the latter's murder trial. There is no currently extant evidence to support Dunham's claims of a pre-war association with the Union Secretary of War. (p. 26).

> Department, and Col. Lafayette Baker, a shrewd, ruthless Stanton man who had been hired to root out disloyalty and became one of the hardest of the group of hard men wielding arbitrary wartime powers.[24]

There are a number of indicators, however, that Dunham was not exclusively nor even primarily an agent for the North, but may have been acting for even deeper handlers, and playing the entire Union as a pawn.

3. Coming Full Circle: Dunham, Blair, Stanton, Johnson, and Canada

We also find Dunham lurking in the background of the Blair peace plan and its "geopolitical" solution to the war, for under his alias of Harvey Birch, Dunham advanced the same idea in a newspaper article in *The New York Herald* on September 23, 1863, almost a year before Blair proposed the idea to President Lincoln. This suggests once again that Dunham is acting as an *agent provocateur*, planting ideas in the public consciousness to prepare the public for the eventual adoption of the idea, while simultaneously sewing the idea in the minds of those able to bring it about. In the article, Birch-Dunham argued that a solution to the war lay in the mutual interest that both the Confederacy and the Union had in pushing out the foreign influence and presence on the North American continent, with the Confederacy pushing France out of Mexico, and the Union pushing Great Britain out of Canada. That this was essentially the same idea behind Francis Preston Blair's initial peace proposal to Jefferson Davis and to Abraham Lincoln cannot be denied, and this

---

[24] Carman Cumming, *Devil's Game*, pp. 78-79.

suggests that perhaps Dunham had some other hidden role in Blair's scheme.[25]

The mention of Dunham in connection to Canada brings us to yet *another* strange turn in this maze of mirrors, Dunham's presence in that country in 1864, during the exact same period that the Confederate cell in Montreal was planning its various raids across the border into Union territory, including the infamous raid on St. Alban's, Vermont. There, Dunham's activities in Montreal are again wrapped in mystery, but some light on his presence there is suggested by the fact that after the war, Edwin Stanton sent Major General Dix—the same General Dix that was Stanton's liaison officer controlling the New York City press—to take charge of Dunham, who had been arrested by the Canadian authorities for unpaid bills. But the reason Dunham was sought by the Union at such a high official level (a Major General playing escort and guard duty!) was that Dunham was wanted to give testimony during the trial of the Lincoln assassination conspirators at the military tribunal! "No comparable effort," writes Barry Sheehy, "was made on behalf of any other witnesses at the trial of the Lincoln conspirators."[26] This was putting it mildly, for Stanton effectively authorized an open cheque book to reimburse all expenses that Major General Dix might incur on the trip, including, presumably, the greasing of tongues with financial gifts, a response to Dunham's presence in that country that "appears, at the least, disproportionate."[27]

Not only this, but there may have been more to the raids, and to General Dix's presence in Canada than meets the eye. Stanton, in response to the Confederate cross-border

---

[25] Carman Cumming, *Devil's Game*, p. 88f.

[26] Barry Sheehy, *Montreal, City of Secrets*, p. 155.

[27] Ibid.

raids into Union territory from Canada, authorized Dix to allow the pursuit of Confederate raiders across the border into Canada, an action which viewed against the backdrop of the Blair peace proposals and the Birch-Dunham *New York Herald* article urging a "geopolitical" peace between the Union and Confederacy to drive the British and French from the continent, could easily have functioned as a cover for a Union invasion designed to annex the territory. This is, of course, pure speculation, but it is buttressed by the fact that Radical Republican Michigan U.S. Senator Zachariah Chandler was in favor of the annexation of Canada in order to strengthen the Republican position in Congress in the eventuality of the South's return to Congress, with newly-emancipated slaves tipping the apportionment balance once again in the South's favor.[28]

U.S. Senator from Michigan Zachariah Chandler

[28] Carman Cumming, *Devil's Game*, p. 105.

Chandler was no ordinary Senator nor even senatorial power broker, for he had been Lincoln's 1860 presidential campaign manager, and would become Ulysses S. Grant's Secretary of the Interior, and thus responsible for oversight of the Homestake and Comstock lodes and their development.

In any case, Dunham's activities in Canada once again confront us with the difficulties of interpreting the man. Was he simply a grifter and a swindler, stirring up confusion and trouble solely for personal profit? Or was he working for the Confederacy in helping plan the raids?[29] or for the Union in exposing them? Or was he working for someone else entirely, and playing a dangerous game not of agent or even double agent, but triple agent? Carman Cumming is quite alert to the difficulties, and it is worth citing his survey of these problems at length:

> The best documented of Dunham's games deal with faked raid plans, which he invented, promoted, and reported—for reasons still unclear. Much less certain, but intriguing, is his possible part in the revival of the old scheme... to reunite North and South through a joint campaign of continental conquest.
>
> Various theories on Dunham's Canadian mischief are thus still open. The simplest is that his troublemaking was designed only to make money, by raising interest in his

[29] Q.v. Carman Cumming, *Devil's Game*, pp. 98-99, where Cumming outlines Dunham's plans, which he shared with the Confederate leaders in Montreal, for a raid on Croton, New York. The purpose of the raid was to blow up the dam there, thus flooding New York City, and denying it a water supply. Cumming also notes that Dunham presented himself to the Confederate officials in Montreal *without* showing them the credentials which he had from the Confederate Secretary of War himself, John Seddon, credentials which were issued to yet another Dunham alias, a Colonel Margrave.

territory to promote his work as journalist and spy (sic). That explanation conflicts with the purposeful quality of his earlier writing, however, and the risks he ran also suggest deeper motives. A second theory is that he was working for the North to make trouble that could be blamed on the Democrats, or that he was collecting rebel raiders who could be led into ambush (sic). A third is that he was actually working for the South. The record argues strongly against this, although his mischief making certainly helped the Confederates raise border alarm, forcing the North to move resources back to the Canadian frontier. That was especially true when Dunham wrote a detailed *New York Tribune* story warning of plans for a big rebel raid on Ogdensburg, Plattsburg, and the Clinton State Prison at Dannemora, New York, to be followed by a destructive sweep across Vermont and New Hampshire. In his columns, of course, Dunham could (and did) claim he had foiled such raids by exposing them. But in this case, at least, he himself was said to have talked up the project among Montreal rebels. As in the Croton Dam plot, he created the threats of which he warned.

A fourth possible explanation of Dunham's games is that he was acting for those Americans, some prominent, who for various reasons, including anger over Britain's support for the South, wanted to provoke a war and annex the Canadas before Gen. Ulysses S. Grant's armies were disbanded. And certainly Dunham's stories of Canada-based plots for border raids, poisoning of water conduits, or assassination helped fuel an already hot Northern anger toward Canada. Again, there is no proof—but Dunham's path did touch those of many leading expansionists of the time, including…Horace Greeley,,. Gen, John A. Dix… Benjamin Butler, Edwin Stanton…[30]

---

[30] Carman Cumming, *Devil's Game*, pp. 95-96, emphasis added.

But the logic of Dunham's "method" cuts both ways: if Dunham's exposure" of the various Confederate raiding plots and plans was a factor in their *not* being pursued and executed, then the same applies to his articles—under one of his aliases of course—*exposing* the "peace plan" that included a Union-Confederate military alliance for the purpose of driving British and French influence from the continent. Under that interpretation, the beneficiaries of Dunham's activities are neither the Union nor the Confederacy, but precisely Britain and France.

We may now advance our thesis: Dunham's activities *and their expensive nature* best fit the profile of an accomplished *agent provocateur* acting for other hidden principal actors with deep pockets and subtle agendas. This much Cumming himself states, but believes Dunham to have been acting throughout his career for these interests on behalf of the Union.[31] *But his activities are much more subtly in line with interests wanting to accomplish two basic things: (1) keep the United States divided sectionally and politically, and thus thwart the emergence not only of a new continental power, but of a power that was, effectively, an entire continent, and (2) to make whatever financial profit it could from this division, for as long as it could. To put it succinctly, his activities, their continental extent, his presence in both Union and Confederate corridors of power, and the sheer expense of all these operations, betoken European interests and handlers.* Moreover, given the subsequent events, I believe the best European candidate for this, one with extensive experience in the tradecraft of intelligence, espionage, false flags, forgeries, aliases, legends, all blended into an in-depth knowledge of the interplay of geopolitics and

[31] Carman Cumming, *Devil's Game*, p. 99.

finance—geopolifinance as I have dubbed it—is Great Britain.

In this light, consider yet another lengthy passage from Cumming where he tries to get a firm grasp on the greasy wet soap bar that is Dunham, one that exposes a typical Dunham trick in the bag of the *agent provocateur's* dirty tricks:

> Even the basic question of whether he was actually loyal to the Union is still in doubt. A modern reader shown one set of his letters and articles, those from Richmond and Montreal, would at first glance be certain he was a true rebel. Another reader shown a different set would be equally sure he was working for Washington. (*He must be the only Civil War figure who is on record as accusing each side of atrocities and as calling both ways for invocation of the* ***lex talionis****—the law of retaliation. He may be the only Civil War figure to propose in both (sic) Washington and Richmond plans to raise troops in enemy territory.)*
>
> Despite these ambiguities… A good deal of circumstantial evidence indicates his 1863 Southern adventure may have been undertaken with Union knowledge, if not control. Clear evidence also exists that for an extended period before the 1864 election, his journalistic dirty tricks consistently helped Lincoln's Republican government and damaged his old Democratic allies. In 1864, for instance, posing as George Margrave, he sold to the Copperhead *New York Daily News* a fake letter allegedly written by a prominent Southerner to encourage peace contacts. Them as Sandford Conover, he wrote for the *New York Tribune* an exposé of the *Daily News* article,

> showing how the traitorous paper had been duped by Colonel Margrave.[32]

It should be noted that while these events and activities could be interpreted as those of a Union *agent provocateur*, they could, with equal force, be argued to be those of a *British agent provocateur*, creating stories that will be repeated in the British press and perhaps pushing the Palmerston government to action, the least of which would be to reinforce British garrisons in Canada. In any case, this vignette also shows Dunham using yet another standard tactic in the tradecraft of the *agent provocateur*, the creation and use of multiple aliases and characters, some of whom are used to *argue* with oneself in an entirely faked stream of articles, comments, ripostes, thrusts, counter-thrusts, and so on.

C. The Assassination of Lincoln: Agent of the Radical Republicans, or the Confederates, or "Someone Else"?

Nowhere is Dunham's consummate skill as an *agent provocateur* more in evidence than in his testimony to the military tribunal trying the Lincoln assassination conspirators. As was seen, Union Secretary of War had dispatched his press liaison, Major General Dix, to Montreal with a blank cheque, sparing no expense to repatriate Dunham to Washington where his testimony in the military tribunal was needed. The reason for Stanton's, and Judge Advocate General Joseph Holt's interest in Dunham has already been encountered: it was Dunham who first exposed the Lincoln kidnapping-assassination plot idea in an article in the New

---

[32] Carman Cumming, *Devil's Game*, pp. 9-10, emphasis added.

York City press in 1864! Indeed, in Dunham's original published version of the plot, the scheme was a decapitation strike against not only Lincoln, but his entire cabinet. Under his alias of Sanford Conover, Dunham wrote a draft of an article, found in a trunk of his belongings in Montreal. In the draft, intended for Horace Greeley's *New York Tribune,* Conover accuses "Colonel Dunham"(!) of having orchestrated an entire decapitation strike: "They did not desire the death of the President and Secretary of State merely," Dunham/Conover wrote, "but the destruction of the entire cabinet, Vice-President, Chief Justice of the Supreme Court and others. Had their scheme succeeded fully the nation would have been without a head, would have been paralized (sic) and have become anarchical...."[33] As if this were not enough deliberately sewn confusion, Dunham/Conover then continued by admitting in the draft article that he (Conover) had *no* evidence that either President Davis, or his Secretary of War, John Seddon, had ever authorized the assassination. All that he would say is that he was "sure" that the plan was approved by Judah Benjamin and C.G. Meminger.[34]

Booth's conspirators, needless to say, followed the basic script to a "T," and needless to say, Booth's diary's eighteen missing pages detailed precisely such a wider decapitation plot, one additionally involving "deep players" intending a *coup d'etat* and a radical change of postwar reconstruction policy from which they could, and did, profit financially and politically.

This decapitation operation, however, is exactly the *same* plan, but in reverse, that Dunham had outlined to

---

[33] Carman Cumming, *Devil's Game*, p. 124.

[34] Ibid., p. 125. Benjamin was, of course, the Confederate Secretary of State, and C.G. Memminger was the first Confederate Secretary of the Treasury, preceding Trenholm in that role.

Lincoln for a similar decapitation strike against Jefferson Davis and *his* cabinet, a plan that evolved into the Dahlgren raid! Small wonder that Edwin Stanton wanted to get his hands on Dunham for the conspirators's trial, for Dunham's testimony, which might have exposed things best left unexposed, had to be tightly controlled.

Judge Advocate General Joseph Holt

Chaired the Military Tribunal trying the Lincoln Assassination Conspirators;
He was Stanton's Creature at the Tribunal

1. Dunham at the Assassination Tribunal

Dunham's testimony to the military assassination tribunal, *and the effects it had*, are another strong argument that one is not dealing with a mere scallywag, grifter, and trouble-maker, but with a supremely capable *agent provocateur*. It is important to the story at this juncture to remember that it was under his alias Sanford Conover that Dunham was apprehended in Montreal, and that it was under this alias that Dunham initially testified to the military tribunal. In this testimony, the examiner was not Judge Advocate Joseph Holt, but his assistant, John A, Bingham, who carefully managed to avoid asking certain questions, like, how did "Conover" happen to know that "Colonel Dunham" and "Colonel Margrave" were behind the plan.[35] Under this examination, Conover/Dunham stated that he had known various Confederates in Montreal, including John Wilkes Booth, and John Surratt, son of Mary Surratt who ran the boarding house that hosted some of the conspirators. At this point, Bingham and Conover get into the nasty details, the details that would send Mary Surratt and others to the gallows:

> BINGHAM: John Wilkes Booth?
> "CONOVER": Yes, Sir.
> BINGHAM: State whether you saw either of the persons last named, Booth or Surratt, in Canada more than once?

---

[35] Carman Cumming, *Devil's Game*, p. 130.

"CONOVER": I never saw Booth more than once. I saw Surratt on several successive days.[36]

BINGHAM: With whom did you see them when they were there?

"CONOVER": I saw Mr. Surratt on a number of days in April last. I saw him in Mr. Jacob Thompson's room, and I also saw him in company with Mr. George N. Sanders, at two or three places….

BINGHAM: State whether he gave any communication to Thompson in your presence in his room, and what that communication was.

"CONOVER": There was a conversation there at that time, from which it appeared Mr. Surratt had brought dispatches from Richmond to Mr. Thompson. Those dispatches were the subject of the consultation.

BINGHAM: From whom in Richmond were the dispatches brought?

"CONOVER": From Mr. Benjamin, and I think there was also a letter in cipher from Mr. Davis…. I had some conversation with Mr. Thompson previously on the subject of a plot to assassinate Mr. Lincoln and his Cabinet, of which I had informed the paper for which I was a correspondent, and I had been invited to participate in that enterprise….

…

BINGHAM: did they speak of the persons that the rebel authorities had consented might be the victims of this plot?

---

[36] At this juncture, Cumming inserts an editorial comment that, "A year later, Dunham's memory had advanced to the point of telling the Judiciary Committee that Thompson himself had introduced him to Booth and Surratt." Thompson was one of the Confederate leaders of the Montreal cell. Cumming, *Devil's Game*, p. 130.

"CONOVER": Yes, Sir; Mr. Lincoln, Mr. Johnson, the Secretary of War, the Secretary of State and Judge (Salmon) Chase.

BINGHAM: Did they say anything about any of the generals?

"CONOVER": And General Grant.

BINGHAM: In that connection was anything said, and if so what was said, by Thompson and Surratt or either of them touching the effect the assassination of the officers named would have upon the people of the United States, and their power to elect a President?

"CONOVER": Mr, Thompson said on that occasion (I think I am not so positive that it was on that occasion) but he did say on the day before the interview of which I speak, that it would leave the government entirely without a head; that there was no provision in the Constitution of the United States by which they could elect another President if these men were put out of the way....[37]

This was damning testimony indeed, for it clearly and explicitly implicated Jefferson Davis and his Secretary of State Judah Benjamin in the Lincoln assassination plot, and painted Mrs. Mary Surratt, mother of John Surratt, with a healthy black tar of guilt by association with an alleged member of the plot. Dunham/Conover ended his testimony on May 22, 1865, and Judge Advocate General Joseph Holt expressed its impact by noting that he had been the most important witness of the whole tribunal.[38] His identity, and his entire testimony, had been given and taken in closed door session. No one knew who he was, nor what he had said, except when summaries and snippets began to appear in the

---

[37] Carman Cumming, *Devil's Game*, pp. 130, 133.

[38] Ibid., p. 142.

Northern press, leading many to suspect that Stanton himself was the source of the leaks;[39] the song-and-dance is an old and familiar tune: "we have it from a highly-placed source who must remain anonymous."

It all began to unravel on June 8, 1865, however, when the remaining Montreal Confederates began to examine the records, especially in light of the leaks that were coming out about the Lincoln assassination tribunal, and they began to connect Conover, Wallace, Birch, and Dunham's many other aliases to Dunham himself. What emerges from this "meltdown of the aliases," however, is not only that Holt and Stanton knew about many of them,[40] but that Holt himself, when Dunham was summoned to reappear before the tribunal only ten days before the conspirators would be hung, managed to keep Dunham's collapsing aliases out of the limelight until *after* the hangings! Once Dunham's many aliases, faked stories, claims, counter-claims, faked arguments and dubious character were known, the case against Jefferson Davis himself all but collapsed like a house of cards on a sandy beach during incoming hide tide.[41]

---

[39] Ibid., p. 143.

[40] Carman Cumming, *Devil's Game*, p. 145,

[41] Ibid., p. 189. Dunham actually offered to produce "Anti-Davis" witnesses, whom he himself "trained" how to answer questions, in a literal "school" for suborning perjury, and offered to produce these witnesses for Holt and Stanton. Q.v. pp. 162-165, 179. The whole scheme was eventually exposed and the attempt to bring Davis to trial collapsed as a result. During this episode, Dunham again revealed his ability to switch sides suddenly, and faked even more evidence to imply that Judge Advocate General Holt had himself faked evidence to convict the Confederate President! (p. 181) Again, the pattern is that not of a Union agent, nor a Confederate agent, but of an *agent provocateur* working for someone else, and therefore able and willing to appear to be working for the Union or the Confederacy at different points. Dunham also faked evidence implicating the two prominent Radical Republicans.

D. Dunham's Conviction for Perjury, and the Impeachment of Andrew Johnson

Even the Impresario of Imposture could not avoid trial for perjury once his elaborate tapestry of legends and aliases and contrived "journalistic reports" and faked counter-arguments collapsed. This unfolded just as the great conflict between Andrew Johnson and Congress over reconstruction policies was heating up,[42] and true to form, Dunham managed to inject himself into the very center of that conflict. This in itself is an event which again, as is so often typical of so much in Dunham's life and career, can be interpreted in two basic ways: either Dunham is simply an inveterate grifter, taking advantage of every crisis as an opportunity to cause trouble and advance his own fortunes, or he is an *agent provocateur* acting in that capacity to keep the sectional divisions of the country going, its government weakened, and the field ripe for others to exploit financially and geopolitically.

The trial centered around Dunham's "School for Perury" and his effort to produce—literally to *fabricate*—witnesses to convict Davis, Judah Benjamin, and other Confederate authorities of being directly involved in the plot to murder Abraham Lincoln. In prosecuting the trial Judge Advocate General Joseph Holt had to rely on some of these fabricated witnesses from Dunham's "School for Perjury" to prove Dunham had committed perjury! Two of these witnesses testified that "Dunham had recruited them, fabricated their stories (about the supposed meeting with John Surratt, Judah Benjamin, and Jefferson Davis), rehearsed

---

in these various schemes, Thaddeus Stevens and Senator Benjamin F. Wade. (Q.v. p. 193)

[42] Carman Cumming, *Devil's Game*, p. 199.

them, guided them in their appearances before Holt, and finally had sworn before the (House) Judiciary Committee that he had not committed all these acts."[43]

The trial's farcical nature was best summarized by the charge that its judge made to the jury before it retired to deliberate. The judge remarked that "I have never known or heard of or read of any case of perjury in which the witnesses for the State had necessarily to prove themselves guilty of the crime of perjury in one transaction in order to convict the prisoner of the crime of perjury in another proceeding."[44] Dunham was eventually convicted and sent to prison on the charge, but the trial had effectively resolved none of the old problems and had managed to raise new ones,[45] not the least of which is an issue not noticed by Cumming: if Dunham was merely acting on his own account, a conviction and sentencing to perjury should have ended the matter.

But Dunham managed—from prison—to orchestrate an entirely new campaign of confusion. This campaign included a new effort to implicate President Johnson in the assassination plot,[46] evidence of which he indicated to the Radical Republicans in Congress he would be willing to supply to them in their impeachment efforts—thus unmasking himself as the *source* of those claims by the Radicals—while in the meantime, he promised to supply *Johnson* with evidence exposing the Radicals in return for a presidential pardon.[47] The method was, again, pure Dunham, for he "informed" Johnson of a Radical Republican plot to impeach him using fabricated witnesses who in turn would give

[43] Carman Cumming, *Devil's Game*, p. 205.
[44] Ibid., p. 207.
[45] Ibid.
[46] Ibid., pp. 217-218
[47] Ibid., p. 213.

fabricated testimony about Johnson's high crimes and misdemeanors, and some believed that Dunham specifically implicated Johnson's inherited Secretary of War Edwin Stanton in these schemes,[48] and thus, Dunham may have even played a factor in Johnson's firing of Stanton, the event that unleashed the whole impeachment drama to begin with![49]

The deal was struck, and the Johnson White House released Dunham's documents implicating the Radical Republicans, who responded in kind by publishing the Dunham-linked conspiracy allegations of Johnson being involved with Davis and Booth in the Lincoln assassination.[50] As related in chapter two, Andrew Johnson soldiered through his impeachment(s), and in February 1869, made good on his deal with Dunham and issued a presidential pardon for supplying the government with important information that had proven John Surratt innocent of any involvement in the Lincoln murder. Johnson's statement to this effect was doubtless intended to stick in the craw of Judge Advocate General Holt, and his boss at the time, Edwin Stanton, for Johnson never forgave either man for withholding a clemency plea from Mary Surratt from him until after her hanging. When Johnson found out what had been done, he had determined to dismiss Stanton. As one newspaperman at the time opined, the real dastards throughout the whole business were Holt and Stanton.[51]

But there is one final incident to relate, and a very telling one at that. It is little known but nonetheless true that

---

[48] Carman Cumming, *Devil's Game*, pp. 233-234.

[49] The template appears to have been dusted off, updated a bit to incorporate the most modern techniques and technologies, and used again recently.

[50] Ibid., p. 238.

[51] Ibid., o. 211.

the Union Secretary of War, Edwin Stanton, was himself in favor of American expansion throughout the entire continent, with Mexico and Canada being the principal targets, and together with Johnson impeachment prosecutor, Benjamin Butler, and Michigan US Senator Zachariah Chandler, "had shown unmistakable signs of willing to go to war with Britain for the conquest of Canada."[52] Stanton in particular was privy to, and in favor of, the Blair peace plan, sharing his own thoughts on expansion with Radical Republican Senator Charles Sumner, chairman of the Senate Foreign Relations Committee. Sumner would then write that "Stanton says, 'it is evident we must take possession of Canada.... I anticipate that Jeff. Davis will ask leave to withdraw with his army to Mexico, to side with Juarez. Anything like this will be a great event which will make Europe quiver.'"[53] The final chapter in this part of the story came in 1872, when the Grant Administration paid the hefty sum of $75,000 for four trunks of Confederate archives of its State Department. There were unproven accusations that some of these papers had been forged by Dunham in league with the man who had become Grant's Secretary of the Interior, and who had been a U.S. Senator during the war...

... Michigan Senator Zachariah Chandler.

The documents purported to detail "southern atrocities" which Grant planned to use in his 1872 "Bloody Shirt" campaign against the resurgent Democrats and their champion, newspaperman Horace Greeley.

While much more could, and probably should, be said about the "career" of this remarkable Impresario of

---

[52] Carman Cummin, *Devil's Game*, p. 157.
[53] Ibid., p. 158.

Imposture,[54] I believe that sufficient evidence has been presented that underscores the difficulty of interpreting the man and what he did. *Virtually every major "deep event" and "deep politics" of the War Between the States will be found at have some connection to him, somewhere.* While it remains an entirely plausible interpretation that Dunham was nothing more than a very accomplished grifter, confidence man, fraud, swindler, mountebank, and adventurer plying his trade for personal profit and emotional "kicks," it is equally possible and plausible that he plied his trade in the service of someone. While accustomed to raise his own money in support of his schemes, the sheer scale of his travels, the expenditures they suggest, not to mention the degree of needed connections and networks to sustain them, imply an infrastructure of personnel and finance to support them.

And if his plots and schemes seemed now to benefit the Union, and now the Confederacy, the biggest result in the end was to keep the nation divided for long after the end of the war and well into the presidency of Ulysses S. Grant if not far beyond. With his appearance on the scene, we may have finally met the chief villain of the era, and through him, handlers and chieftans in the very Europe that had a vested interest to keep the country divided and weak, no matter what the geopolifinancial circumstances.

The opera is over.

It is now time for the curtain call, to assemble the principals, and exhibit the argument.

---

[54] It should be stressed that we have but skimmed the surface of a litany and inventory of plots, sub-plots, schemes, spies, and confidence men that populate Cumming's crucial work.

9
CURTAIN CALL:
A SYNTHESIS OF THE ARGUMENT AS REPRESENTED BY ITS PRINCIPALS

"...Nobody can quite pinpoint the moment when Unitarianism spawned the transcendentalist movement. Hints of transcendentalist arguments appeared early in Channing's ideas, but the members of the new movement were so dazzled by so many trends—German scholarship, the philosophy of Swedenborg, the drift toward social reforms and against slavery, worship of dimly perceived paganism, the religions of the Orient— that defining the principles of transcendentalism is like packaging smoke. Yet transcendentalism was real enough to fuel a flight from the church by many of its most articulate and idealistic young ministers. The rebellion was spearheaded by Emerson."

—Otto Scott[1]

THIS BOOK AND ITS PREVIOUS COMPANION VOLUME, *The Rialto in Richmond*, have presented some facts that, while being part of the public record and thus known for some time, have been generally ignored in most histories of the War Between the States. Many of these facts have implied a much deeper financial and geopolitics, a "geopolifinance" as I have called it, that indicate that the events of that war should not be understood in a vacuum, as if disconnected from the financial and political interests of those

---

[1] Otto Scott. *The Secret Six: John Brown and the Abolitionist Movement* (Murphys, California: Uncommon Books, 1993 [ISBN 0-9638381-0-5]), p. 116.

powers and interests not actively involved in the war as belligerents. And some of these facts, those connected to the Impresario of Imposture, strongly suggest that those interests were not only in play both during and after the conflict, but that they were highly influential in guiding it.

The actual nature of the pieces of the argument supporting that thesis may not, however, be particularly apparent. If any one of the pieces or supports collapses, the argument itself does not. For example, if my speculation—and it is pure speculation based on a very different interpretation—regarding the career of Charles A. Dunham should eventually collapse, the argument of deeper "geopolifinancial" agendas and players does not. For example, the collapse of my hypothesis that Dunham was an *agent provocateur* acting for a multitude of interests, but ultimately and always for British interests, does not affect the meeting between Ulysses S. Grant and Otto von Bismarck and the implications that such a meeting entails, for such a meeting implies some relationship of geopolitical (and thus probably financial) interests between the two heads of government. The failure of the Blair peace mission does not mean that the geopolitics upon which he hoped to forge a peace were not actively at work during and after the war, for we found Edwin Stanton and Zachariah Chandler, among other power brokers, involved in promoting the same geopolitical annexations. Their very presence in such ventures may itself constitute yet another motivation of the Lincoln assassination conspirators to murder a stubborn obstacle to their agendas. The failure to impeach Andrew Johnson did not mean the failure of the Radical Reconstructionist agenda, nor invalidate the underlying currency and financial agendas afoot, and so on.

The argument of these two books about the Rialto in Richmond is this analogous to a cantilevered structure: no one element bears the whole load, and a few of the elements can even fail, and the structure will still be intact. But like a cantilevered building or bridge, the elements are carefully balanced and mutually support each other. So it is time for a review of that argument by way of a curtain call of some of the Principals involved in the opera. In doing so, elements of the previous "intermission" are simply repeated here, and some elements of the previous volume are reprised.

A. Andrew Johnson

1) While Lincoln's and the Republicans' decision to choose Southern Democrat and former Tennessee U.S. Senator Andrew Johnson as his 1864 running mate may have been shrewd politics necessary to their victory in the elections that year, the calculation also was likely a profound temptation to the Radical factions within the Republican Party, dissatisfied as they were with Lincoln's lenient proposals for the post bellum South, to risk the murder of the President in order to inaugurate a harsher policy.
2) Initially, while Johnson seemed to be on the side of the Radicals in his announcements that the Confederate leadership should face legal consequences for their treason, the initial brace of support for Johnson evaporated when it became clear that he opposed the Radical plans for southern "reconstruction."
3) The political calculus that the Radicals employed in accepting Johnson as Lincoln's Vice Presidential running mate was revealed during the impeachment

efforts to remove him from office, as the pro-impeachment forces of the Republican party repeatedly stated to the northern press—still controlled by Johnson's Secretary of War Edwin Stanton—that Johnson held the presidency only accidentally and by dint of an assassin's bullet.

4) Thus, the *assassination of President Lincoln and the impeachment efforts against President Johnson should be viewed as two parts of one complex strategic plan, for the possibility must be entertained that in choosing to rid themselves of Lincoln, the plotters knew that in order to press their agenda, they would have to remove Johnson from office, using his party affiliation as a Southern Democrat against him.* Having assassinated one President, the next could hardly be assassinated without raising suspicion, but impeachment lay open as the means to do so without raising suspicion. The means was contrived to hamstring Johnson through a variety of acts, including the Tenure in Office Act, and the various machinations both Johnson and his opponents showed in the attempt to replace Stanton as Secretary of War and curb his, and the Radicals' influence over southern reconstruction and the military jurisdiction over it.

5) At a deeper level, the oppositions and splits within the post bellum Union provided a wide and rich field in which *agents provocateur* could operate, if any were in the field. These fissures became evident when the voting records and positions of Senators and Congressmen during Johnson's Senate trial on the third and final House impeachment indictment were compared to their votes on key financial and

currency matters. While no such *agents provocateur* were covered in the examination of the Johnson impeachment efforts, mention was made of the "Impresario of Imposture," Charles A. Dunham, treated in the previous chapter

B. Ulysses S. Grant

6) When turning to the two Administrations of the 18th President of the United States, Ulysses S. Grant, the indicators of a deep geopolifinancial interest or interest becomes much more visible. The deliberate demonetization of silver during the currency, credit, coinage, and resumption acts that characterize and mark his administrations, when the vast extent of the Comstock Lode(s) discoveries were fully known, means that silver was removed as a potential means of the resumption of specie exchanges for circulating greenbacks. In seeking a monometallic gold standard, the "geopolifinancial" background is exposed in three ways:

a) Firstly, by the presence at that time of a movement in Europe and the United States to define their money on the basis of gold coins, which were fixed in value relative to the French franc. This movement, as was seen, was supported by Republican Radicals such as Senator Sherman of Ohio, brother of Union General W.T. Sherman, close friend of Ulysses Grant.

b) Secondly, by the fact that the *effect* of the Resumption Act entirely changed the character of the Lincoln greenback from a fiat currency designated legal tender without any backing, to a currency exchangeable at par for specie, in effect, making it of the same character as the *Confederate* currency, and suggesting that resumption, coupled with reconstruction, was the means for holders of Confederate debt to recoup their investments and losses; and finally,

c) Thirdly, by the fact that Grant literally contrived various false flag operations and other deceits to create a *casus belli* with the Sioux Indians in order to seize the rich gold vein of the Homestake lode in the Black Hills of the Dakotas.

7) We saw that few of the European powers actively and openly financially supported the Union by extending it credit, with the exception of the Germans, which at that time would have meant principally the larger German states, Prussia, Bavaria, Baden and so on, led of course by Prussia. By the time Grant left office, German unification had been achieved and the German *Kaiserreich* had been formed. That state went to a monometallic gold standard, and it is this possible that Grant's trip was therefore for the purpose of coordinating financial policy, and also for the purpose of coordinating, or reporting on, the progress of aerodynamic research as argued in *The Rialto in Richmond.* These considerations mean that there is *some* element of truth behind Bismarck's alleged remarks about European finance being behind the breakup of the American republic into two sections, North and South, in 1861.

C. Jefferson Davis

8) The Confederate President Jefferson Davis's flight from Richmond in 1865 was a Continuity of Government operation, as was argued in *The Rialto in Richmond*,[2] and was part of a plan to withdraw Robert E. Lee's Army of Northern Virginia and link up with the armies of Generals Joseph Johnston and P.G.T. Beauregard in the Carolinas, and withdraw or fight their way to the Trans-Mississippi Department—Arkansas, Louisiana, Texas, and the Indian territories (Oklahoma) – to continue the war.

D. Francis Preston Blair

9) This plan, as we discovered in this volume, was precisely the "peace" plan first suggested by the Impresario of Imposture, and subsequently actively pursued by Francis Preston Blair, and while President Lincoln refrained from explicitly endorsing it, he did not altogether prohibit Blair from pursuing it. As was also seen, some in the North, including Lincoln's own Secretary of War Edwin Stanton, and his 1860 campaign manager and US Senator Zachariah Chandler were advocates of the idea. This raises the further implication and question of whether the failure of the Blair plan may have been a factor in the

---

[2] Joseph P. Farrell, *The Rialto in Richmond,* pp. 21-74, particularly pp. 51-62.

Radical Republican involvement in Lincoln's assassination.

E. Colonel Ulric Dahlgren

10) Against this wider geopolifinancial context, the raid of Union Colonel Ulric Dahlgren raises a number of important questions and implications. The First Lady of the Confederacy, Varina Howell Davis herself expressed an amazed shock that Ulric Dahlgren could or would have been party to an operation designed to kidnap and kill her husband, based on the ante bellum friendship of the Davis and Dahlrgen families. The principal difficulty is that the orders to kidnap and kill Davis and his entire cabinet which were found on Dahlgren's body after the failure of the raid have no clear provenance. It is doubtful that the Union would have committed such orders to paper, and equal doubts may be raised about the Confederacy's ability to forge, and then plant, orders that could withstand the scrutiny of a skeptical Northern Press, at that time under the tight control of the Union Secretary of War Edwin Stanton.
11) As a speculative hypothesis, however, the cultural and social *result* of the raid should be noted, for from that point on, both the North and the South believed their opponent to be capable of anything, including the most dastardly conduct of war. The result of the raid was thus to *harden* social and cultural divisions, and this is condign to the actions of any putative deeper players and interests seeking to perpetuate such divisions even should the war

end. The orders could thus have been planted on Dahlgren's body not by Confederate forgers, but rather by someone in Dahlgren's own raiding party, acting for that putative deeper player. While there is no evidence of a planted set of orders—Confederate or otherwise – the only complete scholarly account of the raid, that of Duane Schultz, does not rule out the possibility.

12) In this respect it should be recalled that the Impresario of Imposture, Charles A. Dunham himself, openly wrote of kidnapping and assassination plots for *Lincoln* in the Northern press in 1864, and privately suggested a similar plot against Davis a year earlier and to Lincoln himself, who passed the idea along to his Secretary of War, Edwin Stanton. I thus strongly believe that Dunham was the ultimate and real origin of the Dahlgren raid, and was possibly an influential factor in the planning of the Lincoln assassination. This ability to originate operational plans, and then to adapt them to both sides in the conflict for use on the other, is not only a Dunham trademark, but an essential component in the profile of any *agent provocateur*.

F. Lord Palmerston, Gladstone, Disraeli, and Montreal

13) Given Dunham's ability to operate on both sides of the line, and more importantly, his presence in Montreal, seat of the largest Confederate covert operations cell on foreign soil, a city where Union and Confederate intelligence officers, black marketeers, and businessmen mixed and mingled with each other on a regular basis, and given the

fact that many of his operations ultimately benefitted the long term objectives of Great Britain, I believe quite strongly that the possibility that he may have been working for Great Britain as his ultimate loyalty must be entertained. As was seen in this volume, there are strong indicators that the British Prime Minister, Henry John Termple, Lord Palmerstone, and his Chancellor of the Exchequer, William E. Gladstone, and his foreign secretary Lord Russell, were very close to a British intervention in the war on the side of the South, and that the heavy British subscriptions to the Erlanger Cotton loan were made on the basis of insider trading and knowledge of this fact. These efforts were to some extent also thwarted by Tsar Alexander II, who having emancipated his own serfs, sent his fleet to Union ports to indicate his support for the Union and Russia's opposition to British and French designs on North America.

14) The rise of railroad technology and its implications became a chief concern of British geopolitical thought from about this time period to the theories of Sir Halford Mackinder at the end of the nineteenth to the early twentieth centuries. Mackinder pointed out in his public writings that railroads (and then subsequently, air travel) would knit together the Eurasian land mass as never before, and be able to do so without the threat of interdiction by British seapower. But the unspoken and unwritten component of this analysis, which surely must have been part of the political calculus in Whitehall, was that railroads might actually link North America directly to Russia. This was,

> indeed, speculated upon from the mid-nineteenth century on both the Russian and on the American sides, and was the deep geopolifinancial reasoning for "Seward's folly," the purchase of Alaska from Russia by the United States. Such a link had to be prevented at all costs, and this could be done by careful manipulation of tight money policies in the post-bellum United States (designed also to covertly recoup European investments in the Confederacy), and by the creation of a new Pacific power capable of interdiction of such a link—Japan —via British technological transfers to that power.

G. Charles A. Dunham, the Impresario of Imposture

What *does* emerge from this narrative is a highly speculative argument that Charles A. Dunham may have been a truly legendary figure, an accomplished *agent provocateur* of extraordinary stature, perhaps the most gifted such agent who ever lived. He was either that, or he was merely working on his own, an extraordinary grifter, a man with a genius talent for taking advantage of virtually every major situation and turning it to his personal advantage. But I frankly doubt the latter.

1. His Connection to Major Events and the Principals

It is hardly coincidental that at virtually every turn in the previous narrative, we find some sort of connection between events and the Impresario of Imposture, from the Lincoln Assassination, to the Blair Peace project, to the Dunham raid, the Montreal Confederates. He was able to negotiate both with radical congressional Republicans *and* with their arch-nemesis, President Andrew Johnson from a prison cell, and to procure from the latter a presidential pardon. It is difficult to imagine anyone doing this entirely on their own, without a support network with its own powerful connections, sources of information, and deep pockets.

On the same, if not greater level, of importance, we find some sort of connection between the Impresario of Imposture and the major principals: Abraham Lincoln, Jefferson Davis, Edwin Stanton, Lafayette Baker, Zachariah Chandler, Horace Greeley, Francis Blair, Ulric Dahlgren, and even John Wilkes Booth; between all of them and Charles A. Dunham there is some sort of direct connection, no matter how tenuous it may be.

This brings us to the advancement of one final, deeply disturbing and extremely speculative possibility…

2. Dunham, Booth, and Booth's Diary

As has been intimated in this and the previous volume, Edwin Stanton, the Union Secretary of War, spared no effort to track down Booth, identify his corpse, round up the assassins, try, convict, and hang them, and to that end, he spared no effort nor expense to find Dunham and bring him to Washington to testify at the military tribunal, which he did under his Sanford Conover alias. But as was seen in *The Rialto in Richmond*, there was some question—never adequately resolved—over the identification of the corpse that the Union authorities claimed to be that of Booth. As was also seen, Stanton took extreme measures not only to recover the "diary" found on Booth's body, but probably he or some agent acting in his behalf, may have removed the infamous eighteen pages of the diary that were only recovered a century later. Those pages, it will be recalled, implicated "Booth" in a much wider plot than simply that involving the four individuals who were hung (and the other four who were sentenced to long prison terms).

Thus, one has to admit the possibility that "Booth" was not Booth at all, but a body double, switched out at some point during the assassin's confused and confusing flight from Washington. But there is another possible source for the information to be found in those lost-and-recovered pages of the "Booth" diary, and that is, of course, Charles A. Dunham, the Impresario of Imposture. Was "Booth's" diary *itself yet another one of Dunham's clever forgeries, planted on him at some point during the confusion at Garrett's Farm where Booth was supposedly shot?* We will never know, but the mere presence of Dunham in all these events means that the possibility, however slim, cannot for the moment be completely discounted nor rejected.

H. Epilogue:
1. The Indissoluble Union

In the end, the War Between the States resolved little but the issue of slavery itself. All the other underlying issues were not resolved, but merely exacerbated, with Reconstruction only enhancing the already existing racial tensions by throwing the bulk of southern blacks *and* whites into a new form of debt peonage and poverty: sharecropping. The great constitutional issues surrounding states' rights and sovereignty versus an all-powerful, all-consuming national government were, in the final analysis, not resolved at all; Union cannon and bayonets only put polite and philosophical discussion on hold for a period. Was a strong General Government or Union really possible if, when events or policies turned out not to be to the liking of a state or region, it could be shattered by a state legislature? Conversely, were states really sovereign if, once they joined the union voluntarily, they could never leave it? If so, then why talk of "union" at all? It was merely a suicide pact, a kind of political version of a Roman Catholic marriage, something indissoluble, and "dissoluble" only by an authoritative pronouncement from some secular Rota that it had never really been consummated in the first place. The questions are with us still; it is only the circumstances of the issues raising these questions that have changed. In the terms of these issues, Abraham Lincoln, Henry Clay, Daniel Webster, and Alexander Hamilton did not lose the war; but then again and in the final analysis, neither did Jefferson Davis or John C. Calhoun.

2. The "American Way" of War, The Great Alibi, The Treasury of Merit, and The Secret Six

It should therefore come as no surprise, then, that the famous twentieth century southern American man of letters and novelist Robert Penn Warren couched his famous essay on the implications of the war in quasi-theological and metaphysical terms, because in the final analysis, those terms were what it was ultimately about. While the war may have "claimed the Confederate States for the Union," at the same time it "paradoxically made them more Southern,"[3] to the extent that "We may say that only at the moment when Lee handed Grant his sword was the Confederacy born; or to state matters another way, in the moment of death the Confederacy

---

[3] Robert Penn Warren, *The Legacy of the Civil War* (Lincoln, Nebraska: The University of Nebraska Press, 1998 [ISBN 0-]), 803209801-3), p. 14.

entered upon its immortality."[4] The war forever fixed in the American imagination even the way America would fight all future wars. The War Between the States

> Formed… the American concept of war, and since the day when Grant tried his bold maneuver in the Wilderness and Lee hit him, military thinking at Washington has focused as much on problems of supply, transport, materiel, and attrition, as it ever did on problems of slashing tactics and grand strategy.[5]

This effect of the war on war-making itself also carried with it an indelible, and ineluctably dialectical, imprint on the "American way" of governance and social order, for the pre-bellum tendencies were magnified and hardened, with the always moralizing North eager to remake everyone in its own morally superior virtue-signaling image, and to do so quickly and without regard for the speed with which its neighbors could adapt, while the South—for all its advocates of "the high road" to manumission, the road advocated by Davis himself—temporized and resisted the implementation of any practical steps to rid itself of the institution its own statesmen supposedly deplored.

Penn summarized all this social dialectic with a lapidary sentence elegant for its simplicity: "If in the North the critic had repudiated society, in the South society repudiated the critic; and the stage was set for trouble."[6] The War, writes Penn, gave America its two great moral postures, The Great Alibi, and The Treasury of Virtue, or, as it is more commonly known, the Treasury of Merit. The Great Alibi

---

[4] Ibid., p. 15.
[5] Robert Penn Warren, *The Legacy of the Civil War,* p. 15.
[6] Ibid., p. 36.

was particularly applicable to the post-bellum South, but it also became a convenient way to explain, or explain away, the failures of wider culture and society:

> The race problem, according to the Great Alibi, is the doom defined by history—by New England slavers, New England and Middle Western Abolitionists, cotton, climate, the Civil War, Reconstruction, Wall Street, the Jews. Everything flows into the picture.[7]

The Treasury of Virtue, or Treasury of Merit, is even more insidious, and more theological, for it is indeed a uniquely secularized American version of the Roman Catholic doctrine of the Treasury of Merit, the idea that, because Christ's Sacrifice and Resurrection not only meet but exceed all the requirements of divine justice and punishment for sin, a superabundance of merit, a "treasury" of virtue exists (consisting in the virtues and merits of the saints, super-added to that already existing super-abundance). According to this notion implanted in the American psyche by the War, the country is inherently virtuous, especially in its wars, which are always signaled as being undertaken in the service of some virtue: "defeating fascism," spreading "democracy" or "equal rights" or "women's suffrage" or any number of things, even if those to whom it is being spread and upon whom America is showing its blessings don't want it. Then, they're showered with bombs.

> ...The War appears, according to the doctrine of the Treasury of Virtue, as a consciously undertaken crusade so full of righteousness that there is enough overplus stored in Heaven, like the deeds of the saints, to take care of all small

---

[7] Ibid., p. 55.

> failings and oversights of the descendants of the crusaders, certainly unto the present generation. From the start America had had adequate baggage of self-righteousness and phariseeism, but with the Civil War came grace abounding for the least of sinners….
>
> But what the Yankees achieved—for their generation at least—was a triumph not of middle-class ideals but of middle-class vices. The most striking products of their crusade were the shoddy aristocracy of the North and the ragged children of the South.[8]

While we have not spoken of it in these two volumes, behind *The Rialto in Richmond*, and *The Rialto in Richmond, Reconstructed*, there is yet another hidden layer, "The Secret Six," the group of transcendentalists, preachers, ministers, and above all, "market players" determined to end slavery even with violence, and in the name of the Angry God of Puritan and Unitarian New England, determined to remake all in their very "progressive" and "enlightened" vision, bringing "their democracy" to all.

Their footprints and monuments were once to be found around the country, from the horrors of "Bloody Angle" at Spotsylvania Courthouse to the "Sunken Road" at Antietam.

Small wonder they are always trying to erase their footprints by taking down the statues and erasing the names of their victims, the Ulysses S. Grants, Robert E. Lees, Abraham Lincolns, Jefferson Davises, Tecumseh Shermans or Braxton Braggs or Joseph Johnstons or Hiram Revels of history, for it will never do for the success of whatever miserific projects they are still engaged upon, to have people be able to know and learn from their history, especially from its grimmer details, for the ideologies of universal perfection

---

[8] Robert Penn Warren, *The Legacy of the Civil War*, pp. 64-65.

and utopia must ever war against the reality of the specific good and its very real imperfections and its always personal struggle of confession and repentance.

The love of money is, indeed, the root of all evil, and so much more so when it becomes the token of the election of God.

Ralph Waldo Emerson

BIBLIOGRAPHY

Allen, Felicity. *Jefferson Davis: Unconquerable Heart.* Columbia. University of Missouri Press. 1999. ISBN 0-8262-1219-0.

Benedict, Michael Les. *The Impeachment and Trial of Andrew Johnson.* New York. W.W. Norton & Company, Inc. 1973, ISBN 0-393-05473-X.

Bennett, John D. *The London Confederates: The Officials, Clergy, Businessmen and Journalists Who Backed the American South during the Civil War.* Jefferson, North Carolina. McFarland and Company, Inc., Publishers. 2008. ISBN 978-0-7864-6901-7.

Bigelow, John, LL.D. *Lest We Forget: Gladstone, Morley and the Confederate Loan of 1863: a Rectification.* New York. No Imprint. 1905. (University of California Library Reprint.) M0D1004954752.

Buck, Paul H. *The Road to Reunion 1865-1900.* Boston. Little, Brown and Company. No Date, but probably ca. 1905-1910. ISBN 978-1406749885.

Conroy, James B. "The Hampton Roads Peace Conference." *Essential Civil War Curriculum.* https://www.essentialcivilwarcurriculum.com/the-hampton-roads-peace-conference.html

Conroy, James B. *Our One Common Country: Abraham Lincoln and the Hampton Roads Peace Conference of 1865*. Guilford, Connecticut. Lyons Press, 2014. ISBN 978-0-7627-7807-2. (A valuable and must-have book for anyone interested in the intricacies of the end of the War Between the States.)

Cumming, Carman. *Devil's Game: The Civil War Intrigues of Charles A. Dunham.* Urbana and Chicago. The University of Illinois Press. 2004. ISBN 978- 0-252-

07519-3. An indispensable source for the machinations of one of the era's greatest covert operatives.

Davis, Jefferson. *The Rise and Fall of the Confederate Government.* New York. Thomas Yoseloff. No ISBN.

Edwards, William C. and Edward Steers, Jr., eds. *The Lincoln Assassination: The Evidence.* Urbana, Illinois. The University of Illinois Press. 2009. ISBN 978-0-252-03368-1. (This massive 1450 page volume is a must-have treasure trove of little known documentation and evidence concerning Mr. Lincoln's murder and the conspiracy behind it.)

Ehret, Matthew, and Chung, Cynthia. *The Unfinished Symphony: The Clash of the Two Americas, volume 1* (Canadian Patriot Org., 2021 [ISBN 979-8541-003543.

Nugent, Walter T. K. *The Money Question During Reconstruction.* New York. W.W. Norton and Company, Inc. 1967. Obsolete Standard Book Number (SBN) 393-09759-5. An excellent and indispensible overview of the role and interplay of cultural, social, and monetary policy that resulted from Reconstruction.

Scott, Otto. *The Secret Six" John Brown and the Abolitionist Movement.* Murphys, California. Uncommon Books. 1993. (Reprint of 1979 New York Times Book edition.) ISBN 0-9638381-0-5. Another indispensable book probing the secularized Calvinst-Unitarian financial roots and backers of radical Abolitionism and John Brown's terror campaigns in Kansas and his infamous raid on Harper's Ferry.

Schultz, Duane. *The Dahlgren Affair: Terror and Conspiracy in the Civil War.* New York. W.W. Norton and Company. 1998. ISBN 0-393-31986-5.

Seabrook, Lochlainn. *The Hampton Roads Conference: The Southern View*. Park County, Wyoming. Sea Raven Press. 2024. ISBN 978-1-955351-34-8.

Sheehy, Barry, with Photographer Cindy Wallace. *Montreal, City of Secrets: Confederate Operations in Montreal during the American Civil War*. Montreal. Baraka Books. 2017. ISBN 978-1-77186-123-6. (A crucial and indispensable book, full of details that illuminate the darkest corners of the War Between the States, that connect many dots, and that raise even more questions.)

Stewart, David O. *Impeached: The Trial of President Andrew Johnson and the Fight for Lincoln's Legacy*. New York. Simon and Schuster. 2009 ISBN 978-1-4165-4750-1.

Thomas, Don. *The Reason Lincoln Had to Die*. Chesterfield, Virginia. Pumphouse Publishers. 2013. USBN 978-0-9894225-2-9.

Trefousse, Hans L. *Impeachment of a President: Andrew Johnson, the Blacks, and Reconstruction.* New York. Fordham University Press. 1999. ISBN 978-0-8232-1923-0.

Warren, Robert Penn. *The Legacy of the Civil War*. Lincoln, Nebraska. The University of Nebraska Press. 1998. ISBN 978-0-8032-9801-3.

Wikipedia. *Hampton Roads Conference.* https://en.wikipedia.org/wiki/Hampton_Roads_Conference.

Get these fascinating books from your nearest bookstore or directly from: Adventures Unlimited Press

www.adventuresunlimitedpress.com

COVERT WARS AND BREAKAWAY CIVILIZATIONS

By Joseph P. Farrell

Farrell delves into the creation of breakaway civilizations by the Nazis in South America and other parts of the world. He discusses the advanced technology that they took with them at the end of the war and the psychological war that they waged for decades on America and NATO. He investigates the secret space programs currently sponsored by the breakaway civilizations and the current militaries in control of planet Earth. Plenty of astounding accounts, documents and speculation on the incredible alternative history of hidden conflicts and secret space programs that began when World War II officially "ended."

292 Pages. 6x9 Paperback. Illustrated. $19.95. Code: BCCW

THE GIZA DEATH STAR REVISITED

An Updated Revision of the Weapon Hypothesis of the Great Pyramid

By Joseph P. Farrell

Join revisionist author Joseph P. Farrell for a summary, revision, and update of his original *Giza Death Star* trilogy in this one-volume compendium of the argument, the physics, and the all-important ancient texts, from the Edfu Temple texts to the Lugal-e and the Enuma Elish that he believes may have made the Great Pyramid a tremendously powerful weapon of mass destruction. Those texts, Farrell argues, provide the clues to the powerful physics of longitudinal waves in the medium that only began to be unlocked centuries later by Sir Isaac Newton and Nikola Tesla's "electro-acoustic" experiments.

360 Pages. 6x9 Paperback. Illustrated. $19.95. Code: GDSR

THE DEMON IN THE EKUR

Angels, Demons, Plasmas, Patristics, and Pyramids

By Joseph P. Farrell

Farrell looks at the Demon in the *Ekur* (the gathering place of the gods in Sumerian tradition) and the Great Pyramid Weapon Hypothesis. He delves deep into the realm of angels, presenting John of Damascus' Angelology and examines the "Immaterial Materiality" of angels; their ability to penetrate ordinary matter and "unlimited" nature; their ability to shapeshift; and the everlasting temporality, or "Sempiternity," of angels. Farrell also explores "Plasma Cosmotheology" and the Plasma Life Hypothesis. He presents intriguing pictures of nuclear detonations and discusses the Hyper-Dimensional Transduction Hypothesis. He includes a discussion of crystals as tuners and transducers, and explores the planetary associations of crystals with angels.

160 Pages. 6x9 Paperback. Illustrated. $16.95. Code: DITE

HESS AND THE PENGUINS

The Holocaust, Antarctica and the Strange Case of Rudolf Hess

By Joseph P. Farrell

Farrell looks at Hess' mission to make peace with Britain and get rid of Hitler—even a plot to fly Hitler to Britain for capture! How much did Göring and Hitler know of Rudolf Hess' subversive plot, and what happened to Hess? Why was a doppleganger put in Spandau Prison and then "suicided"? Did the British use an early form of mind control on Hess' double? John Foster Dulles of the OSS and CIA suspected as much. Farrell also uncovers the strange death of Admiral Richard Byrd's son in 1988, about the same time of the death of Hess.

288 Pages. 6x9 Paperback. Illustrated. $19.95. Code: HAPG

HIDDEN FINANCE, ROGUE NETWORKS & SECRET SORCERY

The Fascist International, 9/11, & Penetrated Operations

By Joseph P. Farrell

Farrell investigates the theory that there were not *two* levels to the 9/11 event, but *three*. He says that the twin towers were downed by the force of an exotic energy weapon, one similar to the Tesla energy weapon suggested by Dr. Judy Wood, and ties together the tangled web of missing money, secret technology and involvement of portions of the Saudi royal family. Farrell unravels the many layers behind the 9-11 attack, layers that include the Deutschebank, the Bush family, the German industrialist Carl Duisberg, Saudi Arabian princes and the energy weapons developed by Tesla before WWII.

296 Pages. 6x9 Paperback. Illustrated. $19.95. Code: HFRN

THRICE GREAT HERMETICA & THE JANUS AGE

By Joseph P. Farrell

What do the Fourth Crusade, the exploration of the New World, secret excavations of the Holy Land, and the pontificate of Innocent the Third all have in common? Answer: Venice and the Templars. What do they have in common with Jesus, Gottfried Leibniz, Sir Isaac Newton, Rene Descartes, and the Earl of Oxford? Answer: Egypt and a body of doctrine known as Hermeticism. The hidden role of Venice and Hermeticism reached far and wide, into the plays of Shakespeare (a.k.a. Edward DeVere, Earl of Oxford), into the quest of the three great mathematicians of the Early Enlightenment for a lost form of analysis, and back into the end of the classical era, to little known Egyptian influences at work during the time of Jesus.

354 Pages. 6x9 Paperback. Illustrated. $19.95. Code: TGHJ

REICH OF THE BLACK SUN

Nazi Secret Weapons & the Cold War Allied Legend

by Joseph P. Farrell

Why were the Allies worried about an atom bomb attack by the Germans in 1944? Why did the Soviets threaten to use poison gas against the Germans? Why did Hitler in 1945 insist that holding Prague could win the war for the Third Reich? Why did US General George Patton's Third Army race for the Skoda works at Pilsen in Czechoslovakia instead of Berlin? Why did the US Army not test the uranium atom bomb it dropped on Hiroshima? Why did the Luftwaffe fly a non-stop round trip mission to within twenty miles of New York City in 1944? Farrel takes the reader on a scientific-historical journey in order to answer these questions. Arguing that Nazi Germany won the race for the atom bomb in late 1944,

352 PAGES. 6x9 PAPERBACK. ILLUSTRATED. $16.95. CODE: ROBS

THE COSMIC WAR
Interplanetary Warfare, Modern Physics, and Ancient Texts
By Joseph P. Farrell

There is ample evidence across our solar system of catastrophic events. The asteroid belt may be the remains of an exploded planet! The known planets are scarred from incredible impacts, and teeter in their orbits due to causes heretofore inadequately explained. Included: The history of the Exploded Planet hypothesis, and what mechanism can actually explode a planet. The role of plasma cosmology, plasma physics and scalar physics. The ancient texts telling of such destructions: from Sumeria (Tiamat's destruction by Marduk), Egypt (Edfu and the Mars connections), Greece (Saturn's role in the War of the Titans) and the ancient Americas.

436 Pages. 6x9 Paperback. Illustrated.. $18.95. Code: COSW

THE GRID OF THE GODS
The Aftermath of the Cosmic War & the Physics of the Pyramid Peoples
By Joseph P. Farrell with Scott D. de Hart

Farrell looks at Ashlars and Engineering; Anomalies at the Temples of Angkor; The Ancient Prime Meridian: Giza; Transmitters, Nazis and Geomancy; the Lithium-7 Mystery; Nazi Transmitters and the Earth Grid; The Master Plan of a Hidden Elite; Moving and Immoveable Stones; Uncountable Stones and Stones of the Giants and Gods; The Grid and the Ancient Elite; Finding the Center of the Land; The Ancient Catastrophe, the Very High Civilization, and the Post-Catastrophe Elite; Tiahuanaco and the Puma Punkhu Paradox: Ancient Machining; The Black Brotherhood and Blood Sacrifices; The Gears of Giza: the Center of the Machine; tons more.

436 Pages. 6x9 Paperback. Illustrated. $19.95. Code: GOG

THE SS BROTHERHOOD OF THE BELL
The Nazis' Incredible Secret Technology
by Joseph P. Farrell

In 1945, a mysterious Nazi secret weapons project code-named "The Bell" left its underground bunker in lower Silesia, along with all its project documentation, and a four-star SS general named Hans Kammler. Taken aboard a massive six engine Junkers 390 ultra-long range aircraft, "The Bell," Kammler, and all project records disappeared completely, along with the gigantic aircraft. It is thought to have flown to America or Argentina. What was "The Bell"? What new physics might the Nazis have discovered with it? How far did the Nazis go after the war to protect the advanced energy technology that it represented?

456 pages. 6x9 Paperback. Illustrated. $16.95. Code: SSBB

THE THIRD WAY
The Nazi International, European Union, & Corporate Fascism
By Joseph P. Farrell

Pursuing his investigations of high financial fraud, international banking, hidden systems of finance, black budgets and breakaway civilizations, Farrell continues his examination of the post-war Nazi International, an "extra-territorial state" without borders or capitals, a network of terrorists, drug runners, and people in the very heights of financial power willing to commit financial fraud in amounts totaling trillions of dollars. Breakaway civilizations, black budgets, secret technology, international terrorism, giant corporate cartels, patent law and the hijacking of nature: Farrell explores 'the business model' of the post-war Axis elite.

364 Pages. 6x9 Paperback. Illustrated. $19.95. Code: TTW

ROSWELL AND THE REICH

By Joseph P. Farrell

Farrell has meticulously reviewed the best-known Roswell research from UFO-ET advocates and skeptics alike, as well as some little-known source material, and comes to a radically different scenario of what happened in Roswell, New Mexico in July 1947, and why the US military has continued to cover it up to this day. Farrell presents a fascinating case sure to disturb both ET believers and disbelievers, namely, that what crashed may have been representative of an independent postwar Nazi power—an extraterritorial Reich monitoring its old enemy, America, and the continuing development of the very technologies confiscated from Germany at the end of the War.

540 pages. 6x9 Paperback. Illustrated. $19.95. Code: RWR

SECRETS OF THE UNIFIED FIELD

The Philadelphia Experiment, the Nazi Bell, and the Discarded Theory

by Joseph P. Farrell

Farrell examines the now discarded Unified Field Theory. American and German wartime scientists and engineers determined that, while the theory was incomplete, it could nevertheless be engineered. Chapters include: The Meanings of "Torsion"; Wringing an Aluminum Can; The Mistake in Unified Field Theories and Their Discarding by Contemporary Physics; Three Routes to the Doomsday Weapon: Quantum Potential, Torsion, and Vortices; Tesla's Meeting with FDR; Arnold Sommerfeld and Electromagnetic Radar Stealth; Electromagnetic Phase Conjugations, Phase Conjugate Mirrors, and Templates; The Unified Field Theory, the Torsion Tensor, and Igor Witkowski's Idea of the Plasma Focus; tons more.

340 pages. 6x9 Paperback. Illustrated. $18.95. Code: SOUF

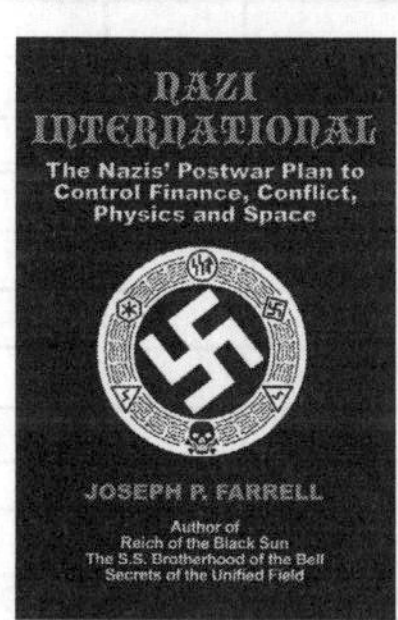

NAZI INTERNATIONAL

The Nazi's Postwar Plan to Control Finance, Conflict, Physics and Space

by Joseph P. Farrell

Farrell covers the vast, and still-little-known recreation of Nazi Germany in South America with help of Juan Peron, I.G. Farben and Martin Bormann. Farrell then covers Nazi Germany's penetration of the Muslim world including Wilhelm Voss and Otto Skorzeny in Gamel Abdul Nasser's Egypt before moving on to the development and control of new energy technologies including the Bariloche Fusion Project, Dr. Philo Farnsworth's Plasmator, and the work of Dr. Nikolai Kozyrev. Finally, Farrell discusses the Nazi desire to control space, and examines their connection with NASA, the esoteric meaning of NASA Mission Patches.

412 pages. 6x9 Paperback. Illustrated. $19.95. Code: NZIN

THE RIALTO IN RICHMOND

The Money War Between the States & Other Mysteries of the Civil War

By Joseph P. Farrell

Farrell examines the Confederate and Union monetary systems, the flight of the Confederate President Jefferson Davis the assassination of Abraham Lincoln and more. Why did Confederate President Jefferson Davis never stand trial for treason, in spite of being in federal custody for two years after the War Between the States had ended, and in spite of being implicated in the conspiracy that murdered Union President Abraham Lincoln? What did money and finance have to do with all of it, and where did all that missing Confederate silver and gold disappear to? How did the South and North finance their war efforts, and what were the differences and similarities between their systems?

236 Pages. 6x9 Paperback. Illustrated. $19.95. Code: TRIR

ORDER FORM

10% Discount When You Order 3 or More Items!

One Adventure Place
P.O. Box 74
Kempton, Illinois 60946
United States of America
Tel.: 815-253-6390 • Fax: 815-253-6300
Email: auphq@frontiernet.net
http://www.adventuresunlimitedpress.com

ORDERING INSTRUCTIONS

- ✓ Remit by USD$ Check, Money Order or Credit Card
- ✓ Visa, Master Card, Discover & AmEx Accepted
- ✓ Paypal Payments Can Be Made To: info@wexclub.com
- ✓ Prices May Change Without Notice
- ✓ 10% Discount for 3 or More Items

SHIPPING CHARGES

United States

- ✓ POSTAL BOOK RATE
- ✓ Postal Book Rate { $5.00 First Item / 50¢ Each Additional Item
- ✓ Priority Mail { $8.50 First Item / $2.00 Each Additional Item
- ✓ UPS { $9.00 First Item (Minimum 5 Books) / $1.50 Each Additional Item

NOTE: UPS Delivery Available to Mainland USA Only

Canada

- ✓ Postal Air Mail { $19.00 First Item / $3.00 Each Additional Item
- ✓ Personal Checks or Bank Drafts MUST BE US$ and Drawn on a US Bank
- ✓ Canadian Postal Money Orders OK
- ✓ Payment MUST BE US$

All Other Countries

- ✓ Sorry, No Surface Delivery!
- ✓ Postal Air Mail { $29.00 First Item / $7.00 Each Additional Item
- ✓ Checks and Money Orders MUST BE US$ and Drawn on a US Bank or branch.
- ✓ Paypal Payments Can Be Made in US$ To: info@wexclub.com

SPECIAL NOTES

- ✓ RETAILERS: Standard Discounts Available
- ✓ BACKORDERS: We Backorder all Out-of-Stock Items Unless Otherwise Requested
- ✓ PRO FORMA INVOICES: Available on Request
- ✓ DVD Return Policy: Replace defective DVDs only

ORDER ONLINE AT: www.adventuresunlimitedpress.com

10% Discount When You Order 3 or More Items!

Please check: ☑

☐ This is my first order ☐ I have ordered before

Name

Address

City

State/Province | Postal Code

Country

Phone: Day | Evening

Fax | Email

Item Code	Item Description	Qty	Total

Please check: ☑

Subtotal ▸

Less Discount-10% for 3 or more items ▸

☐ Postal-Surface — Balance ▸

☐ Postal-Air Mail (Priority in USA) — Illinois Residents 6.25% Sales Tax ▸

Previous Credit ▸

☐ UPS (Mainland USA only) — Shipping ▸

Total (check/MO in USD$ only) ▸

☐ Visa/MasterCard/Discover/American Express

Card Number:

Expiration Date: Security Code:

✓ SEND A CATALOG TO A FRIEND: